About Island Press

Island Press is the only nonprofit organization in the United States whose principal purpose is the publication of books on environmental issues and natural resource management. We provide solutions-oriented information to professionals, public officials, business and community leaders, and concerned citizens who are shaping responses to environmental problems.

In 2006, Island Press celebrates its twenty-second anniversary as the leading provider of timely and practical books that take a multidisciplinary approach to critical environmental concerns. Our growing list of titles reflects our commitment to bringing the best of an expanding body of literature to the environmental community throughout North America and the world.

Support for Island Press is provided by the Agua Fund, The Geraldine R. Dodge Foundation, Doris Duke Charitable Foundation, The William and Flora Hewlett Foundation, Kendeda Sustainability Fund of the Tides Foundation, Forrest C. Lattner Foundation, The Henry Luce Foundation, The John D. and Catherine T. MacArthur Foundation, The Marisla Foundation, The Andrew W. Mellon Foundation, Gordon and Betty Moore Foundation, The Curtis and Edith Munson Foundation, Oak Foundation, The Overbrook Foundation, The David and Lucile Packard Foundation, The Winslow Foundation, and other generous donors.

The opinions expressed in this book are those of the author(s) and do not necessarily reflect the views of these foundations.

MEASURING
LANDSCAPES

MEASURING LANDSCAPES

A Planner's Handbook

André Botequilha Leitão, Joseph Miller,
Jack Ahern, and Kevin McGarigal

ISLANDPRESS

Washington • Covelo • London

Library of Congress Cataloging-in-Publication Data.
Measuring landscapes : a planner's handbook / André Botequilha Leitão ... [et al.].
    p.   cm.
Includes bibliographical references and index.
ISBN 1-55963-899-0 (pbk. : alk. paper)
  1. Landscape ecology. 2. Land use—Planning. 3. Sustainable development.
4. Ecological landscape design. I. Leitão, André Botequilha.
QH541.15.L35M43 2006
333.95'16—dc22

                                                                2005031586

British Cataloguing-in-Publication Data available.

Design by Brighid Willson

Printed on recycled, acid-free paper ✪
Manufactured in the United States of America

09 08 07 06 05 04 03 02   8 7 6 5 4 3 2 1

André Botequilha Leitão dedicates this book to
Fernando H.D.O. Muge, Associate Professor with Aggregation
of Instituto Superior Técnico (IST), Technical University of Lisbon
who had a decisive influence in his academic career,
and for his friendship over many years.

Contents

Foreword

Land planning often resembles a multi-legged stool, with each leg a major goal and its thickness determined by the planner's expertise and perspective. A three-legged stool is also common, for instance, reflecting economics, social pattern, and environment. Alas, too often such approaches are strongly anthropocentric with natural systems receiving superficial attention. In contrast, consider mimicking a seesaw on the playground. Too much weight on either side brings unhappiness. The only stable point balances both sides . . . effectively integrating land and people, nature and humans, or culture and ecology.

Consider the vision: mold the land so nature and people both thrive long-term. Frederick Law Olmsted and other planning pioneers brilliantly knit people and nature together in large visible solutions that achieved top grades in the test of time. Not surprisingly, attempting to substitute short-term economics or public policy for the longer-term ecology produces results that fail the test.

Planning and design are normally considered "good," and done by optimists to help society. Objects are arranged at any scale, from continent or region to backyard or vase. Lack of planning generally leads to unsuitable spaces, such as fishing spots that become polluted, building sites that flood, and wildlife reserves cut off by busy highways. But a completely designed place seems sterile, controlled, boring. So, how much of the land should be planned, or designed? I'd say: "Plan most of the land at a broad scale, then design key places within it, and let the interplay of nature and people create the rest in ways that they both thrive."

The gaping lacuna in wise planning is not more knowledge, but rather the scarcity of accessible, informative and (especially) compelling syntheses and handbooks. The authors, from ecology, landscape architecture, and land-use planning, are experts in spatial pattern and landscape metrics, and have blended their expertise into this handy, readable book. Hopefully analogous collaborations will proliferate, with the land around us being the big beneficiary.

The authors highlight the importance of absorbing landscape ecology principles and then applying them in spatial planning. That has been, and is, exactly the growing success story in strengthening forestry (e.g., watershed management), biological conservation (rare species protection), transportation (road ecology), and wildlife management.

Landscape metrics, the measures of spatial pattern, are indicators of many human and natural conditions on land, from built-area patterns and built-system flows to the big three habitat issues: loss, degradation, and fragmentation. The pages ahead lucidly portray landscape metrics and their application, effectively sorting a large number in the literature down to a core set of ten. Both opportunities and caveats are explained. For the first time this scientific area is made available and readable.

Landscape structure is a key indicator of how the land works for people and for nature. Thus, changing landscape pattern emerges as a convenient "handle" for planners, and for each of us, to improve the planet. Over years, scholars will study the effects of landscape structure on function. But, over minutes and weeks, planners can and must help guide society by highlighting specific salutary changes in landscape structure. In effect, landscape metrics represent a "pre-handle," or primer, for the planners' handle for change.

Finally, what would you say if asked to develop a long-range plan that strengthens both natural systems and their human uses for the region around a growing major city? Give me funds and a couple of years to collect much-needed information? The Chief Architect/Planner for the Mayor of Barcelona visited me and posed the basic question at our first encounter. He said the work should be based on the book, *Land Mosaics: The Ecology of Landscapes and Regions*,[1] and added powerfully: "We're wasting land!" I suspected that no comprehensive model or case study existed for the task, and knew that "the bulldozers are running," as my students often hear. After emphasizing that I was a scientist, not a planner, had barely been to Spain, and never in the Greater Barcelona Region, the only response was, "I can do that. I've never done such a plan but, based on landscape ecology, I can envision what it might look like." The project took fifteen months and opened many doors. Unique solutions resulted from meshing stated principles with spatial patterns on the land.[2]

The experience also made me see cities as the key expanding powerhouses across the land, affecting everything, and that the ecology and planning of urban regions is ready to emerge as one of the great challenges of history. For most people the urban region is beyond understanding and defies optimism. Yet outlining a spatial vision, where both

---

[1]Forman, R. T. T. 1995, Cambridge University Press, New York.

[2]Forman, R. T. T. 2004, *Mosaico territorial para la region metropolitana de Barcelona*, Editorial Gustavo Gili, Barcelona.

nature and people thrive long-term, may provide a promising, tractable trajectory for cities. Landscape ecology is the only central paradigm I can find for such a vision.

The pages in your hand reveal a rich array of insights and an important big-picture perspective. Planners and ecologists, and indeed all who think about changing the land, will be enriched by the exploration ahead.

January 2006
Richard T. T. Forman
Harvard University

Preface
The Need for Sustainable Planning

Sustainability is a powerful but hard-to-define concept that is addressed by many disciplines, including planning. Sustainable planning is a multi-dimensional activity, which aims to assure the viability of ecological, social, and economic systems. Many scientists believe that planning for conservation and the protection and appropriate use of land and natural resources is the overarching goal of landscape planning (Forman 1995). According to Van Lier (1998a, 81), "the notion to create more sustainable systems in the countryside has become a leading principle for all those scientists that are involved in planning future land uses." To some, sustainability is the major objective of any planning (Grossman and Bellot 1999).

From an ecological point of view, sustainability can be defined as the capacity of the earth to maintain and support life and to persist as a system (Franklin 1997). This concept is relevant globally as well as for smaller ecosystems (Jongman 1999). Sustainability involves the maintenance of spatial patterns of land cover types that are ecologically beneficial. The spatial dimension of planning for sustainability is strongly related to the interdependence of land uses, and to spatial processes such as fragmentation (Bryden 1994 cited in Van Lier 1998, 79).

Sustainability also recognizes the interdependencies between ecosystems and human culture. Therefore, sound planning cannot be achieved without due consideration of ecology. Ecology and planning share many common characteristics. Ecology is concerned with the functioning of systems and resources, and planning focuses on their use for human benefit. However, planning has only recently accepted ecological principles, and ecology has traditionally focused on the biophysical dimension where humans were viewed as separate from natural systems.

To plan an ecologically sound human habitat, it is essential for ecology to provide clear linkages to planning by explicitly addressing the spatial dimension and adopting a more anthropocentric perspective. Planning a landscape is inherently a spatial problem. Plans for watershed management, wildlife conservation, housing development, and public recreation all share a fundamental concern for the spatial component. Plans attempt to influence specific changes in the pattern of landscapes with particular consequences for ecosystem structure and function. For example, when new housing is built in a forested landscape, water flows and wildlife movements may be interrupted, and important habitats may be displaced.

Landscape as an Appropriate Unit to Plan for Sustainability

Due to the interdependencies of ecosystems, a planning approach is needed that examines a broad context: the landscape. An ecosystem's external linkages with the landscape are as important to proper functioning as the internal ecosystem environment (Odum 1989). Some even argue that landscape context is more important than content (Dramstad et al. 1996). This recognition of the importance of context supports a hierarchical or systems view in which landscapes are nested within larger regions and are themselves composed of lower-order ecosystems.

Landscape is arguably the optimal scale for sustainable land planning for two reasons. First, landscapes are usually large enough to contain many different ecosystems with enough redundancy in ecosystem composition, structure, and function to accommodate natural variability in the system while maintaining the flow of ecosystem goods and services. Second, landscape is consistent with the scale of human perception, decision making, and physical management (Forman 1995; Ahern 2002). Many conservation and land management organizations, both public and private, now view a landscape perspective as essential for sound resource management (Wallinger 1995; Wigley and Sweeney 1993 cited in Gustafson 1998, 144).

Landscape Ecology as an Integrative Science

Science needs to inform planning in a more effective way. Science is evolving to help society move towards a more sustainable condition (Lubchenco 1998 cited in Nassauer 1999, 131). The relatively new interdisciplinary science of landscape ecology is particularly well poised to address this challenge. In landscape ecology, human activities are considered an integral part of ecosystems, not a separate component. Landscape ecology addresses issues related to the understanding, analysis, planning, design and management of natural systems at the landscape and regional levels. A transdisciplinary perspective considers the principal landscape dimensions—spatial, temporal—as the nexus of nature and culture, and as a complex system (Tress and Tress 2001). New methods have been proposed to apply landscape ecological knowledge to landscape planning. Across the world, landscape ecology is beginning to provide a scientific basis for landscape and natural resource planning and management.

The Role of Landscape Metrics in Planning

Landscape ecology focuses on three main characteristics: structure, function, and change. Landscape ecology-based metrics quantify landscape structure or pattern. Structure relates to the composition and spatial distribution patterns of landscape elements: ecosystems, or, at a coarser level, land cover types (LCTs). For example, picture a map representing agricultural fields, forests, urban areas, roads, wetlands, lakes, ponds, and rivers. Structure has two dimensions. One dimension is composition: the number, type and extent of these elements without explicit consideration of their spatial distribution. For example, the number of LCTs and the proportion of each type are measures of landscape composition. The other dimension is configuration, which is the spatial character, arrangement, position, or orientation of landscape elements. For example, the distance from one pond to another, the shape and complexity of forest patches, and the clumpiness of landscape elements are measures of landscape configuration.

Some ecologists view landscape functions as the flows of animals, plants, energy, mineral nutrients, and water between landscape elements (Forman and Godron 1986; Forman 1995). For example, a river transporting dissolved nutrients from its headwaters downstream across a diverse landscape, a young animal dispersing across a landscape from its natal site, and the spread of wildfire disturbance across a landscape are all considered landscape functions. Besides the flow of water, rivers and streams serve as a transport media for dissolved nutrients and soil particles.

Landscape structure and function influence one another; when structure changes, functions change, and vice versa. Consider a stream located in an urban watershed. Imperviousness affects both the physical (channel stability and water quality) and biological (stream biodiversity) qualities of stream habitat (Center for Watershed Protection, 1998). In this case, the structure of the watershed, characterized by sizeable urban areas located upstream (size and location of urban areas), affects the downstream flow of water and nutrients (landscape function).

The need for flood control and navigational improvements in riverine systems also illustrates the relationship between landscape structure and function. Channelization causes drastic alteration and simplification of rivers, as opposed to the original, complex, meandrous, and remarkably self-organized structures of riparian corridors (Bell 1999, 156). River channelization causes serious disruptions of the natural functions of these hydrological systems by decreasing their capacity for storage, nutrient cycling, and riparian processes (Bell 1999).

When significant relationships between structural landscape features and ecological functions are established, landscape metrics-based approaches can constitute useful tools for planning. They can contribute to an understanding of ecological processes, allowing for the construction of models, and the comparative evaluation of planning alternatives. The establishment of relationships between landscape structure and function can help planners to predict the impacts of planned activities on ecological systems. By looking at landscape structure, planners can gain insights into landscape functioning in a holistic manner.

Landscape metrics measure the geometric properties of landscape elements, and their relative positions and distributions (composition and configuration). At this point one might ask, so what? How are metrics useful for planning? The answer lies at the core of landscape ecology in the fundamental relationships between landscape structure and function. Spatial structure influences ecological functions and processes, and is therefore highly relevant for landscape planning and management (Turner 1989; Ahern 1999). For example, there is strong empirical evidence that landscape structure has a close relationship with biodiversity (McGarigal and Marks 1995). These structure and function relationships help to anticipate the ecological consequences of plans and designs of the landscape, and ultimately help to make landscapes more sustainable.

A wide gap still exists between science and planning. Science in general, and ecology in particular, has developed much knowledge about the functioning of landscapes. However, only a small proportion of this information makes its way through the decision-making arenas where the future of landscapes is debated and decided (Rockwood 1995). Opdam et al. (2002) argue that planners do not use the current body of knowledge on species and landscapes and thus future landscape plans are not tested against criteria based on ecological processes. Planners simply do not have the knowledge or time required to put it into a form that they can apply (Meredith 1996 cited in Theobald et al. 2000, 36). In order for planners to use the existing science successfully, ecologists need to understand the goals of planners and design ecological research to produce both data and findings that are directly relevant to planning.

Planners should acquire an appropriate level of landscape ecological literacy and numeracy as a prerequisite to understanding the fundamental principles of landscape ecology (Ahern et al. 1999). This would provide planners with a conceptual basis for holistic, transdisciplinary planning of multifunctional landscapes of a total human ecosystem (Naveh 2001, Tress and Tress 2001). It is therefore crucial to improve the flow of information between science and planning. A way to help to bridge the gap is to develop tools for planning informed by landscape ecological principles that will help practitioners relate landscape patterns to both natural and cultural processes (Botequilha Leitão 2001).

Purpose and Organization of the Handbook

This handbook will introduce the ecological and spatial dimensions of sustainability and focus on a particular tool (landscape metrics) to support planning for sustainability. We provide linkages between the concepts and tools presented, which are derived from multidisciplinary literature and from professional practice.

This handbook aims to promote awareness, understanding, and application of landscape metrics by planners, and thus facilitate interdisciplinary communication and collaboration. This handbook is a primer designed to help planners acquaint themselves with landscape metrics and thus help promote more ecologically sustainable planning solutions. We emphasize the application of metrics by planners and managers of landscapes across a reasonable spectrum of resources. In any landscape we can recognize three principle types of resources: Abiotic, Biotic, and Cultural (ABC). These have been traditionally addressed in three discrete planning sectors: watershed planning and management, conservation planning, and urban and recreation planning. In the application examples provided in this handbook, we address each of these sectors from a holistic perspective.

Chapter one provides an introduction to landscape ecology and explains how to quantify landscape structure. Chapter two presents an overview of planning categories and stages, and describes how planning can relate to landscape ecology. It also identifies a core set of landscape metrics for planning, and introduces some technical issues and data models for mapping a landscape. Chapter three presents a selected set of ten metrics, each explained in terms of concept, metric equation and calculation, application(s), limitation(s), recommendations, related metrics, and selected references. Chapter four includes a broad application of landscape metrics to spatial planning, focusing on the three ABC resources: water (abiotic), biodiversity/wildlife (biotic), and human habitat (housing and recreation) (cultural). Chapter five provides a summary and conclusions.

Acknowledgments

André Botequilha Leitão thanks his parents and friends for their continued support and friendship throughout the preparation of this book, without which it would not have been possible.

Financial support of André Botequilha Leitão is gratefully acknowledged from the Fundação da Ciência e Tecnologia (FCT) under a PhD grant (PRAXIS XXI/BD/9209/96) and a Post-Doctoral grant (SFRH/BPD/11620/2002), from the Fundação Luso-Americana para o Desenvolvimento (FLAD) under a research grant, and from the CVRM - Centro de Geo-Sistemas do Instituto Superior Técnico. André would also like to acknowledge the institutional support of the Faculty of Engineering and Natural Resources (FERN), University of Algarve.

Joseph Miller thanks his wife Sallie for her continued love, support, and enthusiasm—none of this would have been possible without her.

1

Landscape Ecology
A Spatial and Human-Oriented Ecology

During the eighteenth and nineteenth centuries, many scientists developed the basis for what would become the science of *ecology* (Forman and Godron 1986). Haeckel introduced the term ecology in 1866, originally meaning "knowledge of the house (hold)" (Capra 1996), as a sister science of economy, which is literally "the management (and counting) of the house (hold)" (Zonneveld 1995).

Ecology is concerned with the interactions between organisms and their environment and how those interactions determine the distribution of both plants and animals (O'Callaghan 1996).

Ecology focuses on the study of ecosystems, and on the vertical relationships (topology) between the different components of ecosystems, such as climate, water, soil, bedrock, flora, and fauna.

1.1. Foundations of Landscape Ecology

Landscape ecology emerged in Europe in the 1950s and shares its heritage with the related disciplines of biogeography and ecology. One of the principal distinctions between landscape ecology and other branches of ecology is the emphasis and focus on the spatial patterning of multiple ecosystems in heterogeneous landscapes.

Landscape ecology introduced several perspectives and principles that have become fundamental for planners. One such perspective is the spatial dimension of ecological processes. Vertical (topological) relationships are considered together with horizontal (chorological) relationships between the ecosystems that comprise a landscape. Landscape ecology offers theory and empirical evidence that enables scientists and planners to understand and compare different spatial configurations of land cover

1

types (Forman 1995), and enables planners to anticipate and manage the ecological consequences of a plan.

A second fundamental perspective is the focus of landscape ecology on human ecology, and on the application in planning and management. In landscape ecology, human activities are considered part of ecosystems, not as a separate component.

A third perspective consists of adopting the landscape as the principal unit of study. Together with a systemic, holistic approach, landscape ecology provides an integrated analysis of the complex, human-made landscapes that are fast becoming dominant worldwide.

In nature, form and function constitute a unity because they are reciprocally influential in a closely integrated relationship responsible for landscape evolution. In this context, the form and function principle is particularly useful to planning since it allows one to relate physical characteristics of the landscape and the spatial configuration of a plan with landscape functions and the processes that shape and alter those same characteristics. Although these might have slightly different meanings, land use, land cover, spatial structure, and pattern are fundamental concepts for both landscape ecologists and planners (Antrop 2001). Landscape ecologists focus on detecting structure where planners work on creating new structures. The former look at spatial patterns to learn about landscape processes and functions, the latter focus on guiding these according to planning goals (Antrop 2001).

1.2. A Landscape Perspective

There is enormous global diversity in landscape types, from grasslands and deserts, to forests and tundra, with many gradations between these types and the level of human activity occurring within them—activities such as agriculture, urban and suburban development, forestry, and mining. Each of these landscape types has several dimensions: ecological, economic, social, cultural, and aesthetic. Depending on one's professional or disciplinary viewpoint, landscapes can be seen from multiple perspectives. One perspective views the visible component of the landscape, the so-called "phenosystem" (González Bernáldez 1981), primarily as an aesthetic phenomenon as in the seventeenth century landscape painting. Another perspective views landscapes as "closer to the eyes than to the mind, more related to the heart, the soul, the moods than to the intellect" (Hardt 1970 cited in Bastian 2001, 758). Others view landscape as a socio-spatial entity (Linehan and Gross 1998), or as landscape products (Taborda 2000). Others perceive landscapes as geographic surface units, focused on their natural components including: water, hills, fields, and forests (Wascher 2000). Since the beginning of the twenty-first century, the landscape concept has been evolving towards a transdisciplinary perspective (Naveh 1991; Tress and Tress 2001) (see Box 1.1).

Box 1.1. Landscapes as Multidimensional Entities

Landscape ecology originally focused on three landscape characteristics: structure, function, and change. And respectively on (1) the distributional patterns of landscape elements or ecosystems, (2) the flows of animals, plants, energy, mineral nutrients, and water between these elements, and (3) the ecological changes in the landscape mosaic over time. Forman and Godron (1986) defined three fundamental elements of landscape structure: patches, corridors, and the matrix. Together these constitute the widely accepted "patch-corridor-matrix" or mosaic model (Forman 1995).

However, landscapes are more than biophysical elements. Both nature and culture interact to produce patterns, to influence functions and to effect change. Some argue that if we are to promote an integration of biophysical and cultural approaches, we should be focusing on commonalities instead of focusing on differences (Botequilha Leitão 2001). So what do natural sciences (e.g., ecology) have in common with social sciences (e.g., sociology), or humanities (e.g., history)?

Marcucci (2000) argues that a historical model is best to integrate a spatial, geographical dimension and to allow cultural systems to be represented as sequential phenomena related to place. He also emphasizes the significance of geography in history that, by accounting for the profound impact of ecological flows on landscape evolution, helps place it in a regional context and supports the recreation of ecological stages of the land. According to Cronon (1990 cited in Marcucci 2000, 75) "landscape ecology is that form of ecology which is credited with bringing ecology and history together." Other authors found social system variables to have a clear influence on spatial differentiation of ecological impacts (Pickett et al. 1997; Grove and Burch 1997).

Thus it seems that the spatial dimension could provide for a common linkage among several disciplines. Spatially-explicit landscape models can articulate the linkages between natural and cultural variables. As Brandt (2000) states, it is not a matter of opposing the human mind to nature, but to stress the important and special dynamics between them (Brandt 2000). Close cooperation is needed to transcend the realms of natural sciences and reach out to human and social sciences, which are connected with

(continues)

Box 1.1. *Continued*

human land uses (Naveh 1998 and 2001; Marcucci 2000). Although the transdisciplinary challenge is being addressed by different disciplines, a truly integrative approach is yet to be fully developed and achieved, one that would consider the different landscape dimensions equitably, in one single model, and that should prove to be operational and applicable to planning. Recently a transdisciplinary landscape model was proposed by Tress and Tress (2001), which considers five landscape dimensions: spatial, temporal, mental, as the nexus of nature and culture, and as a complex system. Although promising, this approach is at an early stage of development.

The message to take home is that nature and culture are complementary, not counterparts, and the landscape represents the very point of contact between them (Naveh 1998; Tress and Tress 2001).

1.3. Main Characteristics of Landscape Ecology

To use landscape pattern metrics appropriately, it is important to understand their scientific context. While the range of applications for landscape metrics may be diverse, most metrics were developed and adapted specifically for landscape ecological research applications. Therefore, the more knowledge planners possess about landscape ecology principles and concepts, the easier it becomes for them to use landscape metrics appropriately.

In this handbook we have adopted a widely accepted definition of landscape: a kilometer-wide mosaic over which particular local ecosystems and land uses recur (Forman and Godron 1986; Forman 1995). A landscape mosaic is comprised of spatial elements (e.g., patches, corridors, and matrices, described below), and landscape metrics help to measure, describe, and understand the significance of these elements or their spatial pattern. Although we focus on a spatial approach to understand landscapes, we acknowledge the need to perceive landscapes as multidimensional entities that can be understood from a transdisciplinary perspective (see Box 1.1). Additionally, we find the spatial approach to understanding landscapes to be compatible with other approaches from other disciplines including: anthropology, sociology, history, and economics.

Landscape ecology focuses on the relationship between landscape structure and function and the ways landscapes change over time. To introduce this we will first examine the conceptual fundamentals of landscape structure and function. Then we will examine fundamental conceptions of landscape change, focusing on issues that are highly relevant for planning.

1.3.1. *Landscape Structure*

Landscape structure is a description of the spatial relationships among ecosystems, or more specifically the distribution of energy, materials, and species in relation to the size, number, types, and configurations of ecosystems.

There are several principal ways to describe the structure of landscapes, each using different kinds of data. With point data, the property of interest is usually the geographic location of each point, although measured attributes at each location may also be of interest. Linear networks within a landscape may be useful in the study of hydrologic systems (such as rivers and streams), wildlife corridors, or transportation and energy networks. Surficial, or continuous surface data is useful to address landscape variability as gradients (McGarigal and Cushman 2005). Categorical data assumes a patchy landscape structure, as commonly seen in soil or land cover maps. In this handbook the categorical data model is used, which has been widely adopted by planners.

Forman and Godron (1986) use three fundamental landscape elements to define landscape structure: patches, corridors, and the matrix. With these three elements any landscape (e.g., urban, agricultural, forested) can be described. According to Forman (1995, 7), the model that coalesces these landscape elements, the *mosaic model*, has analogies in other disciplines such as art, architecture, urban planning, and medicine. In the circulatory system of the human body, an organ (heart) and tubes (veins, arteries) together form a structure that allows blood to move (flow) and transport oxygen (function) within an overall context of other systems in the body (matrix). Over time body shape and size changes, thus altering body functions. Another example of this analogy is provided by Kevin Lynch's typology of urban form including: districts, edges, nodes (patches), paths (corridors), and landmarks (Lynch 1960).

In addition to landscape elements *per se*, it is important to account for the spatial relationships among the elements that make up a landscape. Are they clustered and adjacent to one another, or dispersed and far apart? In a landscape ecological approach, landscape elements can only be fully understood by understanding their context. The ecological significance of spatial characteristics (size, shape, or spatial distribution) of landscape elements is given not by these characteristics *per se*, but by considering the effect of those characteristics on each other and on other elements of the landscape. All landscape elements, regardless of their specific land cover type, influence landscape functions through their spatial characteristics. This is a fundamental interrelationship applicable to any landscape type—urban, rural, or natural (see Box 1.2).

Box 1.2. Structure as a Holistic Property of Landscapes

Many contemporary landscape ecologists argue that a holistic conception of landscapes is needed to understand how landscape elements relate to each other (Naveh and Lieberman 1994; De Leo and Levin 1997; Antrop 1998; Tress and Tress 2001). By definition, holism states that the sum is more than the mere sum of their parts (Figure 1.1). Holism provides a new way to analyze; it argues that landscape elements receive their meaning or significance by their context, or their position within the whole (Antrop 1998, 157).

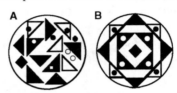

Figure 1.1. *Holism*. The significance of spatial structure and relationships between components in a given system, e.g., landscape elements in a given landscape. B is not the mere sum of the components in A due to different interactions across system components, changed by an alteration on the spatial organization of the elements, i.e., structure. *With permission from Bòlos 1992*

Additionally "systems thinking is a method of scientific enquiry that allows one to understand and investigate complex realities" such as landscapes (Tress and Tress 2001, 149). Holistic thinking "provides the basis for studying certain wholes or systems, without knowing all the details of its internal functions" (Zonneveld 1988, 8).

The modelling approach used to study the dynamic interactions between landscape spatial structure and functions is similar to those so-called black box models, which are useful to model complex systems. In these we know both the inputs (change in structure, e.g., shape of a patch), and the outputs (change in a certain function, e.g., increase in movement of a certain species of interest, or an ecological process), but we do not comprehend entirely the mechanisms of this relationship (what is behind what happens between input and output) (Figure 1.2).

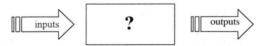

Figure 1.2. *"Black box" modelling approach*. Both input and output are known, but often the mechanisms or the causal relationships that operate between inputs and outputs are not well understood.

Isolation is a landscape characteristic emerging from a given landscape structure, measurable by particular landscape metrics. Ecological significance of isolation of a certain patch only has meaning if the patch is considered within its landscape context. For example, what is the relationship of the patch to other patches in its neighborhood? (Figure 1.3).

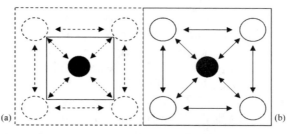

Figure 1.3. The concept of isolation is understood differently at the patch and landscape (context). The box represents the focus of the analysis, i.e., our landscape; circles represent landscape spatial elements, and the arrows represent landscape flows between elements. Solid lines represent elements and flows that are being considered, dashed lines represent those that are disregarded. Note that in the left diagram (a) the focus is on the central patch. Landscape context, including all other patches around it and the relationships between these, is ignored. Thus the ecological significance of the isolation of the central patch in (a) only makes sense if we consider what is going on outside of the solid line box, as in (b). Landscape elements are not islands; to understand their dynamics, one needs to consider the context, as proposed by R.H. MacArthur and E.O. Wilson in *The Theory of Island Biogeography* (1967).

According to McGarigal et al. (2002) "isolation deals explicitly with the spatial and temporal *context* of habitat patches, rather than the spatial character of the patches themselves." For example, there has been a proliferation of mathematical models on population dynamics and species interactions in spatially subdivided populations (Kareiva 1990), and results suggest that the dynamics of local plant and animal populations in a patch are influenced by their proximity to, or isolation from, other subpopulations of the same or competing species. Isolation is particularly important in the context of habitat fragmentation. Several authors have claimed, for example, that patch isolation explains why fragmented habitats often contain fewer bird species than contiguous habitats (Moore and Hooper 1975; Forman et al. 1976; Helliwell 1976; Whitcomb et al. 1981; Hayden et al. 1985; Dickman 1987; in McGarigal et al. 2002, 45). Therefore, the importance of a given patch for habitat conservation is dependent on the relationships with other patches of a similar nature (landscape context). Isolation metrics such as the *nearest neighbor distance* or the *proximity index* provide ways to quantify these structural characteristics.

Landscape Structural Elements:
Patch, Corridor, and Matrix

A patch is defined as a relatively homogeneous nonlinear area that differs from its surroundings (Forman 1995). Patches provide multiple functions including wildlife habitat, aquifer recharge areas, or sources and sinks for species or nutrients. A parcel of native forested land surrounded by farm fields is a patch, as is a large asphalt parking lot surrounded by golf courses. Thus, there are many kinds of patches: agricultural fields, wood lots, or villages (Figure 1.4). What constitutes a patch ultimately depends on the application and what is deemed meaningful as a way of representing the landscape mosaic in the context of that application.

A corridor is defined as a linear area of a particular land cover type that is different in content and physical structure from its context (Forman 1995). Corridors serve many functions within the landscape including habitat for wildlife, pathways or conduits for the movement of plants, animals, nutrients, and wind, or as a barrier to such movement. There are many types of corridors, ranging from riparian or river corridors, to interstate highway systems, to canals within an agricultural landscape (Figure 1.5).

The matrix is the dominant land cover type (LCT) in terms of area, degree of connectivity and continuity, and control that is exerted over the dynamics of the landscape (Forman 1995) (Figure 1.6). Examples of

Figure 1.4. A village (urban patch) embedded in a matrix of mixed agriculture in Portugal. *Courtesy of A. Silva*

Figure 1.5. Corridors in the landscape can be either natural (the river corridor), or human made (the road or the bridge). *Courtesy of A. Silva*

Figure 1.6. A forest matrix that surrounds a village with its agricultural fields, in plateaus (maize fields and vineyards).

matrices include: a city with patches of parkland, forest with patches created by timber harvesting, agricultural fields with occasional small woodlots, or an agricultural landscape with a dense network of hedgerows and riparian vegetation (Figure 1.4). In the last example, hedgerows may exert significant control over the functioning of the landscape by controlling the movement of nutrients, wind, water, and wildlife across the landscape, as well as controlling the movement of people in the landscape. This control is accomplished without being the proportionately dominant land cover type—spatial arrangement of the hedgerow is key.

The spatial arrangement of patches, corridors, and matrices, and their profound interactions are, in a sense, the hallmarks of landscape ecology.

1.3.2. *Landscape Function*

Landscape function can refer to the broad categories of "services" that landscapes provide: production, protection, and regulation. Production services support the human needs for food, wood, recreation, and transport. Landscape protection provides for natural functions, such as rainfall infiltration, oxygen production and absorption of carbon dioxide, water cleansing by soils and wetlands, nutrient buffering by riparian corridors, and maintenance of biological diversity. Landscape regulation provides negative feedback loops that assure the overall stability of a landscape (Naveh 1994; 1998, 9; 1999).

Landscape function can also refer specifically to the flows of energy, materials, nutrients, species, people, and finally to ecological processes such as the production of biomass or the infiltration and percolation of rainfall. Materials like water or nutrients like carbon, phosphorus, and nitrogen either cycle within or flow through ecosystems, either between air and organisms (carbon), soil and organisms (phosphorus), or between air, soil, and organisms (nitrogen) (Forman 1995).

1.3.3. *Relationships Between Landscape Structure and Function*

Structure and function relationships are illustrated by the form and function principle, which states that the interaction between two objects is proportional to their common boundary surface (or edge) (Forman and Godron 1986, 177). The size and shape of patches determines to a large degree their ecological and functional characteristics. Large agricultural fields, for example, have greater evapotranspiration rates per unit of area than small fields. This is due in part to the greater expanse of vegetation (crops) that the wind may travel over, and the large proportion of topsoil exposed to wind and sunlight. Large forests, on the other hand, may serve to protect water and soil resources by providing vegetative cover for an entire aquifer, and by limiting the amount of soil that is exposed to weathering forces of wind and sunlight.

Large patches of native ecosystems are more likely to possess a greater variety of habitats than small patches, and therefore are more likely to support greater biodiversity (Dramstad et al. 1996). More food, fiber, and biochemical products are likely to be found in large patches (Forman 1995). Ecosystem services such as moderating fluctuations in surface water levels, the recycling of minerals and nutrients, and the removal of toxins from circulation in the environment are also more likely to be achieved as the size of the patches is increased. In addition, the inspirational and aesthetic experiences of the public may be greater when experienced in larger patches, such as wide-open spaces, spacious urban parks or gardens, or even urban neighborhoods of high aesthetic quality.

Variation in the size and shape of patches and corridors, and the area of the matrix, has a strong influence on the resulting landscape pattern. Size and shape determine the amount of boundary shared with other patches, corridors, and the matrix. Linear patches and corridors have greater amounts of boundary than compact, rounded patches. And complex, convoluted patch shapes have greater amounts of boundary than simple patch shapes. The boundaries between landscape elements are termed "edge" by ecologists, and they have significant implications for how a patch, corridor, or matrix ecosystem will function. For example, Hardt and Forman (1989) found that natural succession of a reclaimed strip mine site or other open area could be managed by manipulating the boundary (edge) shape at the scale of tens of meters. Planting trees and shrubs to form concavities along a straight forest boundary proved to effectively enhance the colonization of a mine. In fact, reclaimed mine areas where forest patch perimeters were characterized by concavities experienced more colonization than those by straight boundaries or convexities.

Spatial distribution, the relative location of patches and corridors within the matrix, matters as well. Each type of land cover has distinct physical characteristics. For example, a parking lot or a pasture exposed in the sun is hotter than the adjacent woods or a pond. Flows are created by measurable differences, such as those in pressure and temperature, across the landscape (Forman and Godron 1986). Wind is caused by a differential of air pressure, flowing from high pressure to low pressure areas. Landscape flows behave and move differently throughout the landscape depending on what land cover types (LCTs) are adjacent or near to one another.

LANDSCAPE CONNECTIVITY

Connectivity is a landscape property that nicely illustrates the relationship between landscape structure and function. In general, connectivity refers to the degree to which the landscape facilitates or impedes the flow of energy, materials, nutrients, species, and people across the landscape. Connectivity is an emergent property of the landscape that results from the interaction between landscape structure (i.e., the composition and configuration of the landscape mosaic) and landscape function (e.g., water flow, nutrient cycling, maintenance of biological diversity). Because connectivity is essential to proper ecosystem functioning, it is of great relevance in conservation planning and management (Naveh 1994; Forman 1995; Bennett 1999). For example, the greenway concept recognizes connectivity as key to providing multifunctional corridors for hydrological management, species movement, recreation, and cultural landscape preservation (Ahern 2004).

The concept of connectivity is perhaps easiest to understand in the context of plant and animal movement. In this context, connectivity refers to the degree to which the landscape facilitates or impedes movement of individuals among habitat patches. Connectivity affects the rate of movement among local populations in a spatially-structured population (or metapopulation) and is therefore critical to the persistence of populations in fragmented landscapes (Forman and Godron 1986; McDonnell and Pickett 1988; Opdam 1991; Opdam et al. 1993; Naveh 1994; Forman 1995; Bennett 1999). By affecting movement rates and patterns, connectivity also affects gene flow, which is essential for the long-term survival of populations (Selman and Doar 1992). An abrupt change in the connectivity of the landscape may interfere with dispersal success such that formerly widespread populations may suddenly become fragmented into small, isolated populations. This may in turn lead to an abrupt decline in patch occupancy and ultimately to the extinction of the population in the landscape. Thus, connectivity is often a critical issue regarding the conservation of populations.

Connectivity for populations may be achieved in many ways. The size, number, and distribution of habitat patches influence the physical connectedness of habitat across the landscape, and may be the primary determinant of connectivity for some species (Fritz 1979; Opdam 1988 cited in Selman and Doar 1992). This is most likely when there is a discrete patch structure in which the landscape is comprised of habitat and nonhabitat— at least as perceived by the species. In this situation, when habitat is abundant and widespread, connectivity is virtually assured. Habitat loss results in a simple loss of suitable habitat and the effect on landscape structure is a quantitative one: a reduction in the proportion of habitat on the landscape. A qualitative change in landscape structure and connectivity occurs at a critical threshold, beyond which any additional loss of habitat produces a fragmented landscape in which habitat is dissected into multiple small, isolated patches. The pattern of habitat destruction and the dispersal capabilities of the species determine the level of habitat loss at which this threshold in landscape connectivity occurs.

Physical connections between habitat patches via corridors may also affect connectivity for populations (Baudry and Merriam 1988). Corridors have different functions with respect to connectivity: (1) they may provide breeding habitat for individuals and thus serve to connect larger population units by maintaining gene flow, (2) they may provide only dispersal habitat and thus serve only to facilitate movement among larger habitat patches, and (3) they may serve as barriers or filters that prevent or impede the movement of organisms across the corridor (Forman and Godron 1986). Empirical evidence that corridors actually facilitate landscape connectivity is equivocal (Simberloff and Cox 1987; Simberloff et al. 1992; Hobbs 1993; Mann and Plummer 1995; Rosenburg et al. 1997). Nevertheless, in conservation practice it is generally assumed that corridors mitigate the effects of habitat fragmentation by facilitating connectivity between habitat patches, and therefore have an important role in the maintenance of biological diversity (Forman 1995; Linehan et al. 1995; Bennett 1999; Jongman and Pungetti 2004) and ecosystem functioning (Chapin et al. 1998; Bennett 1999).

Lastly, the character of the intervening matrix between habitat patches may also affect connectivity for populations. Organisms do not restrict their movement to suitable habitat and the physical connections (e.g., corridors) among those patches, but move throughout the entire landscape mosaic to find suitable habitat. The matrix is often a composite of patches with varying levels of permeability. Consequently, as with corridors, conditions in the matrix may affect movement rates and patterns, and therefore they are the ultimate criterion of successful movement among habitat patches. Unfortunately, like corridors, the evidence in support of the matrix concept is not based on extensive experimental support.

Ultimately, as With (1999) notes: "What ultimately influences the connectivity of the landscape from the organism's perspective is the scale and pattern of movement (scale at which the organism perceives the landscape) relative to the scale and pattern of patchiness (structure of the landscape)."

The concept of connectivity also applies to other flows across the landscape. Water flow is arguably the most important flow in any land-scape. It is important by itself, as a source of water to all life in the land-scape, and for the transport of materials, nutrients, and species, including humans, across a landscape. Consequently, disruption of hydrologic con-nectivity is a major concern when planning for sustainability. Human land use activities that disrupt the flow of water are a major concern for plan-ners. For example, dams disrupt the flow of water and, as a result, can serve as traps for nutrients, pollutants, and sediments, and can impair the movement of fish downstream and upstream during migrations. In the same manner that dams disrupt surface water flows, underground devel-opments (e.g., basements, underground parking, and subways) constitute barriers to groundwater flows.

1.3.4. *Landscape Change*

The surface of the earth is constantly undergoing change resulting from the cumulative effect of a variety of disturbances, and the growth and development of ecosystems and human culture. Landscape change can be understood as the alteration of landscape structure and function over time. The most effective manner for landscape planners to deal with land-scape change is to develop a basic understanding of it, and to understand options and consequences associated with alternative plans for the future.

In many landscapes that are relatively untouched by human manage-ment, it has long been observed that the vegetation present at individual locations in the landscape changes in response to disturbance and succes-sion, but, if averaged over a sufficiently long time or large area, the pro-portion of the landscape in each stage of development remains relatively constant. This "shifting mosaic" concept of landscape change emphasizes that even systems with a high disturbance frequency could be in a steady state or equilibrium if the creation of new patches is balanced by the mat-uration of old ones (i.e., a balance between disturbance and succession on a larger scale). Aubreville was one of the first (1938) to describe and con-ceptualize this process, using as an example the forest in (what was then) French West Africa (Remmert 1991). These forests normally do not uni-formly pass from one stage of development to another in one develop-mental direction. Instead, different portions of the forest are in different stages of growth and decline. As one portion of the forest is reaching a mature state, another portion may only be starting its development after a disturbance. The result is a landscape with different patches in differing stages of development at any point in time, and in which the spatial dis-tribution of stages shifts over time, but the overall composition (in terms of the proportional representation of stages) remains relatively constant.

Watt (1947) referred to any patch mosaic exhibiting this property as the "unit pattern," which he defined as the full representation of the pattern in all its stages. Moreover, Watt suggested that the stages should be present in relative abundances corresponding to the duration of each stage. This is often heralded as one of the earliest and most lucid translations of temporal dynamics into spatial pattern.

There have been several other variations on this theme, most notably the "climax pattern" of Whittaker (1953) and the "shifting mosaic steady-state" of Borman and Likens (1979). Importantly, this form of landscape change is not limited to forests or other unmanaged landscapes. Portions of grasslands in many parts of the world may burn periodically, thus creating a mosaic of differently-aged plant communities. Selective harvesting or replanting of trees in forests may also create a shifting mosaic pattern. And a predominantly agricultural landscape in which farmers practice crop rotation could be seen as a shifting mosaic as well.

Many landscapes, especially those substantially altered by human intervention, do not exhibit shifting mosaic tendencies. Instead, landscapes may undergo a major transformation from one dominant land use to another. A forested landscape can be transformed into an agricultural landscape by human intervention. However, as human populations recognize the benefits associated with forested areas, some of these agricultural systems now incorporate woodlands or even large tracts of forest. This is true in many European forests such as the Veluwe in the central Netherlands. Some landscapes have reverted back to largely forested landscapes, as in New England. The same changes can occur between predominantly mixed agro-forest systems and suburban-urban areas, but in this case the reverse process is more difficult due to the frequently permanent and almost irreversible changes related to urbanization.

Disturbances are important drivers of landscape change. A disturbance is any relatively discrete event (natural or anthropogenic) in time that disrupts an ecosystem, community, or population structure, and changes resources, substrate availability, or the physical environment, including both destructive, catastrophic events as well as less notable, natural environmental fluctuations (White and Pickett 1985). Typically, a disturbance causes a significant change in the system under consideration (Forman 1995, 351). Fires, hurricanes, floods, insect outbreaks, volcanic eruptions, landslides, and land clearing for development can all be considered disturbances because they cause a change in the system.

Natural disturbances can be localized, such as small fires and storms, or cover large areas, such as insect defoliations and hurricanes. Some elements of the landscape may be resistant to certain natural disturbances, such as water being resistant to fire. Other landscape elements may facilitate certain disturbances, revealing an actual ecosystem dependency upon periodic disturbance, such as the chaparral in California where dry vegetation accumulates as fuel for wildfires. These ecosystems have evolved in response to fire, taking advantage of the release of nutrients after a fire occurs. Species may adapt reproductive and physiological strategies in order to survive and take advantage of environmental conditions created by the disturbance.

Anthropogenic disturbances can assume many forms, e.g., pollution, alteration of the rate of ecological processes, habitat destruction and fragmentation. In this handbook we emphasize fragmentation as an important landscape process that affects wildlife habitat. Some forms of anthropogenic disturbance may be linear in form, such as roads, railway lines, foot trails, and canals. Such transportation corridors, in addition to inhibiting movement of wildlife and nutrients, may represent a chronic form of disturbance where noise, litter, and chemical pollutants are introduced into the adjacent landscape elements (Forman and Deblinger 2000; Forman et al. 2003).

Disturbance is a normal part of every landscape that must be taken into account when plans are developed. Complete suppression of natural disturbances is, by definition, impossible. Understanding the disturbance regime, the spatial and temporal characteristics of disturbances (both natural and anthropogenic), is critical to the ecological and cultural success of a proposed plan. Landscapes should be managed to maintain ecosystem processes and the range of natural variability across scales. Events that characterize the variability found in natural ecosystems should be present and functioning. Resource managers often attempt to reduce the probability of events that are considered destabilizing to a landscape, such as floods and fires. Unfortunately, these attempts often lead to undesirable outcomes, namely dramatic changes in the natural cycles. These changes can be the cause of impacts much more damaging in the long term than the events themselves (De Leo and Levin 1997). For instance, flooding holds important consequences for nutrient inputs to surface water, as well as the social and cultural costs incurred when flooding displaces people. Also, disturbance can be critical to enhancing biodiversity by presenting opportunities for a variety of species to colonize a landscape. The suppression of disturbance, therefore, can have several deleterious effects, the most important of which may be the development of a homogenous landscape that is less resistant to future disturbance.

LAND TRANSFORMATION, HABITAT LOSS AND FRAGMENTATION

To provide for basic human needs like food, fuel, and housing, natural ecosystems are converted either to managed forest systems, agricultural systems, or residential systems. In fact, humans have converted 95% of the earth's terrestrial ecosystems to managed forest, agricultural, rural, and urban landscapes (Kim and Weaver 1994).

Loss and fragmentation of habitat is a typical process of landscape change and is one of the greatest threats to biodiversity worldwide (Sorrell 1998). In the last decades of the twentieth century, suburbanization around major cities occurred with significant impacts on forested areas and wildlife habitat. Suburbanization is spreading dramatically and affecting rural landscapes (Antrop 2000). Life-support systems are basically formed by agricultural systems and natural systems; the former providing food, the latter providing other physiological needs by purifying and recycling the air and water, and by stabilizing the climate (Odum 1989). Since cities are highly dependent on their surrounding countryside (Odum 1971; Rees 2003), it is crucial to acknowledge the importance of rural landscape conservation for human society. Even in urban planning *per se*, planners must acknowledge the relationships with the surrounding countryside and its multiple resources, and plan it as a whole unit, as illustrated by Ribeiro Telles' (1998) Global Landscape Concept.

During land transformation three main stages can be identified (Figure 1.7). *Dissection* and *perforation* dominate in the first stage. The construction of roads, power lines, corridors, or other linear features *dissect* the landscape. *Perforation* is caused by the introduction of nonlinear patches (e.g., agricultural fields, houses) within the matrix. In the second stage, the processes of *fragmentation* and *shrinkage* dominate, and the former processes decrease in importance. Fragmentation occurs when continuous natural areas are broken up or subdivided into disjunct fragments as development progresses. Shrinkage is the gradual reduction in area and increased isolation of remaining fragments as development increasingly dominates the landscape. In the third and final stage, *attrition*, i.e., the gradual loss of remaining fragments, leads to a new matrix of a developed land cover type (LCT), such as agricultural or urban residential.

Consider a binary landscape with only two land cover types: (1) forest, and (2) urban. In a simple land transformation process, forest is slowly replaced by urban development (Figures 1.8 and 1.9). In the relatively intact landscape, the majority of the landscape is occupied by forest. During the initial stages of land transformation, small amounts of forest are

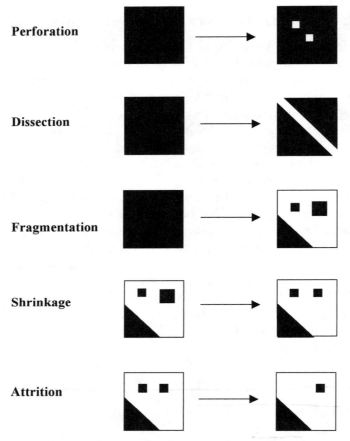

Figure 1.7. Forman's spatial stages of landscape transformation: perforation, dissection, fragmentation, shrinkage, and attrition. Forest habitat cover is represented in black; urban areas, including roads, are represented in white. *Forman 1995, 407*

incrementally lost. As perforation and dissection continue, individual patches of forest begin to appear (fragmentation). As development continues, the distance between forest patches increases. The forest patches then begin to diminish in size (shrinkage) and eventually disappear altogether (attrition) (Figures 1.7, 1.8, and 1.9).

Fragmented landscape patterns hold consequences for many aspects of the environment and human culture. Landscapes that are highly fragmented may have increased rates of soil erosion via wind and water, as well as increased rates of stream and river sedimentation. Fragmented landscapes are less likely to possess long tracts of land suitable for public

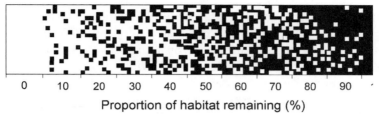

Proportion of habitat remaining (%)

Figure 1.8. Depiction of habitat fragmentation and loss in a simulated landscape. Forest habitat cover is represented in black; urban areas, including roads, are represented in white. *Adapted from Andrén 1994*

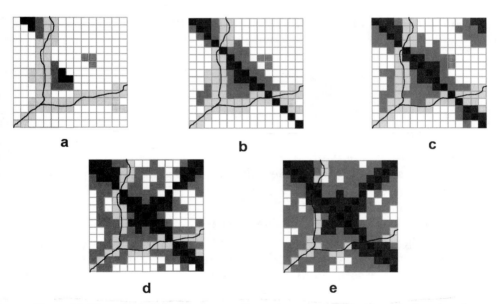

a

b

c

d

e

Figure 1.9. Hypothetical landscape transformation associated with agricultural and urban development. The landscape is composed of seven land cover types: road (black), urban (dark gray), agriculture (medium gray), riparian (light gray), forest (white), wetland (stipple), and meadow (cross hatch). The sequence illustrates a typical transformation in which the landscape changes from a forested landscape (a) to an agricultural/urban landscape (e).

recreation, such as riparian corridors. Wildlife populations are likely to suffer dramatic effects in fragmented landscapes (Andrén 1994). Human activities such as agriculture and urban development are obvious causes of habitat loss and fragmentation. Roads can also be a significant fragmenting factor, because they create access for humans to engage in extraction, recreational, or residential development activities. Roads can have several effects, namely the isolation of wildlife species that depend on core area habitat and/or are unwilling to cross open areas (Garland and Bradley 1984; Mader 1984 cited in Sorrell 1998). Roads also create artificial edges that opportunistic wildlife species exploit, and can be a major cause of mortality when individuals attempt to cross roads.

Forman (2000) and Forman and Deblinger (2000) estimate that transportation infrastructure in the U.S.A. affects one third of its total mainland. A similar impact exists in Europe where roads, waterways, and railways have been affecting landscapes for centuries, resulting in loss of habitats, fauna casualties, disturbance (noise and light), and local pollution influencing many animal species (IENE 1997, Ministry of Water Traffic Management, cited in Jongman 2002, 215).

1.4. Quantifying Landscape Structure

1.4.1. *What Are Landscape Metrics?*

Landscape metrics measure and describe the spatial structure of patches, classes of patches, or entire patch mosaics (i.e., landscapes). Metrics provide useful information about the composition or configuration of a landscape, e.g., the proportion of each land cover type present, or the size or shape of landscape elements. A major value of landscape metrics lies in their usefulness for comparing alternative landscape configurations, e.g., comparing different landscapes mapped in the same manner, evaluating the same landscape at different times, or comparing the same landscape under alternative scenarios (Gustafson 1998).

Landscape metrics measure two fundamental aspects of landscape structure: composition and configuration. *Landscape composition* refers to the variety and abundance of patch types without regard to their spatial character or arrangement. Composition metrics measure the number of patch types (i.e., patch richness), the proportional abundance of each patch type (i.e., class area proportion), and the overall diversity of patch types (e.g., Shannon's and Simpson's diversity indices). Although composition metrics are not spatially explicit, they still have important spatial effects (Gustafson 1998). *Landscape configuration*, in contrast, refers to the spatial character and arrangement, position, or orientation of landscape elements. Configuration metrics measure things such as patch shape and compactness, the distance between patches of the same class (i.e., nearest neighbor distance), the clumping of patches and patch types, and the degree of contrast along patch edges. Landscape composition and configuration affect ecological processes independently and interactively. Therefore it is especially important to understand what component of landscape pattern is being quantified by a particular metric (McGarigal et al. 2002).

1.4.2. *Patch, Class, and Landscape-Level Metrics*

Landscapes can be analyzed at four levels depending upon the desired emphasis: cell (available only when using raster, or grid, data), patch, class, and landscape (Figure 1.10). Cell-level metrics have not yet been well-developed or applied in landscape ecology, so we will limit our concern to the other three levels:

1. Patch level: a patch is a relatively homogeneous area that differs from its surroundings. In vector data, a patch is a polygon, classified as a specific land cover type. In raster or grid data, a patch is a cluster of like-valued cells based on either a four or eight neighbor adjacency rule. Patch-level metrics quantify characteristics of individual patches, such as size, shape, and nearest neighbor distance, and return a unique value for each patch (i.e., one record per patch). In many applications, patch-level characteristics are not interpreted directly, and instead they function simply as the basis for computing characteristics of an entire class of patches (i.e., land cover types) or of the entire patch mosaic. However, in some cases, a planner may be interested in the patch-level characteristics themselves. For example, one could be interested in identifying the largest single patch in a landscape to prioritize for biodiversity conservation.

2. Class level: a class is a set of patches of the same type (i.e., a land cover type). In vector data, a class is a set of polygons classified as the same patch type. In raster or grid data, a class is a set of like-valued cells, regardless of their patch affiliation (i.e., all cells with the same cell value). Class-level metrics quantify characteristics of an entire class (i.e., patch type), such as total extent, average patch size and degree of aggregation or clumping, and return a unique value for each class (i.e., one record per class). Most of the class-level metrics can be interpreted as fragmentation indices (in the broadest sense) because they measure the configuration of a particular patch type. In most applications, class-level characteristics are the primary focus because

the extent and fragmentation of a particular class (or classes) is the principal concern. For example, a planner may be interested in knowing the total area of forest, the average size of forest patches, the average distance between forest patches, or in comparing the total area of forest to the total area of other cover types (e.g., residential or urban). Note that many of the class-level metrics are derived from the patch-level metrics by summing or averaging over all patches of the corresponding class. For example, mean patch size is based on the size of individual patches of the corresponding class.

3. Landscape level: a landscape is a set of all patches within the area of interest. In vector data, a landscape is the entire collection of polygons, regardless of patch type. In raster or grid data, a landscape is the entire collection of cells, regardless of class value. Landscape-level metrics quantify characteristics of the entire patch mosaic, such as the diversity of patch types, average patch size and degree of clumping, and return a unique value for the entire landscape (i.e., one record per landscape). Landscape-level metrics characterize the overall composition and configuration of the patch mosaic without reference to individual patches or patch types. Most of the landscape-level metrics can be interpreted broadly as landscape heterogeneity indices because they measure the overall landscape pattern. Like class-level metrics, many of the landscape-level metrics are derived from patch or class-level metrics by summing or averaging over all patches or classes.

There are a few important caveats regarding the patch-class-landscape hierarchy. First, because all patch-level metrics can also be summarized at the class and landscape levels, it is important to interpret each metric in a manner appropriate to the level. For example, at the patch level, patch area describes the size of a patch in isolation, but denotes nothing of fragmentation *per se*; whereas, at the class level, mean patch area (in conjunction with total class area or number of patches) describes an important aspect of fragmentation of the corresponding class. Similarly, at the landscape level, mean patch area (in conjunction with total landscape area or number of patches) describes the overall patchiness or heterogeneity of the landscape, but denotes nothing of fragmentation *per se*, which is a class-level phenomenon. Thus, the same basic metric (patch area) has a different interpretation at each level of the hierarchy.

Second, not all metrics have counterparts at all three levels of the hierarchy. In particular, some metrics are unique to the class or landscape levels. For example, the number of different patch types (i.e., patch richness)

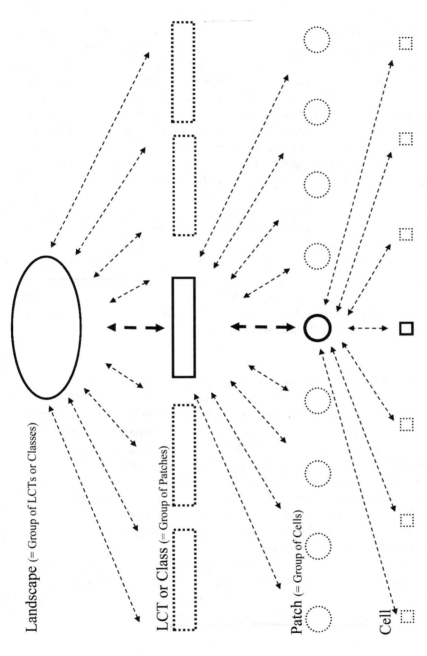

Figure 1.10. Conceptual diagram of the four levels of analysis provided in the metrics included in the handbook: cell, patch, class/land cover type (LCT), and landscape.

and their degree of clumping (i.e., <u>contagion</u>) are only relevant at the landscape level. Similarly, the proportion of the landscape comprised of a particular class (i.e., class area proportion) is only relevant at the class level.

Lastly, despite the use of the patch-class-landscape hierarchy for organizing the quantification of landscape structure, not all metrics are inherently patch based. That is, not all metrics are derived from the spatial properties of patches *per se*, which are aggregated into classes and then into the landscape. For example, the total length of edge or the degree of contrast along those edges does not depend explicitly on the patch structure *per se*; the same total edge length could be derived from wildly varying numbers and shapes of patches. In addition, with raster or grid data, it is possible to derive characteristics from the spatial properties of individual cells, regardless of their patch affiliations. For example, the degree of clumping at the landscape level (i.e., contagion) is derived from the matrix of cell adjacencies, which shows the frequency with which different pairs of patch types (including like adjacencies between the same patch type) appear side-by-side on the map. Thus, while all metrics are tied to one or more levels of the patch-class-landscape hierarchy for purposes of reporting, they are not all formulated based on the patch mosaic organization on which the hierarchy is based.

1.4.3. *Variability*

In many applications, second order statistics, such as the variation in patch size, may convey more useful information than first order statistics, such as mean patch size. Variability in patch size measures a key aspect of landscape heterogeneity that is not captured by mean patch size and other first order statistics. Measuring variability is useful since averaging statistics can camouflage important phenomena, such as an uneven distribution of values and the occurrence of outliers (e.g., very small or very large patches). For example, consider two landscapes with the same patch density and mean patch size, but with very different levels of variation in patch size. Greater variability indicates less uniformity in pattern, either at the class level or landscape level, and may reflect differences in underlying processes affecting the landscapes. However, even second order statistics such as the variance can be difficult to interpret as they mask the details of the exact underlying distribution. Ultimately, it may be most informative to <u>evaluate the actual distribution itself.</u>

1.4.4. *Computing Landscape Metrics*

In the last two decades significant advances have been made in computing, mathematical theory, and systems analysis. These theories and tools are promising for addressing the level of complexity associated with sustainability. As the scale of planning moves from the site or ecosystem level, to the landscape or regional level, data volume increases exponentially. Holism and systems theory have become central paradigms in ecologically-based planning to address the horizontal dimensions and hierarchical (vertical) levels inherent in natural systems. To address the huge volumes of data, the complexity of planning issues, data visualization requirements, and public involvement in the planning process, tools such as Geographic Information Systems (GIS), Artificial Intelligence Systems, and Spatial Decision Support Systems have become more and more common in planning.

In landscape planning, GIS has become a fundamental tool not only for the storage and management of information (cartographic and alphanumeric) that results from spatial analysis, but also in the processing of this information to construct and analyze alternative future landscape scenarios (Burrough 1986; Steinitz 1993; Haynes-Young et al. 1994; Hulse et al. 1997; Steinitz et al. 1998; Ahern et al. 1999; Hanna 1999; Theobald et al. 2000; Botequilha Leitão 2001; Botequilha Leitão and Ahern 2002; Hulse et al. 2002; Steinitz et al. 2003). GIS can play an important role in all phases of planning and decision making:

Data Input, Storage and Management: creating and updating spatial data layers (e.g., topography, land cover, etc.) and managing the spatial database.

Analysis: analyzing spatial relationships within or among data layers (e.g., terrain analysis, landscape pattern analysis, etc.).

Modeling/Simulation: modeling/simulating spatial relationships (e.g., creating alternative planning scenarios, simulating visual impacts of proposed projects, etc.).

Outputs: creating maps to facilitate the planning and decision-making process and to communicate results (e.g., public presentations).

In this handbook, we use the software FRAGSTATS for computing landscape metrics (McGarigal et al. 2002). We adopted FRAGSTATS for several reasons: (1) it contains the most relevant landscape metrics, (2) it supports distribution statistics such as median, average, range, standard deviation, etc., (3) it includes a complete user's guide with a description of the theoretical and mathematical basis for each metric, (4) inputs/outputs are compatible with a wide range of GIS software including ArcGIS (ESRI), and (5) it is available online as freeware at the FRAGSTATS web site at the University of Massachusetts, Amherst (http://www.umass.edu/ landeco/research/fragstats/fragstats.html). In addition, FRAGSTATS is the tool of choice in basic and applied ecological literature as in Diaz (1996), Zorn and Upton (1997), Hargis et al. (1998), Tinker et al. (1998), Tischendorf (2001) and others.

GIS has several imbedded functions that support the gauging of some of the ten metrics without the use of FRAGSTATS. The computation of polygon area (patch size) and perimeter length (patch edge), and the number of polygons (patch number), either disaggregated by land cover type, or computed for the entire landscape map, is relatively easy to compute in most GIS software. They are the basis for computing an entire range of metrics included in the FRAGSTATS software, for example:

- Patch Richness (PR) is readily available in GIS maps, either in raster or vector format, as the number of LCTs or land use classes that show up in a legend of a particular mapped landscape.

- Class Area Proportion (CAP) is calculated by averaging the area of all polygons (patches) of a same LCT.

- Patch Number (PN) is simply the number of patches of an LCT, or for all patches, of all LCTs, across the entire landscape.

- Mean Patch Size (AREA_MN) is computed by calculating the average of polygon areas for a specific LCT.

- Euclidean Nearest Neighbor Distance (ENN) is usually a built-in option in standard spatial analysis GIS software menus.

- The remaining five metrics proposed in this handbook, shape (SHAPE), radius of gyration (GYRATE), proximity index (PROX), edge contrast (ECON) and contagion (CONTAG), are not readily available in most GIS software packages, but are calculated by FRAGSTATS.

2

Planning the Landscape
A Spatial Ecological Approach

First and foremost, approaches to planning for sustainable landscapes and regions involve the maintenance of natural resources. This form of sustainability planning also tries to manage the spatial patterns of land use and land cover to address ecological, social, and economic components of a landscape. Although the principle of sustainability is challenged by virtually no one, many challenges and questions arise with its implementation (Ceña 1999). Landscape metrics are useful tools to address these challenges.

2.1. Planning and Landscape Ecology

Planning seeks to optimize the distribution of land uses in a limited space (van Lier 1998b). In other words, the goal of planning "is to organize functions and space in such a way that it shows the best mutual relationship, or to develop human and natural potentials in a spatial framework in such a way, that all can develop as well as possible" (Buchwald and Engelhardt 1980, cited in Jongman 2002, 217).

Until recently, it was uncommon for ecological theory to be applied in spatial planning (Botequilha Leitão and Ahern 2002; Ndubisi 2002). Moreover, planning was rather sector-oriented, more likely to be single-purpose (Fabos 1985) than holistic.

2.1.1. *Single-Purpose Planning*

The spatial realm of planning can be represented as a triangle (Figure 2.1). The multiple activities and approaches of planning lie along a continuum defined by the three principal types of landscape resources: abiotic, biotic, and cultural (ABC); each type of resource is located in one

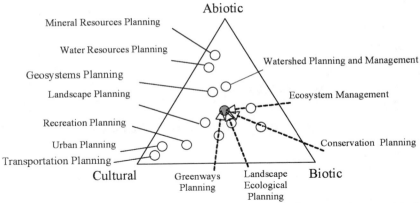

Figure 2.1. The abiotic, biotic, and cultural resource continuum and representative planning disciplines. Differences are largely a matter of the degree of emphasis on particular landscape components. This diagram must be understood as dynamic as several disciplines (dashed arrows) are evolving towards a more integrated perspective as represented by the center circle.

pole of the triangle. Abiotic resources include water, mineral resources, and soils. Biotic resources include flora (e.g., forests, prairie, shrublands), and fauna (e.g., game, fish and wildlife). Finally, cultural resources include places where people live and work, communication networks, recreation, and those more intangible human values such as providing for scenic beauty, and preserving human cultural diversity (e.g., sacred places, some cultural landscapes, and historical buildings and sites).

2.1.2. *Going Beyond Single-Purpose Planning*

Historically, planning along the resource triangle (Figure 2.1) has not been static. In the early 1990s, traditional approaches to natural resource management were widely considered ineffective for promoting the goal of sustainability (Szaro et al. 1998). In planning, as in contemporary science, a paradigm shift has occurred to encompass a broader, more comprehensive vision for human development (Capra 1996; Botequilha Leitão 2001; Naveh 2001; Ahern 2002; Steiner 2002). Thus, planning activities have been converging towards the center of the triangle, which represents a more integrated approach.

For example, water resource planning has evolved towards a watershed approach in which all ABC resources are considered together (Ferreira and Botequilha Leitão 2006), thus taking into account the relationships with other activities such as forest management, recreation, and urban development.

Mineral resource planning has evolved towards a more integrated approach based on the concept of a geosystem (Pereira 2000; Botequilha Leitão and Muge 2001; Botequilha Leitão 2001).

Similarly, conservation biology has moved from single-species management to ecosystem management, and from a focus on isolated reserves to the management of the entire landscape (With 1999; Müssner and Plachter 2002). Although often originating with a recreational focus, greenways planning also combines planning for cultural and natural goals (Ahern 2002).

Ecosystem management emerged for land use management in the United States with sustainability as its overall goal (Grumbine 1994). Federal land use management agencies, collectively responsible for approximately thirty percent of the landmass of the United States, have implemented ecosystem management widely (Coulson et al. 1999). While each agency or organization defines ecosystem management somewhat differently, at least two characteristics are common: (1) management must be built on ecological science and on understanding ecosystem function, and (2) humans are integral components of ecosystems (Bartuska 1999).

Landscape ecological planning and ecosystem management share similar goals and tools (Botequilha Leitão and Ahern 2002). However, the former derives from land use planning, which is typically human-oriented, and the latter originates from natural resource management. In the last decade we have seen the increasing integration of ecological values in the planning and management of both natural resources and human habitat. This convergence around environmental awareness, together with more comprehensive planning, has reduced the gap between landscape ecological planning and ecosystem management. They coalesce into a common body of theory and goals identified under the idea of sustainable land use planning (Botequilha Leitão 2001; Botequilha Leitão and Ahern 2002). They both incorporate new paradigms such as the evaluation of alternative future scenarios, adaptive management and monitoring, and collaborative methods to allow for citizens' participation in the planning process (Hulse et al. 1997; Theobald et al. 2000; Botequilha Leitão 2001; Hulse et al. 2002).

In a broader perspective, planning is practiced to resolve the majority of land use issues simultaneously. Planners label this approach "comprehensive planning." Alternatively, planning can focus on a limited range of goals such as water quality protection, the protection of biodiversity, or the enhancement of recreation. It can also encompass overlapping goals and objectives. Not all planning activities are comprehensive, but that does not mean that the single-purpose planning should not be framed by a broader vision and consider the interrelationships with the environment and with other planning activities and land uses.

2.1.3. *Applying Scientific Principles in Planning*

Planning is both a science and an art, with synthesis as a cornerstone (Costa Lobo 1997). However, the gap between basic science and its application is wide and complex (Ahern 1999; Opdam et al. 2002; Müssner and Plachter 2002). And there is an urgent need to counteract this trend and promote cooperation between these disciplines (Botequilha Leitão 2001; Ferreira and Botequilha Leitão 2006).

One reason for planning to incorporate science is to be more replicable, systematic, and consistent. This would lend transparency to the planning process, and contribute to a wider public acceptance of planning recommendations. Engineering sciences as well as agriculture and forestry have a long tradition of applying quantitative scientific methods and standards with a wide range of acceptance (Müssner and Plachter 2002). This effort would also serve to provide a common language and improve dialogue between planning sectors that generally do not apply quantitative scientific methods.

For some time, planners have applied quantitative techniques (Fabos 1985). Spatial pattern statistics, including landscape metrics, are important quantitative tools that can support the application of ecological principles to planning in a more rigorous manner (Botequilha Leitão 2001). Landscape metrics can be valuable planning tools that provide for a rich source of objective, quantitative, and replicable information.

An important role for landscape metrics is to provide indicators for decision making and planning that reflect some of the important pattern-process relationships within the landscape (Opdam 1997; Verboom 2001). Indicators, in general, focus on relevant characteristics of a system and provide a way of assessing a larger suite of resources, species, or processes (Müssner and Plachter 2002; Botequilha Leitão 2001).

Planning involves making decisions about how a landscape will be used and transformed. The level of detail may vary from a general policy to explicit manipulations of landscape features. Ultimately, planning anticipates and guides change. Without change, there is no need for planning. In order to manage landscape change, the planner must be aware of the characteristics that are likely to change. In order to detect these changes, measurements of these factors must be performed before, during, and after the change has occurred. Planners can more fully appreciate and understand the consequences of their actions upon a landscape by adopting many of the measurement tools available from landscape ecology.

Landscape ecology provides useful conceptual and analytical tools, particularly landscape metrics, to bridge the gap between planning and ecology. Pattern-process relationships are a crucial prerequisite to ecological planning as they form the basis for understanding the functioning of landscapes, and the information needed to model and anticipate ecological consequences of planning and design alternatives. Table 2.1 illustrates

Table 2.1. Landscape functions and processes can be understood as the relationships between landscape structure (matrices, patches, and corridors) and abiotic, biotic, and cultural (ABC) resources. These relationships are considered to work both ways, such as the influence of roads on wildlife (pollution), and of wildlife on roads (car accidents).

Structure	Abiotic Resources (Water)	Biotic Resources (Vegetation, Wildlife)	Cultural Resources (Housing and Recreation)
Matrix Urban	Consumption: drinking water, industry, etc. Cleansing of buildings and pavements Comfort, e.g., cooling Intangible values, such as aesthetics Imperviousness—less infiltration and increased runoff, and depletion and lowering of groundwater levels Surface and ground-water pollution	All urban ecosystems, including urban parks and gardens, provide for numerous functions such as climate regulation, air recycling, water infiltration, wildlife habitats, recreation, diversity and aesthetics, increase of property value, etc. Pollution source (air, water, noise, aesthetics)	Human habitat and movement Recreation and leisure Production of information and cultural artifacts (construction materials, clothing, computers, TV sets, etc.) Scientific research (universities, laboratories, etc.)
Forest	Infiltration and filtration of rainfall flowing into aquifers Water cycle regulation Pollution buffering by riparian forests	Main habitats to wildlife species, mainly interior species	Timber as a construction material Recreation Functions associated with urban ecosystems (see above) Aesthetics Scientific research for forestry and wildlife management
Patches Agriculture	Irrigation Surface and ground-water pollution	Pest control (integrated protection) Habitat for generalists Intensive agriculture: potential source of disturbance for specialists (pesticides, noise from heavy machinery, etc.)	Food production Aesthetics (rural landscapes)—if intensive can turn landscapes rather homogeneous Scientific research

(continues)

Table 2.1. *Continued*

Structure	Abiotic Resources (Water)	Biotic Resources (Vegetation, Wildlife)	Cultural Resources (Housing and Recreation)
Wetlands	Filtration Infiltration Water cycle regulation	Habitat for wetland species Water source for terrestrial species	Control for point and non-point pollution Flood control Recreation and aesthetics Scientific research
Corridors			
Roads	Cleansing of roads Car pollution source Increase run-off concentration times Erosion Flooding due to culverts	Car accidents by medium to large terrestrial mammals Tree shading in parking lots Flood control (parking lot islands—see Low Impact Development techniques) Corridor and barrier, Major cause for habitat fragmentation, Perturbation source, facilitating penetration by people, Pollution source (air, water, noise, aesthetics)	Movement Transport Recreation
Major Rivers	Water movement Flood control Nutrient and materials movement Interface between surface and groundwater	Habitat for larger species, bird and other small to medium sized riparian species Important corridor for movement of other species, especially large mammals, Plant seed dispersion Barrier	Movement Transport Recreation Aesthetics Comfort, e.g., air cooling Media where sewers are rejected

Source: Adapted from Botequilha Leitão 2001; Botequilha Leitão and Ahern 2002

how a landscape ecological perspective can help to relate landscape functions, flows, and processes to landscape structural elements, as referenced to the three selected ABC resources: abiotic, biotic, and cultural.

2.2. Planning Landscape Resources

Below we provide a brief discussion of the three ABC resources, introduced earlier (section 2.1.1). These are also used in the planning examples in chapter four. For our discussion, we will use the following sequence template: (a) definition of the resource, (b) importance of the resource, (c) threats to the resource, and (d) planning the resource, and questions planners might ask that could benefit from landscape metrics. The ABC resources have traditionally been addressed in three major planning sectors: watershed planning and management, conservation planning, and urban and recreation planning.

2.2.1. *Abiotic Resources (Water)*

Water resources are an essential component of any sustainable natural or human system (CO-DBP 2001, 1). Water resources include surface features such as rivers and streams, water bodies such as ponds and lakes, wetlands, and groundwater systems, such as water tables and aquifers. Water resources also include the entire stream corridor ecosystem, which includes the floodplain and the transitional upland fringe (Wells et al. 1998). An even wider perspective would address water resources at the watershed level, and consider the interactions between aquatic and non-aquatic components (e.g., France 2002), both below and above ground (Ferreira and Botequilha Leitão 2006).

Water is the most fundamental resource in any landscape. It provides for linkages between all landscape components that otherwise could be disconnected or isolated. The Scottish geologist James Hutton compared the earth's waters to the circulatory system of an animal (Capra 1996). The hydrological network forms the living vascular system for ecosystems, and water flows are critical for all processes (e.g., nutrient transport, animal movement, and the aesthetic and cultural enhancement of human life). Landscape ecological concepts and metrics can play a critical role by analyzing land use and land cover (the landscape pattern) and critical flows (landscape processes or function), and help to establish relationships between them. This is critical if planners strive to plan for sustainability.

Fresh water constitutes only 2.7% of the earth's overall water mass, and to a large extent it is in a frozen state in the polar caps and the snow cover of high mountains (CO-DBP 2001). According to Vitousek et al. (1997) and Rosen (2000), more than 50% of all accessible surface fresh water is currently used by humanity. The quantity of water available per capita is now no more than 7,000 m^3, as against 17,000 m^3 as recently as 1950 (CO-DBP 2001). By 2025 demand for fresh water is projected to increase by more than 70%. A substantial amount of this water (70%) is withdrawn for agricultural uses, with significant costs to downstream ecosystems and users (Vitousek et al. 1997; Rosen 2000), 6% of world consumption is for domestic use, and 20% is for industry (CO-DBP 2001).

There is a change of paradigms in water resource planning which

includes watershed management (Ferreira and Botequilha Leitão 2006).
Watershed management is being adopted to improve and sustain water
quantity and quality. An example is the Quabbin Reservoir in central
Massachusetts. This 24,000-acre reservoir is the major source of drinking
water for the greater Boston area. The Massachusetts Department of
Conservation and Recreation manages Quabbin with multiple objectives
including watershed protection, water yields, watershed forest management, minimizing air pollution impacts, and wildlife conservation (MDC
1995; Barten et al. 1998).

To provide some simple guidelines to plan and manage water
resources more sustainably, we use Forman's (1995) indispensable patterns as a framework that will be used to address all ABC resources in this
handbook:

1. Maintain large patches of native vegetation. Large patches support
   the most important water resource functions: interception and infiltration of rainfall and runoff, and filtration and cleansing by soil.
   These ecological processes can be particularly important if the large
   patches are located above aquifer recharge areas. When located in the
   headwaters, large patches promote water infiltration at the highest
   altitude in the watershed. In this way overall flows through the watershed are regulated and stabilized.

2. Maintain wide riparian corridors. These support the major flows
   across the landscape of energy, water, nutrients, and wildlife species.
   They also serve as major transportation corridors, and as a source of
   aesthetic experiences (Linton et al. 1974; Saraiva 1999). Riparian corridors also stabilize stream flow and buffer nutrient movements from
   adjacent land uses.

3. Maintain connectivity between important resource patches to allow
   for water to flow freely and continuously across the landscape.
   Obstructions to hydrological connectivity, such as dams, can serve as
   obstacles both to water flow and to aquatic species including salmon
   that require hydrological network continuity to migrate and spawn.
   Roads often intersect the hydrological network impairing the profile
   and natural regime of streams.

4. Maintain heterogeneous bits of nature throughout human-developed
   areas. This refers to the need to assure smaller, isolated water features
   throughout production landscapes such as farmland and managed forest. These bits of nature can provide stepping stones for wildlife
   species, thus allowing species to survive even in these mostly human-

dominated environments. They bring diversity, of both an ecological and aesthetic nature, and can contribute to the enrichment of landscape experiences such as recreation, birdwatching, contemplation, etc. In arid climates such as the Mediterranean, isolated water features introduce a vital feature in the wide rural landscapes dominated by vineyards and cereal fields (e.g., wheat).

Landscape metrics can support the application of landscape ecology concepts for water resource planning. Questions that watershed managers and other ecosystem managers can pose and could be supported by landscape metrics include (see Table 2.4 for information about which metrics could be of use in responding to these questions):

- What is the relative importance of the many aquatic resources in the landscape?
  - Do aquatic or terrestrial features dominate the landscape?
  - Are wetlands large and numerous or small and rare?
  - Are aquatic features, e.g., lakes and ponds, concentrated in one part of the landscape, or dispersed throughout?

- How does the spatial distribution of land cover types and land uses influence water quality and quantity?

  - Do the headwaters of the watershed include land uses that represent a potential hazard for water supply and control (e.g., impervious areas, and/or land uses with industrial hazards)?
  - Are the main rivers and streams bordered by land uses or activities that generate high pollution levels?
  - How have land use changes affected water quantity and quality in the past?
  - Are there better landscape patterns to protect water resources?

2.2.2. *Biotic Resources (Wildlife and Biodiversity)*

The Convention on Biological Diversity defines biological diversity, or biodiversity, as "the variability among living organisms from all sources, including terrestrial, marine and other aquatic ecosystems and the ecological complexes of which they are part; this includes diversity within species, between species and of ecosystems" (UNEP 1995, 8). More simply stated, biodiversity is the variety of life and its processes (Peck 1998, 3). From a strictly operational point of view, biodiversity is approached in this handbook mainly at the landscape level, i.e., diversity between ecosystems or land cover types.

At all times, the maintenance of life support systems depends on the proper functioning of biological and ecological cycles (O'Callaghan 1996, 7). Since human culture is ultimately dependent upon the proper functioning of ecosystems worldwide, changes in biodiversity are particularly important to continued human well-being. People are as much a part of the ecosystems within the landscape as other species; therefore a plan for the conservation of biodiversity is incomplete if it doesn't consider the interaction of human culture and activity with wildlife biodiversity, and the consequences of these interactions.

The maintenance of biodiversity is crucial to the supply of food and pharmaceuticals, and also contributes to wealth and economic stability, ensuring the viability of ecosystems, and from a purely ethical perspective biodiversity holds intrinsic value (Freemark et al. 1996). Planning for biodiversity simultaneously provides important collateral benefits for people including: access to outdoor recreation, educational opportunities, improved water quality, and economic health (Ahern et al. 1998; White et al. 1999).

Common issues that are related to biodiversity and to broadscale landscape pattern include:

• Survival of rare plant and animal species, communities, and ecosystems
• Nutrient cycling
• Water quality
• Control of plant and animal populations
• Preservation of genetic information
• Preservation of pharmaceutically-valuable plants and animals
• Preservation of culturally-important species
• Preservation of the wild ancestors of present-day crop plants

Human impact on biological diversity is manifold. Habitat loss, primarily from urbanization and agriculture, is the single largest cause of species endangerment globally (Wilcove et al. 1998; Czech et al. 2000; Hilton-Taylor 2000, cited in Groves et al. 2003, 5). Forest cover has been reduced worldwide by at least 20%, and perhaps by as much as 50%. Some forest ecosystems, such as the dry tropical forests of Central America, are virtually gone, and grasslands have been reduced by more than 90% in some areas. Approximately 25% of the bird species on earth have been driven to extinction, and 20% of the freshwater fish species have become extinct, threatened, or endangered in recent decades (Rosen 2000).

In the United States the number of species listed as threatened and endangered under the Endangered Species Act (ESA) has increased sevenfold from 174 in 1976 to 1,244 in 2001 (USFWS Service, http:// endangered.fws.gov, cited in Groves et al. 2003, 4). Several initiatives have been put forward to counteract the trend of biodiversity loss at the continental scale, such as the national GAP Analysis Program (Scott et al. 1993; Davis et al. 1998; Jennings et al. 2000). Biodiversity is also a major concern in the European Union where nature conservation is embodied in several directives, and has led to the development of the NATURA 2000 European-wide ecological network (Devillers and Beudels 2001; Opdam 1997).

Biodiversity protection can be achieved at several different levels of organization ranging from species to communities of organisms to ecosystems and landscapes. In addition, the relative richness and proportions of different land cover types, and their spatial arrangement over the landscape have important implications for ecosystems, communities, and species. Since landscapes can be conceived of as broad-scale patterns of ecosystems, the proportionality and number of different types of ecosystems within the landscape is another form of biodiversity.

Landscape ecology offers a scientific framework to plan for biological diversity (Forman 1995; Peck 1998; Botequilha Leitão 2001). Forman's four indispensable patterns (1995) referenced earlier also provide some useful guidelines to plan and manage biotic resources under a landscape perspective (Table 2.4):

1. Maintain large patches of native vegetation (forests, shrubs, grasslands, and wetlands). These plant communities provide habitat for animal populations. The quantity and quality of the large patches have a direct and indirect influence on the total number and diversity of species in these systems. As a general rule, the larger the patch, the better it is for wildlife conservation.

2. Maintain wide riparian corridors. In addition to the functions already mentioned for water resources, riparian corridors provide important habitat for both aquatic and terrestrial species, e.g., for invertebrates, fish, amphibians, reptiles, birds, and mammals. Corridors also serve as conduits for species to move across the landscape.

3. Maintain connectivity between important resource patches to allow

for key processes to flow freely across the landscape, and to support the survival of spatially segregated populations in fragmented landscapes.

4. Maintain heterogeneous bits of nature throughout human-developed areas. Important small patches can serve as stepping stones between large areas of habitat. Patches of natural vegetation, be they forest, grassland, or meadows of wildflowers, can provide for the presence of nature and diversity in more human-dominated environments, particularly in suburbs and cities.

In *Drafting a Conservation Blueprint*, Groves et al. argue that although Forman's guidelines are oversimplified from a biodiversity standpoint, they may prove useful "in the face of limited biological information for assisting the design of a network of conservation areas," and "in portions of the world in which very little is known about the biodiversity other than different types of major ecosystems that dominate the large remaining patches in a matrix of otherwise semi-natural or anthropogenically converted habitats" (Groves et al. 2003, 253–254). Planners frequently deal with situations where data is available but not in a form that provides useful information to integrate the planning and decision-making process (Botequilha Leitão 2001). By looking at landscape structure, planners can gain insights on landscape functioning. Thus, a landscape ecological approach based on structure-function relationships can be extremely useful when species-specific data is limited due to its focus on functional relationships with habitats. These relationships can be established based on land use and land cover maps, which are frequently more available than species-specific habitat maps (Fernandes 2000).

Some specific questions that can be raised by conservation planners and wildlife biologists where landscape metrics can have a supporting role include (see also Table 2.4):

- What is the relative importance of the several biotic resources in the landscape?
  - Are there many land cover types or just a few? Are there any particularly dominant land cover types?
  - How many patches of the habitat type of interest, e.g., oak forest, are available?
  - How many patches of the habitat type of interest fulfill the minimum area requirements of the species, or group of species of concern?
- How does the spatial distribution of land cover types influence habitat quality and quantity?
  - How far apart are habitat patches from one another?

– Are there any land cover types located such that they can act as barriers to wildlife movement between major resource patches? Are there patches that can provide for conduits linking them?

• How should a land acquisition program establish priorities for the purchase of land for conservation purposes? Which area(s) should be purchased first, considering the conservation value of the area(s), the proximity of the area(s) to other lands with conservation value, or the isolation of the area(s) from human influence (Miller 2000)?

2.2.3. *Cultural Resources (Housing and Recreation)*

Cultural resources are typically not a priority in natural resource planning. They relate, by definition, to human needs such as cities and suburbs, transportation networks (highways, train lines, etc.), and with less tangible values such as recreation or cultural activities. Landscape cultural features associated with recreation include traditional landscapes including military battlefields, old mill towns, urban neighborhoods, Native American burial grounds, or scenic landscapes such as Yosemite Valley or the Grand Canyon.

Global urbanization is one of the most urgent issues in planning. A rapidly growing proportion of the world's population now lives in or near cities. Urban population multiplied *tenfold* in absolute numbers in the twentieth century. The urban proportion of the world's population has risen from 14% in 1900 to nearly 50%, or three billion people, in 2000 (Rosen 2000). Alig et al. (2004) reports that 80% of the U.S. population in 2000 lived in urban areas, and that number is increasing, whereas the non-urban population is relatively stable. According to Antrop (2000, 257) the world urban population is estimated to reach 4.8 billion in 2025. This rapid increase in urban population has resulted from (1) a natural increase in total population (largely due to a declining death rate), (2) the migration of rural populations to urban places, and (3) the reclassification of rural settlements to "urban" status or the expansion of existing cities (Brown and Jacobson 1987 cited in Platt 1994). Very large urban regions have grown dramatically in number and absolute population. In many less developed countries, primary cities have been growing at twice the rate of national populations, in some cases doubling within a decade, as in Mexico City (Teitelbaum 1992; 1993 cited in Platt 1994). Quality of life and of the environment in general is less and less acceptable for the majority of people living in large metropolitan areas (Platt 1994; Reis, Machado, and Ahern 1997; Pimentel et al. 1999; Swenson and Franklin 2000; Devuyst et al. 2001).

Table 2.2. Expansion of population and urbanized land area in metropolitan areas in the U.S.

Metropolitan Area	Change in Population 1970–1990	Change in Urbanized Land 1970–1990
Chicago	+4%	+46%
Los Angeles	+45%	+300%
New York CIty	+8%	+65%
Seattle	+38%	+87%

Source: Platt 1994

Urban fringe areas are acutely affected by this global trend. "Most habitat loss in the USA during the last 25 years has occurred as a result of urban growth. The nation's metropolitan areas are currently consuming land at a much faster rate than they are adding population. While the USA's metropolitan population increased 28 percent from 1970 to 1990, its metropolitan land area increased 82 percent" (Bureau of the Census, 1990, cited in Landis et al. 1998, 1) (Table 2.2).

Urbanization affects the countryside over increasingly vast areas (Antrop 2000). When competing with urban functions, rural functions will often decline or adapt, causing a number of problems for abiotic resources, biodiversity, agriculture, and outdoor recreation (Jongman 2002).

But urban development is not the only driver of landscape change. Agricultural landscapes are also subject to rapidly increasing rates of change, with negative and positive impacts (Moss 2000). For example, in Portugal, while traditional agricultural practices, like cork production, are being abandoned, industrial pulp production is expanding at the expense of biodiversity and landscape character. This is due to several policies including forestation programs in the 1960s and 1980s (Moreira et al. 2001), and more recently to the Common Agriculture Policy of the European Union (Pinto-Correia 1993; Firmino 1999; Pinto-Correia and Mascarenhas 1999).

Physical planning has historically been preoccupied with urban planning, focusing on urban centers and the suburbs, without much concern for the rural areas or metropolitan regions as a whole. Urban development frequently occupies land in an irreversible manner. Transportation networks divide land that was once continuous. Roads also represent a vehicle for the distribution and penetration of pollution throughout the landscape (Forman et al. 2003). Recreation has impacts on ecosystems, by promoting human activities that disturb and change natural systems, e.g., trampling vegetation, littering, causing noise, starting fires. Urban and metropolitan planning has typically overlooked the interrelationships between urban and other human infrastructure-related functions and the natural environment as well as the ecological functions that sustain human habitat. In recent decades, environmental engineering has made progress in mitigating some of the impacts on the environment by, for example, improving air and water quality, and reducing noise. However, protective measures for separate environmental threats are not sufficient to plan a more sustainable environment, and an integrated approach based on landscape ecological concepts is becoming ever more important (Jongman 2002).

Human activities need not be so aggressive towards nature and can be integrated into the natural ecosystems. Many cultural landscapes provide good examples of the successful integration of cultural and natural heritage. Cultural and natural heritage is increasingly recognized in international documents, culminating recently in the UNESCO statement on Cultural and Natural World Heritage that explicitly states the need for jointly conserving the world's natural and cultural heritage (Barata and Mascarenhas 2002). In response to this new concept, a new classification emerged for UNESCO World Heritage Sites, of which the Sintra landscape in Portugal was one of the precursors (Botequilha Leitão 2001).

Again we use the template followed earlier to provide for some simple guidelines to plan and manage cultural resources more ecologically (Table 2.4):

1. Maintain large patches of native vegetation. In rural landscapes these constitute important scenic resources. Natural landscape diversity and complexity can contribute to richer aesthetic experiences. Additionally, recreation, particularly passive (contemplation, birdwatching, etc.), requires the kind of quiet and sometimes secluded environment found in the core of large forested areas and urban parks.

2. Maintain wide riparian corridors. Besides all the functions mentioned for both water and biotic resources, these areas can provide for important cultural functions, e.g., for recreation, and by providing for cultural identity.

3. Maintain connectivity between important resource patches to provide people with a "continuum" of experiences, when moving from one resource patch to another, or moving across the landscape. Examples of linkages between resource patches include greenways, bikeways, and trails.

4. Maintain heterogeneous bits of nature throughout human-developed areas. Urban parks or public gardens, even roof gardens, are good examples of how an "oasis of nature" in cities can provide contact with the natural environment and for less tangible human needs (Berkowitz et al. 2003).

Some questions that landscape planners can pose and that can be supported by landscape metrics are (see also Table 2.4):

• What is the relative importance of the key cultural resources in the landscape?
  – What is the proportion of different land uses in the landscape under consideration, e.g., urban, suburban, industrial, mixed use, etc.? Is there any particular type that is dominant (the landscape matrix)?
  – How have these proportions changed over time?
• How is the spatial distribution of land cover types and land uses influencing the quality of human habitat and landscape experience?
  – Where are the best places to protect and where should further urban development be permitted?
  – Are intensive land uses or activities too close to recreational areas?
  – Where should new parks be located within an urban park system? How many and at what size; one large park or several smaller parks? And should we promote round, compact shapes, or more linear spaces (e.g., greenways, ecological corridors)? And where should linkages between parks be promoted to improve access?
  – Where are the best scenic locations to restore? How should the restoration of sites be prioritized?

2.3. A Method of Planning for Sustainability

A structure of five planning phases can help to clarify planning theory and its application: *focus, analysis, diagnosis, prognosis, and sinteresis* (Botequilha Leitão 2001; Botequilha Leitão and Ahern 2002) (Figure 2.2). These stages are filtered from a significant body of literature, and represent a new synthesis of ecologically-based planning. Below we provide a brief description for each of these phases.

1. *Focus*

   This first phase defines and addresses the goals and objectives of a plan. As the problem identification phase, it includes scoping by identifying key components and processes (Treweek 1999). Since the sustainable planning process should be highly dynamic and iterative, the goals and objectives may be reviewed as many times as appropriate through the planning process or after implementation by adaptive management. Stakeholder and public involvement is desirable at this early or iterative stage of the process.

An important output of the focus phase is a _preliminary vision_ (Bastian 2001) for the landscape of interest, which synthesizes the overall goals and objectives. It is a first draft of a desirable future for landscape development. Focus also informs analysis by informing planners where they should spend the efforts on collecting and analyzing data.

2. _Analysis_

Analysis focuses on the characterization of the study area and its landscape context in several dimensions, i.e., environmental, economic, and social. It assesses abiotic, biotic, and cultural (ABC) resources through both a parametric approach looking at each resource separately, and through a holistic approach where the focus is on relationships between components and processes. Landscape units provide an integrated tool for holistic landscape analysis. This phase provides information on the key processes: ecological, socio-economic, and cultural, that most determine landscape functions as identified in the former phase, and how these are influenced by the different elements that form the landscape. Landscape perception and cultural patterns and processes should be integrated with ecological pattern-process analyses (Bell 1999). Landscape history and temporal dynamics provide the necessary background to understand past and present landscape change, and support visioning of the future. Public participation is deemed crucial to incorporate local knowledge into these studies.

3. _Diagnosis_

This phase represents a landscape diagnostic, as done by a medical doctor, who after examining a patient gives a first assessment of the patient's health (Bólos 1992). Based on landscape analysis, a diagnostic includes both values and issues of concern, occurring both in the present (strengths and weaknesses) and in the future (opportunities and threats). It attempts to answer the following questions: Is the landscape functioning well? If not, where is it not functioning well and why? Where and how is it functioning well? Will it keep functioning in the future? Final output of this phase is to be able to identify the main landscape values and (spatial) dysfunctions or conflicts, and where these are located in order to be addressed in the final plan.

4. _Prognosis_

Prognosis comes from the Greek words _pro_ (before) and _gnosis_ (knowledge) (Bólos 1992). This phase is directed to develop possible visions on how the landscape could change to meet goals and to assure that

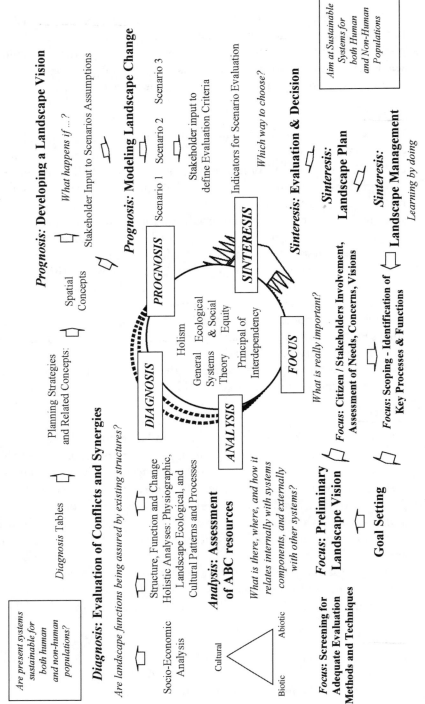

Figure 2.2. The sustainable land planning framework. *From Botequilha Leitão 2001*

the direction of those proposed changes leads overall towards a more sustainable condition. Again comparing with medicine, it forms a landscape prognostic. In this phase we can consider different steps, i.e., designing spatial concepts and supporting criteria for selecting planning strategies, designing planning scenarios, and evaluating and comparing those scenarios against the goals defined in the focus phase. The preliminary vision drafted in the first phase informs alternatives explored and evaluated in this phase.

Ahern (1995) proposed a typology comprised of four planning strategies: protective, defensive, offensive, and opportunistic. For example, an offensive strategy is appropriate when the landscape is already deficient with respect to supporting abiotic, biotic, and cultural (ABC) resources. Guided by a spatial concept, it promotes a "possible" future landscape that can be realized only through restoration or regeneration. Those four strategies are not mutually exclusive. Rather, they are more often used in an integrated manner.

In the prognosis phase we recommend the use of scenarios, based on spatial concepts, as a strategic approach to develop and implement landscape plans. Scenarios can be employed in strategic planning to achieve surprising yet plausible plans and unexpected results. Scenarios can be of two fundamental types: state or process. State scenarios do not specify the required steps to get to the future. Process scenarios specify implementation steps and are classified in two types: (1) in its common usage, as a sequence of events, building on the present and exploring trends into the future-explorative, descriptive, forecasted, or beginning-state driven scenarios, e.g., the "Build-Out" and the "Business-As-Usual" (BAU) or "Trend" scenarios, and (2) those based on a vision of the future-anticipatory, backcasted, end-state driven, prescriptive, or normative scenarios (Ahern 1999; Alcamo 2001).

In order to evaluate planning scenarios, criteria are defined based on previous assumptions or goals for the future landscape. Scenarios are developed according to different strategies that are expressed spatially in a plan or in a spatial concept. Metrics can be applied to assess the potential impacts of the proposed changes on the patterns that affect processes of concern, e.g., biodiversity or hydrological functions. The metrics are first computed on the base scenario and again for comparison with the proposed scenarios (Ahern et al. 1999; Steinitz 1990; Botequilha Leitão 2001; Botequilha Leitão and Ahern 2002). A scenario can then be chosen based on the evaluation of impacts, and on the pre-set goals and objectives for abiotic, biotic, and cultural resources.

5. *Sinteresis*

This term comes from the Greek word *syntereo*, which means to preserve (Bólos 1992). Preservation is not seen as a mere traditional conservative act, but rather as promoting, encouraging, welcoming, and providing guidance for landscape transformation (Corner 1999). In this phase, plans and actions are defined in order to prevent future negative impacts on the landscape and to assure its sustainable functioning. This phase is the time at which the actual plan is designed and implemented. Ultimately, the plan is framed by the goals and objectives identified primarily at the focus stage and refined throughout the entire planning process. The plan aims to respond to the issues identified in the diagnosis stage by exploring the several hypotheses developed at the prognosis stage, and selecting those found most useful to achieve the planning goals. Sinteresis also includes landscape management activities such as adaptive monitoring of the ongoing processes and changes.

"Sustainability is a goal that no one as yet knows how to achieve. The act of sustainable planning and design is a heuristic process; that is, one in which we learn by doing, observing, and recording the changing conditions and consequences of our actions" (Franklin 1997). Within this framework, planning can be approached as an adaptive process where monitoring plays the key role of providing updated information to feed an ongoing process. Therefore, monitoring is essential to design sustainable systems because it allows one to learn through a planning process. For example, in a context of biodiversity conservation, monitoring is defined as the "periodic and standardized measurement of a limited and particular set of biodiversity variables in specific sample areas" (UNEP 1997, 12). It can be done at different levels. Noss and Cooperrider (1994 cited in Lee and Bradshaw 1998) divide monitoring into four basic types: baseline, implementation, effectiveness, and validation.

1. Baseline monitoring is used to establish baseline reference conditions that can be used to quantify a change that might be due to management activities.

2. Implementation monitoring, sometimes called compliance monitoring, is simply tracking to see if management direction is accurately interpreted and followed.

3. Effectiveness monitoring is intended to measure whether progress is being made towards an objective.

4. Validation monitoring seeks to verify the assumed causal linkages between cause and effect.

Landscape ecological concepts and metrics are useful in all types of monitoring:

• Describing patterns (baseline monitoring)
• Allowing for future comparisons (baseline monitoring, implementation monitoring, and effectiveness monitoring)
• Modeling structure-function relationships (validation monitoring)

Additionally, landscape monitoring can be accomplished through different activities, to address multiple aspects, or attributes, of environmental quality, e.g., water quality for human consumption, habitat for selected species, or urban growth around a protected area as proposed or applied by Riitters et al. (1995), Zorn and Upton (1997), Tinker et al. (1998), Botequilha Leitão (2001), Botequilha Leitão and Ahern (2002), and Lausch and Herzog (2002).

Examples of large continental monitoring programs using landscape metrics include the U.S. Environmental Monitoring and Assessment Program (EMAP) (EPA 1994 and 1995), which uses metrics as biodiversity indicators, the Organisation for Economic Co-operation and Development (OECD) program, which uses landscape indicators to measure the environmental performance of agriculture (NIJOS and OECD 2002), and the programs being developed within the European Union to assess and monitor European landscape character and diversity (EC 2001; Wascher 2004; Wascher and Perez-Soba 2004).

2.4. Applying Landscape Metrics in Planning

Landscape metrics are well-known among scientists engaged in landscape ecological research. The intent of this handbook is to facilitate communication between scientists and practitioners and, specifically, to assist planners in the use of landscape metrics in the planning process. Unfortunately, as most landscape metrics were developed for ecological applications, they do not always have a straightforward application for planning. Therefore, we had to go "out of the box" somewhat to extend the use of landscape metrics for planning. Despite these challenges, we believe that there are clear and diverse roles for landscape metrics in planning. In the following sections we briefly describe the role of landscape metrics in planning, introduce a set of ten core metrics, and discuss the proper use and limitations of landscape metrics for planning.

2.4.1. *The Role of Landscape Metrics Applied to Planning*

Landscape metrics measure the composition (i.e., the variety and abundance of patch types) and spatial configuration (i.e., the spatial character and arrangement, position, or orientation) of landscape elements. Moreover, landscape metrics can be used to characterize individual landscape elements (e.g., individual patches), collections of landscape elements of the same type (e.g., unique patch types or land cover classes), and entire collections of diverse landscape elements (e.g., entire patch mosaics). Thus, landscape metrics can be used to characterize a wide variety of spatial patterns. These spatial patterns can affect a wide variety of ecological processes, which, in turn, can affect spatial patterns. Understanding this interplay between spatial patterns and processes is the principal focus of landscape ecology. The versatility of landscape metrics to characterize a broad array of spatial patterns (as a means to facilitate understanding of pattern-process relationships) provides a diverse role for landscape metrics in planning applications.

Because of the relationships between spatial patterns and processes, landscape metrics (i.e., measures of landscape pattern) can inform planners about landscape functions, which are often difficult or impossible to measure directly. In this regard, landscape metrics can help answer questions such as: "which alternative landscape design results in the least habitat fragmentation, or maintains the greatest degree of habitat connectivity?" Planners often work with qualitative relationships in the form of "is scenario one better than scenario two for species *y*?" (Jongman 1999). In such cases, landscape metrics provide quantitative scientific information that can lead to insights about the qualitative relationships (Jongman 1999; Verboom and Wamelink 1999; Botequilha Leitão and Ahern 2002).

Landscape metrics can be particularly useful when planning for natural and cultural resources or planning for sustainable land use. The literature is rich with examples of the use of landscape metrics for resource planning, e.g., water resources (Jones et al. 2001; Ferreira et al. 2003), mining (Hardt and Forman 1989; Botequilha Leitão and Muge 2001), forest resources (Franklin and Forman 1987; Diaz 1996; Moreira et al. 2001), wildlife management and conservation planning (McGarigal and Marks 1995; McGarigal and McComb 1995; Freemark et al. 1996; Schumaker 1996; Pino et al. 2000; Theobald et al. 2000; McGarigal et al. 2002; Botequilha Leitão et al. 2004; Neel et al. 2004; McGarigal and Cushman 2005), rural planning (Dunn et al. 1991), urban development planning (Landis et al. 1998), transportation planning (Forman et al. 2003), environmental impact assessment (Fernandes 2000; Genelleti and Pistocchi 2001), ecological risk assessment (Graham et al. 1991), landscape planning (Iverson 1988; Linehan et al. 1995; Hulse et al. 1997; Ahern et al. 1999a; Miller 2000; Ahern 2002; Botequilha Leitão and Ahern 2002; Varela 2005), landscape monitoring (EPA 1995; O'Neill et al. 1997; Zorn and Upton 1997; EC 2001; Lausch and Herzog 2002; NIJOS and OECD 2002; Wascher 2004; Wascher and Perez-Soba 2004), and cultural resources (Hunziker and Kienast 1999; Palmer 2004).

Landscape metrics can also be particularly useful as environmental indicators, and as proxies or surrogates for difficult-to-measure variables needed by complex ecological models. Similarly, due to the high complexity of natural systems, it is very difficult, if not impossible, to assess every aspect of biodiversity (De Leo and Levin 1997; Simberloff 1998; Treweek 1999). Landscape metrics can provide a measure of the amount and spatial configuration of land cover types (e.g., natural communities), and thereby provide a "coarse-filter" assessment of biodiversity. In addition, as noted above, landscape metrics can provide insights about the spatial distribution of suitable habitat for individual species of concern, and thereby may also serve as part of a "fine-filter" assessment of biodiversity.

Earlier we introduced a five-phase planning method. Table 2.3

Table 2.3. A vertical perspective for the applications of landscape metrics across the five planning (sustainable land planning or SLP) phases.

SLP Phases	Landscape Metric Roles
1. Focus	- Preliminary analysis and diagnosis: describe spatial patterns - In a dynamic (i.e., iterative and cyclic planning process) landscape, metrics are useful to re-evaluate the initial goals according to method updates and monitoring results
2. Analysis	- Describe spatial patterns - Model pattern-process relationships - To be used as an integration tool for different ecological resources
3. Diagnosis	- Identify landscape dysfunctions through interpretation of metrics, i.e., spatial conflicts
4. Prognosis	- Analyze historical patterns and model possible trends in landscape change
4.1 Planning Strategies	- Assist the selection of planning strategies
4.2 Scenario Design—the Spatial Concepts	- Provide insights to assist spatial concept design - Evaluate landscape performance under different
4.3 Evaluation of Scenarios	scenarios; metrics are particularly adequate (but not restricted) to evaluate the ecological component of landscapes
5. Sinteresis 5.1. Monitoring	- Monitor the implementation and success of several management actions under an experimental design, using plans and projects as potential experiments to improve planning solutions for sustainable landscapes

Source: Botequilha Leitão 2001; Botequilha Leitão and Ahern 2002

Table 2.4. The role of landscape ecological concepts and metrics in planning. This table illustrates the potential use of landscape metrics by integrating a horizontal perspective across the planning realm (e.g., planning for ABC resources) and a vertical perspective (e.g., throughout a planning process) under the sustainable land planning (SLP) framework.

SLP Phases/ Planning ABC Resources	Abiotic Resources Water Resources Planning	Biotic Resources Conservation Planning	Cultural Resources Urban and Recreation Planning
1. Focus What are the most important issues? Define planning goals.	Preliminary analysis and diagnosis: describe spatial patterns. In a dynamic, i.e., iterative and cyclic planning process landscape metrics (LM) are useful to re-evaluate the pre-set goals according to methodological updates and monitoring results.		
2. Analysis How does the landscape work? Which are the key landscape elements and functions of concern?	Q: Is the hydrological system dense or sparse? LM: PN/PD, ENN_AM. Is it connected? LM: GYRATE_AM. Are there many wetlands? Are they large or small? LM: CAP; PN/PD; AREA_MN, AREA_AM.	Q: Which are the main and broadest processes of concern? Identify the matrix. –LM: CAP.	Q: What is the matrix? –LM: CAP. Q: What is the historical pattern of land use change, i.e., urban patterns across time? LM: analyze CAP, PN/PD, AREA_MN, AREA_AM for n time periods.
3. Diagnosis Is the landscape functioning at appropriate/ acceptable levels? Identify landscape dysfunctions/spatial conflicts, and opportunities.	Q: How is the water cycle performing overall? Look for the degree of imperviousness as an indicator. –LM: CAP of impervious LCTs (e.g., urban, roads). Q: Are there spatial conflicts between land uses and activities, and water protection requirements? Look at ECON_AM between riparian corridors and potential harmful uses to identify these conflicts. –LM: ECON_AM.	Q: Is the landscape fragmented? How much? Look at overall clustering –LM: CONTAG. Look at LCT of interest, i.e., for the number of patches and its average size: LM: PN/PD, AREA_MN, AREA_AM; and its physical connectivity –LM: GYRATE_AM, and isolation –LM: ENN_AM; PROX_AM.	Q: Is development following any particular spatial trends? Look for concentration of urban LCTs versus their dispersion. LM: CONTAG, GYRATE_AM; for spatial conflicts –LM: ECON_AM. Q: How much is the urban/ suburban landscape humanized? Look for geometric versus irregular/ complex patterns –LM: SHAPE_AM.
4. Prognosis 4.1. Scenario design– spatial concepts 4.2 Scenario evaluation	Q: Which is the more efficient solution to protect water resources? Look for adjacencies of uses that are environmentally conflicting –LM: Compare ECON_AM across alternatives. Compare imperviousness across scenarios –LM: CAP of impervious LCTs (e.g., urban, roads)	Q: Which is the scenario that minimizes important habitat disruption? Use LM to compare area: CAP, size: AREA_MN, AREA_AM, number of patches: PN/PD; patch connectivity: GYRATE_AM.	Q: Where to locate new parks within an urban landscape? Use metrics to identify isolated parks –LM: ENN_AM, PROX_AM.

SLP Phases/ Planning ABC Resources	Abiotic Resources Water Resources Planning	Biotic Resources Conservation Planning	Cultural Resources Urban and Recreation Planning
5. Sinteresis (design and manage final plan) 5.1. Monitoring	Q: Are aquatic habitats decreasing in quantity and quality? Monitor losses (in of number and area) riparian corridors, wetlands, and surface water bodies –LM: PR, CAP, AREA_MN, AREA_AM. Monitor the degree of imperviousness as an indicator of overall impact of urban and roads on water resources quality –LM: CAP.	Q: Are habitats decreasing? Monitor losses (in area and number) –LM: PR, CAP, AREA_MN, AREA_AM and levels of fragmentation –LM: GYRATE_AM, PROX_AM, for the most critical habitats.	Q: How is the city complying in providing open space (OS) areas for recreation? Monitor the amount of open space— LM: CAP, as an indicator for compliance. Are parks close enough to provide for continuity of OS throughout the city? Monitor distance and connectivity between OS patches –LM: ENN_AM, GYRATE_AM.

Source: Adapted from Botequilha Leitão 2001; Botequilha Leitão and Ahern 2002

Note: Q = Questions that planners and managers ask about the landscape; LCT = land cover types; LM = examples of landscape metrics that can be useful to address those questions; CAP = Class Area Proportion; PN = Patch Number; PD = Patch Density; AREA_MN = Mean Patch Size; AREA_AM = Area-weighted Mean Patch Size; SHAPE_AM = Area-weighted Mean Shape Index; ECON_AM = Area-weighted Edge Contrast Index; ENN_AM = Area-weighted Euclidean Nearest Neighbor Distance; PROX_AM = Area-weighted Proximity Index; GYRATE_AM = Area-weighted Mean Radius of Gyration, or Correlation Length; PR = Patch Richness; CONTAG: Contagion.

provides a synopsis of the use of landscape metrics in each planning phase. We also propose that landscape metrics be applied across various types, or sectors, of planning. Table 2.4 provides examples of the use of landscape metrics in several planning phases and applications.

2.4.2. Selecting a Core Set of Landscape Metrics for Planning Applications

There are two major components of landscape pattern—composition and configuration—and only a few aspects of each of these components (McGarigal et al. 2002). Landscape metrics often measure multiple aspects of pattern. Thus, there is seldom a one-to-one relationship between metric values and pattern. Most of the landscape metrics are in fact correlated among themselves (i.e., they measure a similar or identical aspect of landscape pattern) because there are only a few primary measurements that can be made from patches (patch type, area, edge, and neighbor type), and most metrics are then derived from these primary measures. Some metrics are inherently redundant because they provide alternate ways of representing the same basic information (e.g., mean patch size and patch density). In other cases, metrics may be empirically redundant; not because they measure the same aspect of landscape pattern, but because for the particular landscapes under investigation, different aspects of landscape pattern are statistically correlated. Several investigators have attempted to identify the major components of landscape pattern for the purpose of identifying a parsimonious suite of independent metrics (e.g., Li and Reynolds 1993; McGarigal and McComb 1995; Riitters et al. 1995). Although these studies suggest that patterns can be characterized by only a handful of components, consensus does not exist on the choice of individual metrics.

Based on an analysis of the literature and consultation with experts in the field, we reduced the list of potential landscape metrics to a "core set" of ten metrics. We do not claim that the particular metrics included in this set are necessarily the "best," or that collectively they represent a comprehensive set of landscape pattern attributes. However, we expect that this core set of landscape metrics addresses the typical needs of planners and managers to measure and understand landscape composition and configuration.

Core Landscape Metrics

Landscape Composition Metrics:

1. Patch Richness (PR): the number of different patch types (or classes) present in the landscape.

2. Class Area Proportion (CAP): the proportion of the landscape comprised of a particular patch type (or class).

Landscape Configuration Metrics:

3. Patch Number (PN)/Patch Density (PD): the number or density of discrete patches in the landscape or of a particular patch type (or class).

4. Patch Size, e.g., AREA (AREA_MN, and AREA_AM): the size of discrete patches, summarized across all patches of a particular patch type (or class) or across all patches in the landscape as a simple arithmetic mean or as an area-weighted mean patch size.

5. Patch Shape (SHAPE): a standardized measure of patch shape complexity, calculated for each discrete patch and then summarized across all patches of a particular patch type (or class), or across all patches in the landscape as a simple arithmetic mean or as an area-weighted mean patch shape index.

6. Edge Contrast (ECON): a relative measure of edge contrast, where "contrast" is user-defined based on contrast coefficients between each pairwise combination of patch types (or classes) (i.e., each unique edge type), calculated as a percentage of maximum edge contrast. ECON

can be computed for each discrete patch and then summarized across all patches of a particular patch type (or class) or across all patches in the landscape as a simple arithmetic mean or as an area-weighted mean patch shape index. Alternatively, ECON can be computed for each discrete edge segment (without respect to patches per se) and then summarized across all edge segments involving a particular patch type (or class) or across all edge segments in the landscape.

7. Patch Compaction (GYRATE): a measure of patch extensiveness (or, alternatively, patch compaction), calculated for each discrete patch as the mean distance between each cell in the patch and the patch centroid, and then summarized across all patches of a particular patch type (or class) or across all patches in the landscape as an area-weighted mean.

8. Euclidean Nearest Neighbor Distance (ENN): the Euclidean distance between each discrete patch and its nearest neighboring patch of the same patch type (or class), summarized across all patches of a particular patch type (or class) or across all patches in the landscape as a simple arithmetic mean or as an area-weighted mean nearest neighbor distance.

9. Proximity Index (PROX): an index of patch isolation accounting for the amount (i.e., size) and proximity (i.e., distance) of neighboring patches of the same patch type (or class) surrounding a focal patch, calculated for each discrete patch and then summarized across all patches of a particular patch type (or class) or across all patches in the landscape as a simple arithmetic mean or as an area-weighted mean proximity index.

10. Contagion (CONTAG): a measure of the degree to which patch types (or classes) occur in clumped distributions as opposed to being dispersed in many smaller fragments; a measure of the tendency of patch types to be spatially aggregated; that is, to occur in large, aggregated or "contagious" distributions.

2.4.3. *Use and Limitations of Applying Landscape Metrics to Planning*

While landscape metrics can greatly facilitate the job of planning landscapes, they are not without important limitations. It is critical that planners understand these limitations in order to ensure proper use of landscape metrics in the planning process. Several authors have considered in detail issues concerning the use and limitations of landscape metrics, especially as they pertain to planning. For example, Botequilha Leitão

Ahern (2002) discuss the use of landscape metrics in planning and ,vide a set of recommendations and caveats for their use. Based on a ;view of the literature, Varela (2005) discusses the use and misuse of landscape metrics in general and evaluates metric behavior in response to changes in scale. Corry and Nassauer (2005) discuss the limitations of using landscape metrics to evaluate the ecological consequences of alternative plans and designs. Here we provide a brief summary of the most important models and the issues that are most prevalent in the literature. Note, these concerns pertain in general to the application of landscape metrics; limitations pertaining to each metric individually will be discussed in chapter three.

The Categorical Landscape Model

Conventional landscape metrics (i.e., those included in this handbook) measure the composition and spatial configuration of categorical patch mosaics. Under the patch mosaic model of landscape structure, a landscape is represented as a collection of discrete patches. Major discontinuities in underlying environmental variation are depicted as discrete boundaries between patches, while all other variation is subsumed by the patches and either ignored or assumed to be irrelevant. This model has proven to be quite effective. Specifically, it provides a simplifying organizational framework that facilitates experimental design, analysis, and management consistent with well-established tools (e.g., FRAGSTATS) and methodologies (e.g., ANOVA). Indeed, the major axioms of contemporary landscape ecology are built on this perspective (e.g., patch structure matters, patch context matters, pattern varies with scale). However, even the most ardent supporters of the patch mosaic paradigm recognize that categorical representation of environmental variables often poorly represents the true heterogeneity of the system, which often consists of continuous multi-dimensional gradients. Yet, alternative models of landscape structure (McGarigal and Cushman 2005) based on continuous environmental variation are poorly developed. So, for the time being, planners must be content with using landscape metrics based on the patch mosaic model and be cognizant of the implications of assuming a discrete model of landscape structure. Patch-based landscape metrics such as those discussed here are only as good as the model of landscape structure is at representing the real landscape. Thus, the first question one must ask before using landscape metrics in a planning application is: "Does the patch mosaic model represent landscape heterogeneity in a meaningful way?"

THE MAP CLASSIFICATION SCHEME ✳ *Consider for Resistance Values*

Ultimately, as noted above, a landscape metric is only as good as the map it represents, and a critically important aspect of a categorical map is its classification scheme. The categories selected (both the number and variety of classes and the criteria for assigning locations to a class) will have an important influence on the numerical results of any landscape pattern analysis (Turner et al. 2001). In this regard, there are a number of important considerations.

First, does the classification provide a consistent resolution of categories; that is, are the classes discerned at a comparable resolution across the entire classification? For example, does the classification include *wetlands* as a single class, yet break up *forest* into several different forest types? Is *developed* a single class or is it broken down into several different classes, and how does this compare to the classification of *undeveloped* areas? It is not required that the classification resolution be consistent across all classes, only that the relevance of the particular classification to the objectives of the planning application are considered, and that the implications of the particular classification for the quantitative assessment of landscape patterns are recognized.

Second, does the classification include *all* the important landscape elements relevant to your application, especially the fine-scale elements? For example, does the classification include linear landscape features (e.g., roads, streams, hedgerows) and small patch-forming elements (e.g., vernal pools, gravel pits) that may be relevant to your planning application? It is important to determine whether each relevant landscape element is represented in the classification, regardless of whether it is intended as a focus for analysis (e.g., forest as a focal class for considering biodiversity conservation issues) or merely as a landscape feature having a critical effect on a focal class (e.g., roads as fragmenting features of forest).

Third, regardless of the classification scheme, the criteria for interpreting categories should be explicit. For example, the criteria for classifying a forest into deciduous, mixed, or coniferous forest could vary from one application to another depending on the data sources and the objectives of the application, and the differences could lead to very different mapped patterns for the same landscape. To ensure proper interpretation of maps and their patterns, and to facilitate comparison among maps and applications, attention must be given to making the classification criteria explicit.

In summary, the key point is to recognize that map classification is a critical consideration in the interpretation of landscape metrics. Ultimately, the map must be classified in a manner appropriate to the planning application or the computed metrics will have little meaning. For example, if the map represents habitat patches based on species-specific requirements, then landscape metrics such as mean patch size can provide direct information about the capacity of a landscape to provide habitat for those species. On the other hand, if the map represents general land use classes, then landscape metrics may have little meaning regarding habitat conservation for individual species of concern.

THE IMPORTANCE OF SCALE

The following discussion on scale is taken, with permission, from the FRAGSTATS manual (McGarigal and Cushman 2005).

The ability to detect pattern is a function of scale, and the spatial scale of ecological data encompasses both extent and grain (Forman and Godron 1986; Turner et al. 1989; Wiens 1999). *Extent* is the overall area encompassed by an investigation or the area included within the landscape boundary. *Grain* is the size of the individual units of observation. For example, a fine-grained map might structure information into 1-ha units, whereas a map with an order of magnitude of coarser resolution would have information structured into 10-ha units (Fig. 2.3) (Turner et al. 1989). Extent and grain of a particular landscape define the upper and lower limits of resolution in your ability to characterize landscape patterns; you cannot generalize beyond the extent of the landscape and you cannot detect pattern below the resolution of the grain.

It is critical that extent and grain be defined for a particular application and represent, to the greatest possible degree, the phenomenon under study. Otherwise, the measured landscape patterns will have little meaning and there is a good chance of reaching erroneous conclusions. For example, it would be meaningless to define grain as 100-ha units when evaluating forest fragmentation if the sensitive organisms respond to forest patches at a resolution of 1-ha. A strong landscape pattern at the 100-ha resolution may have no significance to the phenomenon (forest fragmentation) under consideration. Similarly, it would be meaningless to define the landscape extent as 1-km^2 when the organisms under consideration only respond to forest fragmentation over much larger areas. Typically, however, it may not be possible to know what the appropriate resolution should be. In this case, it is much safer to choose a finer grain than is believed to be important because the grain sets the minimum resolution of investigation. A general rule of thumb is to use a grain that is two to five times smaller than the smallest landscape element of interest (O'Neill et al. 1997). For example, to

Figure 2.3. Grain is a scale issue in landscape analysis. The images show a fine- and a coarse-grained landscape.

represent linear features (e.g., riparian areas) as narrow as 100 m wide, then the grain should be set to be less than say 30–50 m. Once set, it is always possible to resample to a coarser grain. In addition, a minimum mapping unit can be specified that is coarser than the grain. That is, the minimum patch size can be specified to be represented in the landscape, and this can easily be manipulated above the grain size. Indeed, it may be useful to reanalyze the same landscape using progressively coarser minimum patch sizes to better assess landscape heterogeneity across a range of potentially relevant scales. Thompson and McGarigal (2002) used this approach successfully to define the "best" scale (grain and extent) for representing bald eagle habitat along the Hudson River in New York.

It is important to recognize the practical implications of the choice of grain and extent for a particular application. Many landscape metrics are sensitive to grain. Metrics involving edge or perimeter will be affected (e.g., patch shape index). Edge lengths will be biased upwards in proportion to the grain size; larger grains result in greater bias. Edge lengths can vary by as much as 25–50% over vector calculations depending on grain size. Metrics based on cell adjacency information such as the contagion index will be affected as well, because grain size affects the proportional distribution of adjacencies. In this case, as resolution is increased (grain size reduced), the proportional abundance of like adjacencies (cells of the same class) increases, and the measured contagion increases. Similarly, many landscape metrics vary in relation to extent, especially if the landscape structure is not uniform within the broader geographic context. Intuitively this makes sense, because as the landscape extent increases, new patch types may be encountered and patch configurations may change in response to underlying environmental or land use gradients.

The ratio of grain to extent for a particular analysis warrants consideration as well. If the ratio is very small (i.e., a coarse-grained map), then the landscape dynamics are likely to be dominated by boundary effects, analogous to the bias associated with small sample size in statistics. Moreover, the boundary of the landscape can have a profound influence on the value of certain metrics. Landscape metrics are computed solely from patches contained within the landscape boundary. If the landscape extent is small relative to the scale of the organism or ecological process under consideration, and the landscape is an "open" system relative to that organism or process, then any metric will have questionable meaning. Metrics based on nearest neighbor distance or employing a search radius can be particularly misleading. Consider, for example, a local population of a bird species occupying a patch near the boundary of a somewhat arbitrarily defined landscape. The nearest neighbor within the landscape boundary might be quite far away, yet, in reality, the closest patch might be very close but just outside the designated landscape boundary. In addition, metrics that employ a search radius (e.g., proximity index) will be biased for patches near the landscape boundary because the searchable area will be much less than a patch in the interior of the landscape. In general, boundary effects will increase as the landscape extent decreases relative to the patchiness or heterogeneity of the landscape. The key point is that some landscape metrics are likely to be very sensitive to this ratio (e.g., those based on nearest neighbor distances such as the mean proximity index).

Information may be available at a variety of scales and it may be necessary to extrapolate information from one scale to another. In addition, it may be necessary to integrate data represented at different spatial scales. It has been suggested that information can be transferred across scales if both grain and extent are specified (Allen et al. 1987), yet it is unclear how observed landscape patterns vary in response to changes in grain and extent. The limited work on this topic suggests that qualitative and quantitative changes in measurements across spatial scales will differ depending on how scale is defined (Turner et al. 1989), and that metrics vary markedly in their sensitivity to scale and the nature of the scaling relationships (Benson and McKenzie 1995; Wickham and Riitters 1995; O'Neill et al. 1997; Saura and Martinez-Millán 2002; Saura 2002; Wu et al. 2002; Baldwin et al. 2004). Until more is learned about scaling relationships, any attempts to compare landscapes measured at different scales should be done cautiously.

In summary, the key point here is that any model of landscape structure requires an explicit identification of scale. Unfortunately, in many applications, scale is selected arbitrarily or defined by technical considerations and the significance of the scale-imposed limitations are dismissed or not recognized. In any planning application, it is incumbent upon the planner to select a scale (i.e., extent, grain, minimum mapping unit) that is appropriate to the application, because any interpretation of landscape structure is ultimately constrained by the scale. The scale of change and manipulation being proposed in the landscape plan should guide the choice of scale. In addition, any observed patterns or relationships should be described relative to the limitations imposed by the scale of the investigation.

THE DATA MODEL

There are two basic digital data models relevant to landscape mapping: *vector* and *raster* (Figure 2.4). Each has its strengths and weaknesses. In the vector model, landscape features are represented as polygons, lines, and/or points. The vector model is typically used when the data is derived manually, for example when digitizing landscape features from aerial photos, or when the features of interest are best represented as lines (e.g., roads, streams), and/or points (e.g., groundwater pumping station, fire lookout towers). The vector model is also often used when it is appropriate to represent features that occupy area (e.g., ownership parcel, pond), and when those features are associated with a suite of descriptive attributes (e.g., parcel size, owner, assessed value). The vector model is common in architecture, urban studies, some landscape architecture and land use studies, and agronomy. This data model is frequently advantageous when representing parcel boundaries since the representation by means of a line, or set of lines, is more accurate than the raster, or cell-based format. The vector model is generally more efficient from a data storage and management standpoint than the raster model.

In the raster model, the landscape is represented as a uniform grid of cells, where each cell occupies a fixed area. Each cell takes on a value or

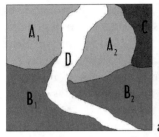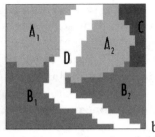

Figure 2.4. Data representation on digital maps: (a) vector-based, and (b) raster- or cell-based.

values based on the character or condition that best describes the landscape at that location. For example, in an elevation grid, each cell takes on a value that represents the average elevation at that location. Similarly, in a land cover grid, each cell takes on a value that represents the land cover class (usually the dominant land cover) at that location. The raster model is frequently used in environmental studies where spatial modeling is often involved. It is also common in environmental studies to use remotely sensed data, which usually has a native raster format.

The raster model has several advantages over the vector model in the realm of spatial data analysis. For example, it is relatively easy to perform calculations such as mathematical operations on a cell-by-cell basis. In addition, it is relatively easy to evaluate the spatial location and context of a cell (e.g., its location relative to another landscape feature) through the use of rows and columns as Cartesian coordinates. These properties facilitate the analysis of spatial patterns using the raster data model.

It is important to realize that the depiction of edges in the raster model is fundamentally constrained by the lattice grid structure. Consequently, the raster model has an inherent bias in how boundaries are represented (Figure 2.5). Vector maps portray lines, including patch edges, in the true form as they are digitized. In contrast, raster models portray lines in a stairstep fashion. The result is an upward bias in the measurement of edge length; that is, the measured edge length is always more than the true edge length. The magnitude of this bias depends on the grain or resolution of the image (i.e., cell size), and the consequences of this bias with regards to the use and interpretation of edge-based metrics must be weighed relative to the phenomenon under investigation.

In some investigations, it may be necessary to convert a vector map into a raster map, for example in order to run FRAGSTATS. It is critical that great care is taken during the rasterization process and that the

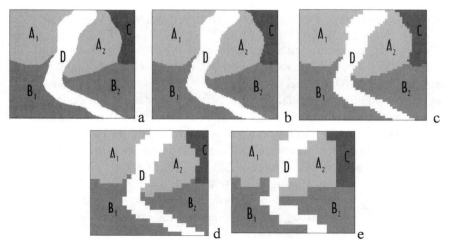

Figure 2.5. Effect of increasing cell size on the representation of boundaries. In map (a), cell size is 0.005; map (b) is 0.010; map (c) is 0.020; map (d) is 0.040; and map (e) is 0.080.

resulting raster image is carefully scrutinized for accurate representation of the original image. During the rasterization process, it is possible for disjunct patches to join and vice versa. This problem can be quite severe (e.g., resulting in numerous 1-cell patches) and lead to erroneous results if the cell size chosen for the rasterization is too large relative to the minimum patch dimension in the vector image. In general, a cell size (as represented by the length of a cell side) less than one half the narrowest dimension of the smallest patches is necessary to avoid these problems. Note, however, that as the resolution increases (i.e., cell size decreases) the grid size increases. Larger grids (in terms of number of cells) require greater disk storage space and are computationally more difficult to process. For extremely large grids, computer processing time (e.g., using FRAGSTATS to calculate landscape metrics) can become prohibitively long.

In summary, the key point is to recognize that any model of landscape structure requires an explicit choice of data formats (vector vs. raster), and that this choice has implications for the measurement of landscape pattern. In any planning application, it is incumbent upon the planner to select a data model that is appropriate to the application, because any interpretation of landscape structure is ultimately constrained by the accuracy of the model. In most cases, practical constraints associated with the measurement of landscape pattern will dictate the use of the raster data model.

Evaluating the Ecological Significance of Metrics

Despite the powerful arsenal of landscape metrics now available to the planner, the statistical properties and behavior of some landscape metrics are not well-known (Neel et al. 2004). In particular, there is a dearth of explicitly documented relationships between landscape indices and ecological functions (Botequilha Leitão and Ahern 2002; Corry and Nassauer 2005). Hence, there is a critical need to build a collective library of empirical studies in which ecological responses are related to particular landscape patterns (e.g., Hargis et al. 1998; Tischendorf 2001; Verboom 2001). Unfortunately, through the use of tools like FRAGSTATS we have the power to measure and report more about landscape pattern than we can interpret in terms of effects on ecological processes (Turner et al. 2001). Despite these limitations, we believe that landscape metrics can provide useful information for planning, even in cases where they cannot provide definitive measures of landscape pattern-process relationships.

Given the limitations above, we contend that the most appropriate use of landscape metrics is as comparative measures of landscape condition. While it is often impossible to relate the absolute value of a landscape metric to an exact landscape condition, it is usually possible to describe the nature and direction of the relationship. For example, it is usually possible to determine whether a larger or smaller value of a landscape metric is associated with a more desirable landscape condition. Therefore, by comparing different landscapes (or landscape scenarios), or the same landscape at different times, the ecological interpretation of landscape metrics can be greatly facilitated.

The interpretation of landscape metrics at any scale is further plagued by the lack of a proper temporal reference framework. Landscape metrics quantify the pattern of the landscape at a specific point in time. Yet it is often difficult, if not impossible, to determine the ecological significance of the computed value without understanding the range of natural variation in landscape patterns. For example, in disturbance-dominated landscapes, landscape patterns may fluctuate widely over time in response to the interplay between disturbance and succession processes. It is logical, therefore, that landscape metrics should exhibit statistical distributions that reflect the natural spatial and temporal dynamics of the landscape. By comparison to this distribution, a more meaningful interpretation can be assigned to any computed value. Despite widespread recognition that landscapes are dynamic, there are few studies quantifying the range of natural variation in landscape pattern metrics (Neel et al. 2004). This remains one of the greatest challenges confronting landscape pattern analysis.

3

The Selected Set of Landscape Metrics

1) COUNTY AS LANDSCAPE

2) CONSERVATION PARCEL AS LANDSCAPE?

In this chapter we review the selected set of ten core landscape metrics. Each metric section is formatted to introduce the concept behind the metric, describe its calculation, provide example applications, discuss limitations on its use and interpretation, provide recommendations for its best use, compare it to related metrics, and provide selected references. Each metric section describes some general applications to planning in addition to a common specific example based on the five stages of land transformation. Importantly, in this chapter we explore planning examples and case studies with a focus on individual metrics. In chapter four, we explore the use of these metrics in conjunction with one another.

3.1. Patch Richness (PR)

3.1.1. *Concept*

Patch Richness (PR) is simply the number of different land cover types (LCTs), or classes, in a given landscape or map extent. PR is a measure of *landscape composition*; it quantifies the variety of LCTs present in a landscape without reference to their spatial character, placement, or location within the mosaic. PR is partially a function of scale, since larger landscapes have a higher probability of having a greater number of LCTs (McGarigal and Marks 1995).

PR has broad utility as an initial measure of landscape diversity. The richness of LCTs within a landscape is an important component of diversity and has significant implications for the diversity of plant and animal communities that occur within the landscape, as well as for the movement of energy, nutrients, and plant and animal species across the landscape.

Consider the two landscapes depicted in Figure 3.1. One landscape is almost entirely forested while the other landscape has a variety of LCTs. The first obvious difference between these two landscapes is the number

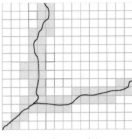 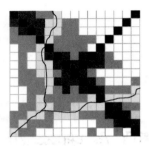

Landscape (1)   Landscape (2)

Figure 3.1. Two landscapes with contrasting levels of patch richness (PR). Landscape (1) has two LCTs (PR=2) while landscape (2) has six LCTs (PR=6). White = forest, light gray = riparian, medium gray = agriculture, dark gray = urban, black = roadway, hatch = wetland.

of different LCTs. Landscape (1) has only two LCTs, while landscape (2) has five different LCTs. While there is significant difference in LCT composition between the two landscapes, there are also similarities. Each landscape has forest and riparian LCTs, so each landscape would be expected to support some of the same species. However, since landscape (2) has more LCTs, the variety of physical and ecological conditions should be greater than in landscape (1), which may lead to significant differences in biodiversity as well as nutrient storage and stormwater retention, for example.

3.1.2. *Metric Equation and Calculation*

PR is simply a count of the number of different LCTs within the landscape.

$PR = m$

m - number of patch types (classes) present in the landscape (McGarigal and Marks 1995)

Units: none
Range of values: ≥1 with no upper limit

There are no differences in counting LCTs in raster or vector datasets, and the range of values is only limited by the number of grid cells (or minimum mapping unit if using a vector dataset) and the spatial extent of the landscape. When the entire landscape has just one LCT, the value of PR is one (the lowest value possible). Note, PR is a landscape-level measure;

there are no comparable measures at the class or patch level. Other subdivisions of the landscape, such as watersheds, could be used to measure the PR of different portions of the landscape for comparative purposes.

3.1.3. *Applications*

Landscape diversity strongly influences several key ecological processes and functions. For example, land cover types have unique physical and environmental characteristics and typically support a unique assemblage of plants and animals. Consequently, greater richness can lead to a greater diversity of environments, which can in turn lead to greater biodiversity. However, the realized biological diversity will largely depend upon the composition of the patch types. For example, an increase in the richness of urban patch types may or may not lead to greater biodiversity, while an increase in the richness of forest or grassland patch types would, with greater certainty, lead to greater biodiversity.

In addition, the diversity of LCTs can affect disturbance processes. Disturbances can be easily propagated across a simple landscape with a lower variety of LCTs. A good example is the 1938 hurricane in central New England that damaged large tracts of forest (Foster 1992; Foster and Boose 1992). The damage was more intense in the areas where the forest was dominated by a single forest cover type, although vegetation height and site exposure were also important factors. Another example is the frequent spread of summer fires through the homogeneous maritime pine forest in the central regions of Portugal.

Figure 3.2 illustrates a landscape in the process of development for human use. The initial landscape is largely untouched, comprised almost entirely of native LCTs. Gradually, other human-created LCTs are introduced into the landscape. The forest, which was once the functional matrix of the landscape, becomes a series of isolated patches within an agricultural matrix.

Examining PR across this transformation process reveals a clear gradient from the first landscape (a) which has four LCTs, to the final landscape (e) which has seven LCTs. Beyond the obvious quantitative differences in PR, an important question arises—which LCTs are present? There is an increase in PR over the land transformation sequence, and with it one must assume that there are at least small differences in the flora and fauna, as well as cultural differences for human beings, but what is the nature of this variety? Are the additional LCTs that appear later in the landscape transformation process of greater contrast with the original suite of LCTs? These questions lead to questions of spatial patterning. Within a given landscape, when additional LCTs are created, there is by default spatial consequence.

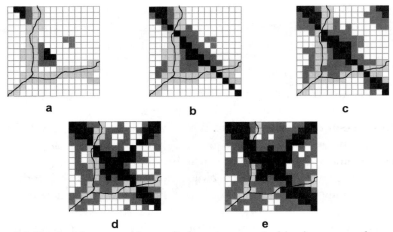

Figure 3.2. Patch richness metrics applied to a prototypical landscape transformation sequence. Seven land use/land cover types illustrate the application of PR: Roads (black); urban (dark gray); agricultural fields (medium gray); riparian (light gray); forest (white). The sequence illustrates a prototypical transformation in which the landscape changes from a forested landscape (a) to an agricultural/urban landscape (e).

The spatial heterogeneity of the landscape (configuration) has increased as well as the variety of content (composition); meadow (cross hatch); wetland (stipple). The specific ecological and anthropogenic consequences of these changes will depend on the specific LCTs present.

3.1.4. *Limitations*

First, PR is sensitive to the land cover classification system being used by the analyst. PR is dependent upon what distinctions among LCTs the analyst is willing to make. Some classification systems may be quite detailed in regards to distinguishing native ecosystems, such as different kinds of forest or wetland, but quite sparse when it comes to categorizing the kinds of urban and suburban land uses. Therefore, be wary of comparing landscapes that have different classification systems for land cover.

Second, PR only provides information about the number of LCTs, rather than their actual identity. To be most useful to the analyst, PR should be coupled with an explicit listing of the LCTs.

Third, PR ignores a critical component of landscape structure: the area occupied by each LCT. The analyst should seek to understand the distribution of patch area by LCT in order to gain a more complete picture of landscape composition and its implications for landscape function. This can be accomplished with Class Area Proportion (CAP).

Finally, PR doesn't provide any indication of how the various LCTs are arranged in space. It only provides a count of patch types within the landscape. Obviously, a greater variety of patch types holds implications for the spatial arrangement of patches, but frequently the analyst will have to probe more deeply than simply PR in order to gain insight into whether spatial arrangement may or may not be important.

3.1.5. *Recommendations*

PR provides important fundamental information about the composition of a landscape and is relatively easy to interpret. PR can be an important component of a suite of metrics used by the analyst. Given the descriptiveness and the limitations of PR discussed above, we offer the following recommendations:

- Before doing any analysis, identify the source of your landscape data and thoroughly understand the classification system and the process used to classify LCTs. Be aware of the limitations of the classification system and the classification process employed before making any measurements or comparisons.

- Couple PR measurements with information about the actual LCTs present and the area of the landscape occupied by each class area proportion (CAP).

- Identify one or more configuration metrics, such as Euclidean Nearest Neighbor Distance (ENN) or Proximity Index (PROX), and use these with PR in a complementary fashion. Do not rely upon PR as a sole measurement, as it provides an incomplete description of the composition of the landscape, and does not describe any aspect of the configuration of the landscape.

3.1.6. *Related Metrics*

PR can be represented in two other forms that may be more suitable for comparative analyses. Patch Richness Density (PRD) is simply PR expressed as the number of patch types per unit of area, enabling comparative analysis of differently sized landscapes. This is similar to the relationship between Patch Number (PN) and Patch Density (PD) (Section 3.3). Relative Patch Richness (RPR) relates PR to the maximum potential richness. For example, a regional land cover dataset may have fifty LCTs. However, in a subset of this regional dataset, it would be highly improbable that all fifty classes would occur. By comparing the PR of the data subset with the PR for the entire dataset, the analyst gains insight into the particular level of landscape heterogeneity present in their subset or study area.

In addition, patch richness is an important component of landscape diversity, and therefore it is closely allied with a number of other landscape diversity metrics. Landscape diversity is influenced by two components —richness and evenness. Richness and evenness are generally referred to as the compositional and structural components of diversity, respectively. In a landscape context, richness refers to the number of patch types or LCTs present (PR), while evenness refers to the distribution of area (or CAP) among LCTs. There are numerous diversity indices that can be computed from these two basic components, but the most common are the Shannon's Diversity Index (SHDI) and Simpson's Diversity Index (SIDI).

3.1.7. *Selected References for Further Reading*

Iverson, L.R. 1988. Land use changes in Illinois, USA: The influence of landscape attributes on current and historic land use. *Landscape Ecology* 2(1): 45–61.

Pickett, S.T.A. and M.L. Cadenasso. 1995. Landscape ecology: Spatial heterogeneity in ecological systems. *Science* 269: 331–334.

Risser, P.G. 1990. Landscape pattern and its effects on energy and nutrient distribution. In *Changing landscapes: An ecological perspective*, eds. I.S. Zonneveld and R.T.T. Forman, 45–56. Berlin: Springer-Verlag.

Turner, M.G. 1990. Spatial and temporal analysis of landscape patterns. *Landscape Ecology* 4(1): 21–30.

Turner, M.G. and C.L. Ruscher. 1988. Changes in landscape patterns in Georgia, USA. *Landscape Ecology* 1(4): 241–251.

3.2. Class Area Proportion (CAP)

3.2.1. *Concept*

Class Area Proportion (CAP) is simply the proportion of the landscape composed of a particular land cover type (LCT). CAP is a measure of *landscape composition*. It refers to features associated with the abundance of patch types within the landscape, but without considering the spatial character, placement, or location of patches within the mosaic. CAP can be represented alternatively as a percentage, by multiplying CAP by 100. When reported in this form it is usually referred to as Percentage of Landscape (PLAND). The choice between CAP and PLAND is a matter of preference, as these two measures are completely redundant.

CAP represents a fundamental aspect of landscape structure and is perhaps the single most important landscape descriptor. It provides basic information about the landscape that can be useful in a wide variety of applications. Its utility stems, in part, from its ease of calculation

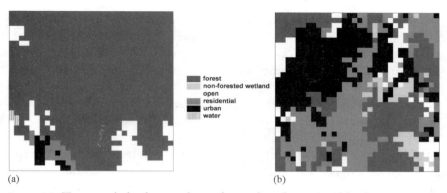

(a)   (b)

Figure 3.3. Two sample landscapes drawn from a broader regional landscape in western Massachusetts undergoing urbanization: (a) a largely undeveloped landscape dominated by forest cover, and (b) a largely urban landscape. Land cover was classified into six broad classes: Forest, Non-Forested Wetland, Open, Residential, Urban, and Water.

and its straightforward and intuitive interpretation. Consider the two sample landscapes depicted in figure 3.3 drawn from the broader regional landscape of western Massachusetts, a largely forested region undergoing urbanization. Here, the landscape is depicted as a mosaic of six LCTs representing broad land use/cover categories. CAP provides a quantitative description of the composition of each landscape, as shown in table 3.1.

CAP reveals some notable similarities and differences in composition between these landscapes that serves to illustrate the broad utility of this metric. First, CAP indicates that landscape (a) is dominated by a single LCT—forest. In this case, forest constitutes a *matrix* because it is extensive and highly connected, and therefore likely to exert a dominant influence on the flora and fauna and ecological processes. Conversely, landscape (b) is not dominated by any one

Table 3.1. Class Area Proportions (CAP) in percentages (%) for sample landscapes A and B in Figure 3.3.

Land Cover Type	Landscape A	Landscape B
Forest	81	35
Non-forested wetland	1	3
Water	1	2
Open (e.g., agriculture)	12	10
Residential	3	30
Urban	2	20

LCT, and therefore does not have a clearly defined matrix. Instead, urban and residential LCTs have increased at the expense of forest, resulting in all three LCTs being co-dominant. Identifying the matrix LCT, or determining whether or not a matrix even exists, is one of the primary uses of CAP.

Second, CAP indicates that some LCTs are poorly represented in one or both landscapes. For example, non-forested wetland is extremely rare in both landscapes. This natural LCT may be extremely important in providing ecological services (e.g., maintaining biodiversity, water storage and purification) and therefore may warrant special consideration during planning. Here, the planning objective might be to maintain or even increase its extent and/or to manage land uses and activities in the surrounding landscape to minimize adverse impacts to this LCT. In contrast, urban land cover is uncommon in landscape (a), indicating that the landscape is still largely non-urban, whereas it is quite common in landscape (b), indicating that the landscape is highly urbanized. Here, the planning objective might be to restrict the potential for urban growth in landscape (a) in order to maximize ecological services, and concentrate urban growth in landscape (b), which is already largely urban. Identifying rare LCTs that may warrant special consideration during planning is another primary use of CAP.

Third, when considered collectively across all LCTs, CAP indicates that landscape (a) is dominated by a single LCT, whereas landscape (b) contains a more equitable distribution of area among LCTs. The distribution of area among LCTs is a particular aspect of landscape composition known as *evenness*, and is one component of landscape diversity (the other being patch richness (PR), the number of different LCTs). Given a constant number of LCTs, greater evenness implies greater diversity. From this perspective, landscape (b) is more diverse than landscape (a). Often maintaining or increasing landscape diversity is a planning objective. However, care must be exercised when using diversity as an objective because the actual composition of the landscape may be more important than overall diversity. In other words, not all LCTs are equal in assigned value or importance. Simple diversity measures, such as evenness, treat all LCTs the same and therefore can be misleading. Note, there are numerous ways to quantify evenness, and most diversity indices have a corresponding evenness index derived from them. In addition, evenness can be expressed as its complement—dominance. Indeed, dominance has often been the chosen form in landscape ecological investigations (O'Neill et al. 1988; Turner et al. 1989; Turner 1990), although we prefer evenness because larger values imply greater landscape diversity.

3.2.2. *Metric Equation and Calculation*

CAP is calculated by computing the area occupied by a particular LCT, expressed as a proportion (or, alternatively, as a percentage) of the total landscape area, as follows:

$$CAP_i = \frac{\sum_{j=1}^{n} a_{ij}}{A}$$

CAP_i equals the Class Area Proportion for the ith LCT, a_{ij} equals the area (m²) of patch j for the ith LCT, and A equals the total landscape area (m²). Thus, CAP_i equals the sum of the areas of all patches of the corresponding patch type, divided by total landscape area. Again, CAP also can be reported as a percentage, by mutliplying by 100, in which case it is usually referred to as a Percentage of Landscape (PLAND). Note, in a raster or grid format, area can be recorded in number of grid cells instead of areal units—the results are equivalent.

Units: none (proportion)
Range of values: $0 < \text{CAP} \leq 1$

CAP approaches zero when the corresponding LCT becomes increasingly rare in the landscape, and equals one when the entire landscape consists of a single patch of the corresponding LCT.

To illustrate the calculation of CAP, consider the simple landscape depicted in figure 3.4 representing a portion of a watershed where two second-order streams combine to form a third-order stream. Here, the landscape is represented as a grid of fifteen by fifteen cells, for a total area of 225 cells, and is composed of four LCTs: urban, agriculture, river, and forest.

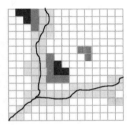

Land Cover Type	Number of Cells	Class Area Proportion
Urban	6	6/225 = .03
Agriculture	9	9/225 =. 04
River	54	54/225 = .24
Forest	150	150/225 = .66
Wetland	3	3/225 = .013
Meadow	3	3/225 = .013
The entire landscape	225	100

Figure 3.4. Hypothetical landscape composed of six land cover types: urban (dark gray), agriculture (medium gray), riparian (light gray), forest (white), wetland (cross hatch), and meadow (stipple).

To compute CAP for each LCT, simply count the number of corresponding grid cells and then divide by the total number of cells in the
landscape, and then round up or down to the desired level of precision. In
figure 3.4 for example, CAP was rounded to two decimal places.

3.2.3. *Applications*

As noted previously, CAP provides basic information about the composition of the landscape. Specifically, CAP allows you to quantify the extent
of each LCT, and thereby discern the presence of a matrix, identify poorly
represented LCTs, and characterize the overall evenness (or its complement, dominance) of the landscape. This information is useful in a wide
variety of applications, including, for example, natural resource planning
and wildlife management (McGarigal and McComb 1995; Gustafson
1998; Atauri and Lucio 2001), land use/cover change analysis (Turner and
Ruscher 1988; Dunn et al. 1991; Moreira et al. 2001), and strategic landscape planning (Steinitz et al. 1997; Botequilha Leitão and Ahern 2002).
In fact, the range of applications of CAP is so great that it is impractical
to discuss them all. Instead, we will illustrate the application of CAP with
a single example.

Consider the hypothetical landscape depicted in figure 3.5. As
described previously, figure 3.5 depicts a globally common sequence of
landscape changes in which the landscape is gradually transformed via
clearing for agriculture and urban development. The physical change in
the structure of the landscape occurring during this transformation
process has significant impacts on landscape function. For example, as the
width of the river corridor is reduced to accommodate expanding urban
land use, and the degree of imperviousness increases in relation to
expanding road and urban cover, stream and riparian functions associated
with the flow of water, nutrients, materials, and species are increasingly
impaired (Nielsson et al. 2003; Center for Watershed Protection 1998).
Scientific research indicates that there may exist ecological thresholds in
watershed imperviousness (e.g., $CAP_{impervious} = CAP_{urban} + CAP_{roads}$) that
affects both physical (channel stability and water quality) and biological
qualities of stream habitat (stream biodiversity). When a threshold of
10% of imperviousness is exceeded, stream channels may become unsta-
ble, although water quality and biodiversity may be relatively unimpaired.
As the percent of imperviousness increases, the quality of water and of
stream habitat declines. Beyond 25% imperviousness, streams are classified as degraded and are characterized by high channel instability, poor to

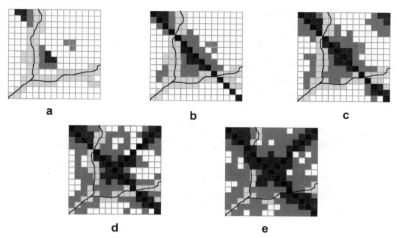

Figure 3.5. Hypothetical landscape transformation associated with agricultural and urban development. The landscape is composed of seven land cover types: road (black), urban (dark gray), agriculture (medium gray), riparian (light gray), forest (white), meadow (cross hatch), wetland (stipple).

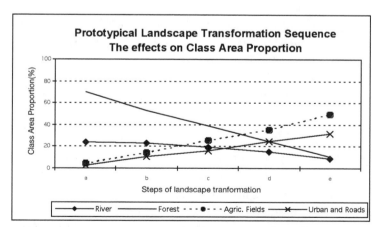

Figure 3.6. Class area proportion (CAP) values for four land cover types associated with the landscape transformation sequence depicted in figure 3.5. The sequence illustrates a typical transformation in which the landscape changes from a forested landscape (stage a; CAP Forest = 0.66) to an agricultural/urban landscape (stage e; CAP Agriculture = 0.50 and CAP Urban and Roads = 0.32).

fair water quality, and poor biodiversity (Center for Watershed Protection 1998).

Consider how CAP can be used as a simple quantitative measure of the structural changes in the landscape undergoing the prototypical transformation (Figures 3.5 and 3.6). The stages of the transformation process can be associated separately with ecological indicators, such as animal movement or stream water quality, which can inform planning as to when and where to mitigate the negative effects of urbanization (Antrop 1998; 2000). Consider the transformation sequence in detail. At the beginning of the transformation process the forest constitutes the matrix ($CAP_{forest} = .66$) and the river corridor (stream plus riparian zone) occupies 24% of the landscape (Figure 3.6). In this largely forested landscape, physical and functional linkages among undeveloped areas maintain natural ecological processes, such as the flow of water, nutrients, and materials through the riparian corridor, and the movement of wildlife species across the landscape. By stage three (Figure 3.5c), forest no longer constitutes a matrix ($CAP_{forest} = .38$) and agricultural fields have expanded ($CAP_{agriculture} = .25$) to support the human population living in the expanded urban areas ($CAP_{urban} = .09$). In addition, roads ($CAP_{roads} = .07$) and agriculture are encroaching on portions of the riparian corridor as competition for space increases. Moreover, the percentage of the landscape covered by impervious surface ($CAP_{impervious} = CAP_{urban} + CAP_{roads}$) exceeds the widely accepted threshold of 10%, which is the point at which watershed function begins to be degraded (Center for Watershed Protection 1998). By stage four (Figures 3.5d and 3.6), the forest has been reduced and fragmented into ten small patches. Consequently, wildlife movements are significantly impaired. Watershed and riparian functions continue to degrade as the riparian area decreases and watershed imperviousness increases ($CAP_{impervious} = .25$); consequently, water quality and aquatic biodiversity are poor (Center for Watershed Protection 1998).

In the final stage of transformation (Figures 3.5e and 3.6), most of the forest has been replaced or has been subdivided into very small fragments ($CAP_{forest} = .10$). Consequently, habitat for forest interior species is minimal, or lost altogether, and edge species predominate. The riparian zone ($CAP_{river} = .08$) has been reduced to a third of its original area and the river has been confined to the riverbed, or channelized to make space for the city and its infrastructure.

3.2.4. *Limitations*

Despite its tremendous utility as a basic descriptor of landscape structure, CAP is not without limitations as a landscape metric. CAP's principal limitation revolves around the fact that it measures landscape composition (i.e., the extent of each LCT), but reveals nothing of the spatial character or configuration of the patch mosaic. For example, a CAP of 0.3 indicates that the corresponding LCT comprises 30% of the landscape, but it doesn't indicate, for example, whether that 30% is aggregated into a few large, contiguous patches or subdivided into several small patches, or whether the corresponding patches are located near each other or widely dispersed across the landscape, or whether the corresponding patches are relatively simple or complex in shape, or whether the LCT contains much core area or is predominantly edge. Clearly, consideration of the spatial configuration of LCTs is critical to understanding the potential ecological consequences of landscape patterns. For this reason, CAP is most useful if used in conjunction with other configuration metrics in a complementary manner.

Also, it is important to recognize that CAP measures the composition of the landscape as it is defined and represented in a categorical map. Often the LCT map is created as a general-purpose map, without any particular application in mind. Thus, the LCT classification scheme may or may not represent the world in a manner relevant to your application. CAP is only meaningful if the LCT is relevant to your application.

3.2.5. *Recommendations*

As noted above, CAP represents a fundamental aspect of landscape structure. It is perhaps the single most important landscape descriptor as it provides basic information about the composition of the landscape that can be useful in a wide variety of applications. Given the applications and limitations discussed above, we offer the following recommendations:

- CAP is most effective when used in conjunction with one or more configuration metrics in a complementary manner. For example, CAP used in combination with mean patch size (AREA_MN) and/or patch density (PD) reveals the overall extent and subdivision of each LCT.

- CAP is only useful if the corresponding LCTs are meaningful to your application (i.e., their classification and categorical representation is relevant).

- CAP is useful for discerning the presence of a matrix. Typically, a matrix exists when a single LCT comprises more than 50% of the landscape and is mostly contiguous. The matrix is the dominant structural element of the landscape and therefore generally plays a dominant role in the functioning of the landscape.

- CAP is useful for identifying and quantifying rare or uncommon LCTs, which may warrant special consideration during planning. For example, rare natural LCTs represent unique landscape features that may be critical to the maintenance of biodiversity in the landscape. In cities these can be represented by more formal open spaces, such as urban parks and public or private gardens, or small, sometimes overlooked urban ecosystems, such as vacant derelict sites. Cities can be great havens for biodiversity, even in industrial areas (Bradshaw 2003, 92).

- CAP is a class metric (computed separately for each LCT), but when interpreted in aggregate across all LCTs, it is useful for characterizing the evenness of the landscape, which is an important component of landscape diversity. Greater evenness implies greater diversity.

3.2.6. Related Metrics

CAP is closely related to a couple of other metrics. Recall that CAP is a *relative* measure of class area because it is reported as a proportion of the landscape. As noted previously, CAP can also be represented as a percentage by multiplying by 100, in which case it is usually referred to as percentage of landscape (PLAND). CAP and PLAND are completely redundant; the choice between them is a matter of personal preference. Class area (CA) is the corresponding *absolute* measure because it is reported in areal units (ha) instead of as a proportion. Although CAP and CA have the same basic utility, CAP may be a more appropriate measure of landscape composition when comparing among landscapes of varying sizes. In addition to its direct interpretive value, CA is used in the computations of many other class and landscape metrics.

As noted above, CAP provides the raw information used in the computation of landscape evenness, a component of landscape diversity and a metric in its own right. Landscape diversity is influenced by two components—richness and evenness. Richness and evenness are generally referred to as the compositional and structural components of diversity, respectively. Richness refers to the number of patch types or LCTs present (see Patch Richness metric) and evenness refers to the distribution of area (or CAP) among patch types (or LCTs).

3.2.7. Selected References for Further Reading

Atauri, J.A. and J.V. de Lucio. 2001. The role of landscape structure in species richness distribution of birds, amphibians, reptiles and lepidopterans in Mediterranean landscapes. *Landscape Ecology* 16: 147–159.

Center for Watershed Protection. 1998. Rapid watershed planning handbook: A comprehensive guide for managing urbanizing watersheds. Maryland: Office of Wetlands, Oceans and Watersheds and Region V, U.S. EPA.

Dunn, C.P., D.M. Sharpe, G.R. Guntenspergen, F. Stearns, and Z. Yang. 1991. Methods for analyzing temporal changes in landscape pattern. In *Quantitative methods in landscape ecology: The analysis and interpretation of landscape heterogeneity*, eds. M.G. Turner and R.H. Gardner, 173-198. New York: Springer-Verlag.

Environmental Law Institute (ELI). 2003. Conservation thresholds for land-use planners. Washington, D.C.: The Environmental Law Institute. Available online at: www.elistore.org.

Gustafson, E.J. 1998. Quantifying landscape spatial pattern: What is the state of the art? *Ecosystems* 1: 143-156.

Moreira, F., F.C. Rego, and P.G. Ferreira. 2001. Temporal (1958–1995) pattern of change in a cultural landscape of northwestern Portugal: Implications for fire occurrence. *Landscape Ecology* 16: 557–567.

Turner, M.G. and C.L. Ruscher. 1988. Changes in landscape patterns in Georgia, USA. *Landscape Ecology* 1(4): 241–251.

3.3. Patch Number (PN) and Patch Density (PD)

3.3.1. *Concept*

Patch Number (PN) is simply the total number of patches. It can be applied at the landscape and class levels. The landscape level includes all patches of all classes. The class level includes all patches within a specified LCT. PN is a measure of *landscape configuration*. It deals with the spatial character of the class or landscape; specifically the degree of subdivision of the class or landscape.

The number of patches likely to occur in a landscape is directly proportional to the extent of the landscape. The larger the landscape, the greater the probability that it will contain a larger number of patches. Therefore, comparing the values of PN among several landscapes of varying sizes poses an inherent problem. To overcome this problem, Patch Density (PD) normalizes PN by dividing it by landscape size. PD has essentially the same utility as PN, except that it expresses the metric on a per unit area basis. If the total landscape area is held constant, then PN and PD express precisely the same information.

Landscape processes such as fragmentation divide large contiguous patches into smaller remnant patches. PN and PD reveal this subdivision aspect of fragmentation, which has important implications for a variety of ecological processes. For instance, within landscapes of comparable area or extent, it appears that a single large patch can support more species than several smaller patches (Forman and Godron 1986).

To aid in illustrating the concept of PN and PD, consider the example landscapes in figure 3.7. Landscape (a) is a relatively simple landscape with relatively few patches, some of which dominate the landscape, while landscape (b) is much more complex. Landscape (b) contains roughly nine times the number of patches than landscape (a). Landscape (b) possesses roughly the same number of LCTs as landscape (a), yet these are distributed in a more fragmented pattern, which results in a greater number of

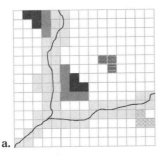 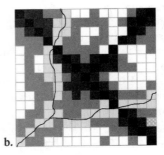

a.   b.

Figure 3.7. A comparison of a landscape (a) with low patch numbers and patch density with a landscape (b) possessing higher patch numbers and patch density. The two landscapes have a mixture of land cover types (LCTs): roads (black), urban (dark gray), agriculture (medium gray), riparian (light gray), forest (white), meadow (cross hatch), and wetland (stipple). Landscape (a) has nine patches (PN) and a PD of 44 patches per 100 hectares, while landscape (b) has 84 patches (PN) and a PD of 415 patches per 100 hectares.

smaller patches. In landscape (a) these same LCTs are in large contiguous patches, often more simply shaped.

3.3.2. Metric Equation and Calculation

PN is simply a count of all the patches within a class or across the entire landscape. PD is the normalized form of PN—achieved by dividing PN by total landscape area.

$$PN = \sum_{i=1}^{n} P_i$$

$P_i = patch\ of\ type\ _i$

$$PD = \frac{PN}{A} \times (10,000)^{m^2}/_{ha.} \times 100$$

A = total landscape area in m^2

Units: None
Range of values: 1, up to the total number of grid cells in the landscape dataset, where each grid cell would be a separate patch.

The following calculation is an example for landscape (a) in figure 3.7. (Note: there are 15 × 15 grid cells, 30 m by 30 m each.)

$$PD = \frac{9}{(202,500 m^2)} \times (10,000)^{m^2}/_{ha.} \times 100$$

$$PD = (0.00004444)^{patches}/_{m^2} \times (10,000)^{m^2}/_{ha.} \times 100$$

$$PD = 44.44^{\ patches}/_{100ha.}$$

The minimum value for PN and PD occurs when the entire landscape is comprised of a single patch, while the maximum theoretical value could be, in a raster map, equal to the total number of cells, each cell representing a separate patch. In vector format, the maximum occurs when all the patches within the landscape equal the smallest resolution possible (i.e., the minimum mapping unit).

PN and PD can be applied at two levels: landscape and class. The landscape level includes all patches of all classes. The class level includes all patches of a particular LCT. At the landscape level, PN and PD provide a broad general characterization of landscape pattern and complexity, while the class-level measurement of PN and PD provides a more resource-specific measurement. When class area is constant, PN serves as a good fragmentation and heterogeneity index by which to compare landscapes (McGarigal and Marks 1995).

3.3.3. *Applications*

PN and PD can reveal important aspects of landscape pattern such as fragmentation. From an ecological perspective, more patches in a single LCT class may assure redundancy within a landscape, thus reducing the risk of loss due to disturbances such as a pest outbreak, hurricane, or flood. According to Franklin and Forman (1987), habitat subdivision, as indexed by the number of patches, may affect the propagation of disturbances across a landscape. If a class is subdivided into a large number of patches, it could be more resistant to disturbances, and thus more likely to persist than a more contiguous patch type (Saunders et al. 1991). Thus, in some cases, habitat fragmentation can be beneficial with respect to particular processes by preventing the propagation of pests or fire, which would spread more extensively in larger contiguous patches. On the other hand, fragmentation can be a contributing factor to such negative effects as wind throw in forested patches.

When considering species that are specific to a certain type of habitat and organized into a metapopulation, PN might serve as a surrogate for the number of subpopulations, which influences the dynamics and persistence of the metapopulation (Hanski and Gilpin 1991). Again, more patches may reduce the risk of loss, in this case the loss of a species from a particular patch. If more patches persist there may be a greater chance that individuals from neighboring patches will recolonize patches where the species has died out.

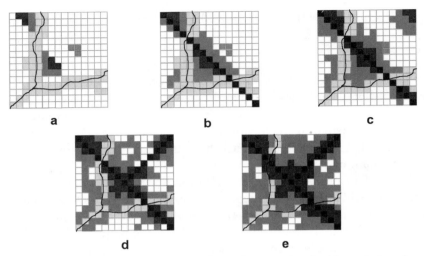

Figure 3.8. Hypothetical landscape transformation associated with agricultural and urban development. The landscape is composed of seven land cover types: road (black), urban (dark gray), agriculture (medium gray), riparian (light gray), forest (white), meadow (cross hatch), and wetland (stipple). The sequence illustrates a typical transformation in which the landscape changes from a forested landscape (a) to an agricultural/urban landscape (e).

The landscapes illustrated in figure 3.8 provide a means of illustrating trends in PN and PD within a landscape undergoing development for human uses.

This landscape transformation process is fairly common in many parts of the world. People subdivide the landscape in order to use natural resources, carry on commerce, and have places in which to live, work, and play.

These subdivisions of use result in different patches of LCTs being created via conversion of one LCT to another or by isolating a patch from its neighbors. Observe the large forest patch in the upper right corner of landscape (b) of figure 3.8. As development proceeds, new urban patches are created (conversion) and agriculture begins to surround portions of the forest (landscapes c and d), isolating it from what was once part of the same patch.

Patch types that represent ecosystems, such as forest, riparian, and agriculture, are in a state of flux, changing from one type to another or having their surroundings change around them. Movement of species and materials across the landscape is directly affected because more patches mean more boundaries between different LCTs, and new intervening LCTs that may pose barriers to movement.

As can be seen in figure 3.8 and graphically in figure 3.9, PD steadily increases due to LCT conversion via development, and then as the urban LCT patches begin to coalesce, PD begins to decline. The same process can be observed in more detail at the class level (Figure 3.10). Forest patches continue to be formed through fragmentation, while other LCT

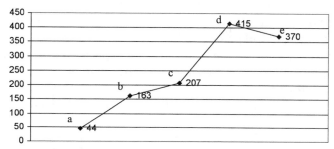

Figure 3.9. This graph shows the landscape patch density (PD), in number of patches/100 ha., for the landscape undergoing transformation depicted in figure 3.8.

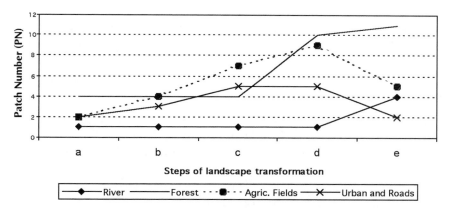

Figure 3.10. Patch number (PN) of landscape (a) through (e), showing a typical transformation from a forest-dominated landscape (a) into an agricultural/urban matrix (e). Notice that the number of forest patches does not decrease from (a) to (c), although forest class proportion decreased from 70% to 39% (see figure 3.6 for forest CAP values). This spatial phenomenon is known as shrinkage and occurs when PN is constant but patch size decreases. In diagrams (c) through (e), PN Forest increases to 10 and then 11 patches as the once connected forested area is fragmented into smaller, increasingly isolated patches. PN can also be understood as a fragmentation index: PN total in (a) is nine, increasing to (d) a PN total of twenty-five, representing an increasingly fragmented landscape. From diagrams (d) to (e), PN decreases as a new agricultural matrix is forming and patches once divided start to coalesce into large single patches. Since the total area of the landscape is constant, PN = PD.

patches that are forming (and continuing to grow) via conversion begin to coalesce into larger patches, with the resultant dip in PN.

3.3.4. *Limitations*

PN and PD offer limited landscape interpretation by themselves because they do not convey any information about area, the distribution of patch areas, or the spatial distribution of patches (McGarigal and Marks 1995). For example, two landscapes that are identical with regard to patch types and number of patches can still be very different. One landscape may have all patches clustered in a specific part of the landscape, while in the other landscape the patches may be scattered evenly across the landscape.

The distribution of patch areas in these two example landscapes may also be quite different. The first landscape may have one very large patch with many smaller patches clustered about it, while the second landscape may have the same number of patches but they may be all approximately the same size and distributed evenly over the landscape.

3.3.5. *Recommendations*

PN and PD quantify fundamental components of landscape structure and fragmentation. They are simple and easy to understand, yet have little utility by themselves. Therefore they are most powerful when used in conjunction with other data and metrics. We offer the following recommendations:

- Use PN and PD in concert with other patch-level metrics such as Patch Area (PA), Class Area Proportion (CAP), Patch size (AREA_AM), Radius of Gyration (GYRATE), Proximity Index (PROX), and Patch Shape (SHAPE). In this way, the spatial complexity of the landscape is more fully described in terms of patches, patch spatial distribution, patch shape complexity, and connectivity.

- Use PN and PD with landscape data that is appropriate for your investigation. PN and PD are limited by the land use/land cover classification of your data.

- PN and PD are best used in comparative analyses between landscapes similar in extent and LCT classification. Analyses of PN and PD for the same landscape over time can be particularly informative.

- Be mindful of the resolution of the landscape data being analyzed. Do not compare PN and PD between landscape datasets of differing resolutions.

3.3.6. *Related Metrics*

PN and PD can be strongly correlated with class area (see previous section on CAP). In many instances, larger values of CAP also coincide with a greater number of patches for those particular LCTs. However, there are also often cases when a single large patch dominates the landscape, thus underscoring the importance of using metrics complementary to PN and PD.

3.3.7. *Selected References for Further Reading*

Franklin, J.F. and R.T.T. Forman. 1987. Creating landscape patterns by forest cutting: Ecological consequences and principles. *Landscape Ecology* 1(1): 5–18.

Opdam, P. 1991. Metapopulation theory and habitat fragmentation: A review of holarctic breeding bird studies. *Landscape Ecology* 5(2): 93-106.

Saunders, D.A., R. Hobbs, and C.R. Margules. 1991. Biological consequences of ecosystem fragmentation: A review. *Conservation Biology* 5(1): 18–32.

3.4. Mean Patch Size (AREA_MN, AREA_AM)

3.4.1. *Concept*

Mean Patch Size (AREA_MN) is simply the average size of patches of a particular LCT (class level) or across the entire landscape (landscape level). Mean patch size is a measure of the subdivision of the class or landscape. According to McGarigal and Marks (1995), patch area is perhaps the single most important and useful piece of information that can be obtained from a landscape analysis. Patches are the basic spatial components of landscapes, and therefore have critical relevance to landscape function for people as well as for natural processes. Consequently, metrics derived from patch area, such as AREA_MN, are extremely useful measures.

The landscapes illustrated in figures 3.11 and 3.12 provide contrasting views of patch size as well as landscape fragmentation. Figure 3.11 shows the pattern of land cover for a typical suburban landscape in the northeastern United States. The dark gray represents remnant patches of what was once a relatively continuous forest. Figure 3.12 depicts a more rural landscape (with extensive areas of agriculture) where the native forest has been more substantially fragmented.

Table 3.2 and Figure 3.13 describe the strong contrast of AREA_MN between these two landscapes.

Perhaps the most noticeable contrast between these two landscapes is the difference in AREA_MN for forest. The Number of Patches (NP) of forest increases from 91 in the rural landscape to 112 in the suburban

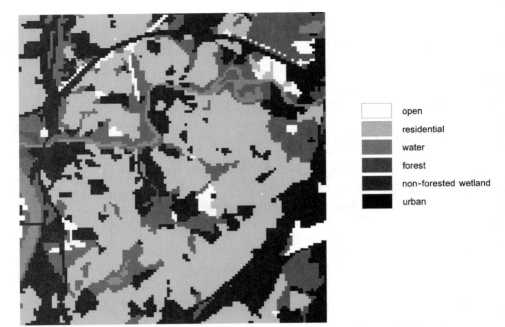

	open
	residential
	water
	forest
	non-forested wetland
	urban

Figure 3.11. A suburban landscape with small remnant patches of forest (dark gray).

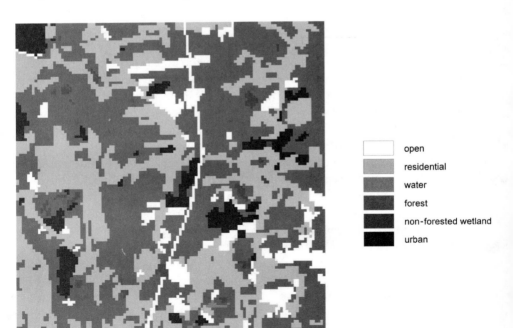

	open
	residential
	water
	forest
	non-forested wetland
	urban

Figure 3.12. A rural landscape with larger remnant patches of forest (dark gray). Note that the sizes of the remaining portions of forest are still large compared to the suburban landscape depicted in figure 3.11.

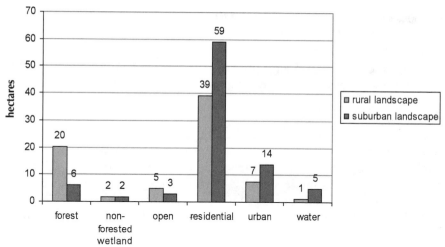

Figure 3.13. Mean patch size (AREA_MN) values for rural and suburban landscapes.

landscape. Significantly, the AREA_MN value for forest drops from just over twenty hectares to six hectares (Table 3.2).

A landscape with more patches of native ecosystems is not necessarily more desirable or ecologically sound than one with fewer patches, particularly if the AREA_MN is smaller for the landscape with more numerous patches. The important functions associated with larger patches include: stormwater management, nutrient recycling, habitat for specialist wildlife

Table 3.2. Number of Patches (NP) and Mean Patch Size (AREA_MN) for each LCT in the example landscapes of Figures 3.11 and 3.12.

Cover Type	Number of Patches (NP)	Mean Patch Size (In hectares)
SUBURBAN LANDSCAPE (Figure 3.11)		
Forest	112	6
Non-forested wetland	7	2
Open	45	3
Residential	27	59
Urban	82	14
Water	26	5
RURAL LANDSCAPE (Figure 3.12)		
Forest	91	20
Non-forested wetland	26	2
Open	62	5
Residential	33	39
Urban	29	7
Water	7	1

species, and recreation for people. These functions are less likely to be supported in smaller patches. The total value and number of benefits provided by these patches are diminished when their area is reduced. Therefore, the area requirements for priority patch functions must be taken into account when planning or managing a landscape for multiple uses.

3.4.2. *Metric Equation and Calculation*

Patch size relates to the area occupied by each patch in the landscape, and it can be summarized at the class and landscape levels. At the class level, AREA_MN is the average or mean patch size for a particular class of LCTs. At the landscape level, AREA_MN is the mean patch size for all the patches of all LCTs contained within the landscape.

In a raster or grid format, area can be recorded in the number of grid cells instead of areal units—the results are equivalent. The range of values for AREA_MN is only limited by the extent of the landscape. For instance, if a patch occupied the entire landscape, the landscape area would be the maximum value for the metric.

Class-level calculation of AREA_MN:

$$AREA\_MN = \frac{\sum_{j=1}^{n} a_{ij}}{n_i}$$

a_{ij} = Area (m^2) of patch$_{ij}$
n_i = number of patches in the landscape of patch type (class)$_i$

Units: square area units (typically m^2 or ha)
Range of values: < 0, without limit

AREA_MN (mean) at the class level equals the sum, across all patches of the corresponding patch type, of the area of the patches, divided by the total number of patches of the same type.

Landscape-level calculation of AREA_MN:

$$AREA\_MN = \frac{\sum_{i=1}^{m} \sum_{j=1}^{n} a_{ij}}{N}$$

N = Number of patches in the landscape (mean) at the landscape level.

AREA_MN equals the sum, across all patches in the landscape, of the area of the patches, divided by the total number of patches N in the landscape. Units and range are the same as above.

Another patch size measurement is an adaptation of AREA_MN, called the Area-Weighted Mean Patch Size (AREA_AM).

Class-level calculation of AREA_AM:

$$AREA\_AM = \sum_{j=1}^{n}\left[a_{ij}\left(\frac{a_{ij}}{\sum_{j=1}^{n}a_{ij}}\right)\right]$$

AREA_AM (area-weighted mean) at the class level equals the sum, across all patches of the corresponding patch type, of patch area multiplied by the proportional abundance of the patch (i.e., patch area divided by class area). Units and range are the same as above.

Class-level calculation of AREA_AM weights each patch on the basis of its relative size; that is, its size relative to the total class area. Thus, larger patches are weighted more heavily than smaller patches. The computed mean is essentially biased towards the larger patches that comprise a disproportionate area of the class and therefore probably have greater ecological importance. The area-weighted mean patch size has a particular advantage over the unweighted version in that it is insensitive to the omission or addition of very small patches. In practice, this makes the results more reproducible as investigators do not always use the same lower limit of patch size.

Landscape-level calculation of AREA_AM:

$$AREA\_AM = \sum_{i=1}^{m}\sum_{j=1}^{n}\left[\frac{a_{ij}}{N}\left(\frac{a_{ij}}{\sum_{i=1}^{m}\sum_{j=1}^{n}a_{ij}}\right)\right]$$

AREA_AM (area-weighted mean) at the landscape level equals the sum, across all patches in the landscape, of patch area multiplied by the proportional abundance of the patch (i.e., patch area divided by the sum of patch areas). Note that the proportional abundance of each patch is determined from the sum of patch areas rather than the total landscape area, because the latter may include internal background area not associated with any patch. Units and range are the same as above.

With the landscape-level calculation of AREA_AM, the area of each patch is weighted by its size relative to the area of the entire landscape instead of the corresponding class. Again, larger patches are weighted more heavily than smaller patches, reflecting the understanding that larger patches often play a more important role in how a landscape functions. This metric can be particularly useful in situations where one or more large patches of a native ecosystem may be dominant within the landscape, despite the presence of numerous small patches. Any area effects associated with the large patches may have more of an impact on the ecology of the landscape than edge effects associated with the very small patches (small patches having less habitat value for fewer species).

AREA_AM at the landscape level has an interesting interpretation as a measure of overall patchiness. AREA_AM is directly related to the probability that two randomly chosen pixels in the landscape are situated in the same patch. Specifically, as AREA_AM increases, the probability that any two pixels will be physically connected (i.e., contained within the same patch) increases, which is not necessarily true of the unweighted mean patch size.

3.4.3. *Applications*

As described earlier, mean patch size (AREA_MN and AREA_AM) is one of the most important pieces of information an analyst acquires about a landscape. Patches are major physical and functional components of most landscapes, and as such they exert significant control over landscape functions, abiotically, biotically, and culturally. According to Forman and Godron (1986), patch size affects biomass, primary productivity, nutrient storage per unit area, as well as species composition and diversity. Large patches of native vegetation protect larger areas from soil erosion. They function as large "sponges" promoting rainfall infiltration and serve as habitat patches for interior species that require relatively undisturbed habitat.

Patch size and its derivatives (e.g., AREA_MN and AREA_AM) may serve as rough indicators of landscape function. For example, mean patch size (weighted and unweighted) can serve as an indicator of habitat fragmentation. A landscape with a smaller mean patch size for the target patch type than another landscape may be considered more fragmented if the number of patches is held constant. Similarly, within a single landscape, a patch type with a smaller mean patch size than another patch type might be considered more fragmented if the number of patches is the same (McGarigal and Marks 1995). The size of habitat patches has a close relationship with the population of species that it can support. However, the reduction of patch area does not affect all species equally. Generalist species are not significantly affected by reductions in patch size, while interior species are negatively affected, and edge species are positively affected (Bender et al. 1998). These relative effects will depend on the size of the patches being lost. For example, if the loss of habitat area involves only small patches, edge species will be more affected than interior

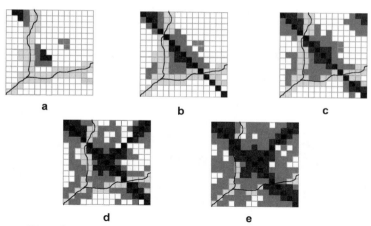

Figure 3.14. Hypothetical landscape transformation associated with agricultural and urban development. The landscape is composed of seven land cover types: road (black), urban (dark gray), agriculture (medium gray), riparian (light gray), forest (white), meadow (cross hatch), and wetland (stipple). The sequence illustrates a typical transformation in which the landscape changes from a forested landscape (a) to an agricultural/urban landscape (e).

species, and conversely if the loss occurs mainly for large patches, interior species will suffer the greater effects (Bender et al. 1998).

In order to illustrate the use and interpretation of AREA_MN and AREA_AM, consider the landscape undergoing transformation in figure 3.14. The landscapes depicted here illustrate a common process in which the landscape is developed for agriculture, urban, and transportation uses. The landscape changes from a forested matrix (a) towards dominance of agriculture and urban uses (e). Two major trends in mean patch size can be observed (figure 3.15). First, the extensiveness of forest and riparian cover types decreases as the landscape progresses through the transformation stages (a) through (e). Second, the extensiveness of agriculture essentially doubles as the landscape is transformed. The road network and urban cover show very little variability throughout the entire process.

Several consequences should be expected as the landscape is transformed and the mean patch size declines for the native forest and riparian patches. First, plant and animal communities which depend on patches of at least three or four hectares or larger will become less diverse and fewer in number. The genetic diversity of these communities will decline as well, as a consequence of reduced population sizes.

Second, as agricultural patches become larger, the number of species that benefit from agricultural land cover can be expected to increase. One

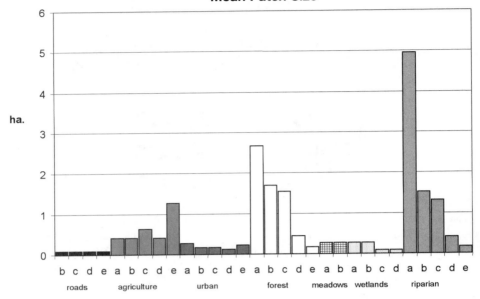

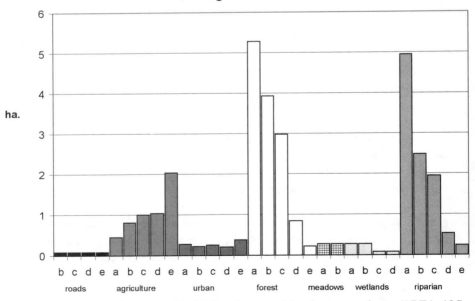

Figure 3.15. Mean patch size (AREA_MN) and area-weighted mean patch size (AREA_AM) values for the landscape of figure 3.14 undergoing transformation.

potential effect of larger agricultural patches and smaller native vegetation patches is larger areas of land devoid of vegetative cover during longer periods of time than would occur with native ecosystem patches. This holds direct implications for stormwater runoff, soil erosion, and nutrient leeching, particularly when riparian patches that buffer streams from agricultural runoff become smaller.

3.4.4. *Limitations*

Mean patch size has three significant limitations. First, it does not address the spatial distribution of patches; for example, how far apart the patches are arranged over the landscape.

Second, mean patch size does not provide information about the distribution of patch sizes. Are there a few very large patches with a multitude of smaller patches, or is the number of patches in each general size class roughly the same? More sophisticated statistical measures may be more descriptive, or even a simple scatter plot of patch sizes can reveal important information about the patches in a particular landscape.

Third, mean patch size reveals no information about the context of the patches. What is the matrix of the landscape? This is at least as important as the size of the patch itself, as the context of the patch determines to a large degree how isolated the plant and animal communities are within the patches. These neighboring patches can be important complementary LCTs that enhance the functionality of the patches, or they can impinge upon the proper functioning of the patch. For example, a grassland adjacent to a forest patch may provide alternative habitat for a forest species, while a residential patch may not.

3.4.5. *Recommendations*

Patch size is a fairly intuitive measure of landscape structure and has many potential applications, both with other landscape data and other landscape metrics. It is with these characteristics in mind that we offer the following principal recommendation.

Mean patch size (AREA_MN and AREA_AM) should not be used without some other indication of required patch size for the landscape functions of interest. For instance, what aspects of landscape function important to the analyst are dependent on or affected by patch size? What are the size requirements for these functions? The more specific the analyst can be about the patch size requirements for various functions, the better they will be able to assess the current state of proposed changes that would affect patch size in the landscape. Formulating the "requirements" and key questions before analysis will provide greater meaning to mean patch size measurements.

Related Metrics

ecological applications, second-order statistics, such as the variation of patch size, may convey more useful information than first-order statistics such as mean patch size. Variability in patch size measures a key aspect of landscape heterogeneity that is not captured by mean patch size and other first-order statistics. Measures of variability are useful since averaging statistics can camouflage important phenomena, such as an uneven distribution of values and the occurrence of extreme values (e.g., very small or very large patches). For example, consider two landscapes with the same patch density and mean patch size, but with very different levels of variation in patch size. Greater variability indicates less uniformity in pattern either at the class level or landscape level, and may reflect differences in underlying processes affecting the landscapes.

Unfortunately, variability is a difficult thing to summarize in a single metric. The two simplest measures of variability are the standard deviation and coefficient of variation. Patch Size Standard Deviation (AREA_SD) is a measure of the absolute variation in patch sizes. For example, a mean patch size of 10 ha could represent a class (or landscape) with six 10-ha patches or six patches of 1-, 2-, 3-, 4-, 10- and 40-ha patches, and the differences between these cases could be important from an ecological perspective. The AREA_SD for the first case is 0, since all patches have the same absolute size. However, the AREA_SD for the second case is 4.34 ha, revealing a significant departure of the individual patch sizes from the average value.

Another useful measure of patch size variability is the Patch Size Coefficient of Variation (AREA_CV). AREA_CV divides AREA_SD by AREA_MN, which normalizes the variability by the mean. Thus, a AREA_SD of 1 ha with a mean of 10 ha has a AREA_CV of 10%, whereas the same absolute variability in patch size (AREA_SD = 1 ha) with a mean of 100 ha has a AREA_CV of only 1%. AREA_CV can be useful when comparing variability among landscapes or among classes with different mean patch sizes.

Patch size is closely related to the concept of interior or core areas. Core Area (CORE) is defined as the central portion of a patch that remains after removing a specified perimeter edge zone. The amount of forest edge vegetation (the transition zone between non-forest and interior forest around a perimeter) is often used to predict species richness (Sorrell 1997). Several bird species are sensitive to patch CORE due to negative intrusions from neighboring areas. Interior species are rare in many human-dominated landscapes and are of high conservation value. Edge species are generally common throughout many landscapes (Dramstad et al. 1996). CORE is a function of both patch size and shape. Its relationship with these two metrics is not linear, due to the shape effect. A patch with a narrow, elongated shape will have a smaller core area than a more compact (rounded) patch with the same area. Shape and core area metrics can be a surrogate measure for the adequacy of a landscape to provide habitat for a particular species. The distance used to define the patch core area must be derived for, or related to, a specific organism or process of interest. Some examples of edge distances are 30–60 m for plant species and 60–600 m for animals (Pearce 1993 referred in Sorrell 1997). Sorrell (1997) and McGarigal and McComb (1995) used 100 m as forest edge width, whereas Tinker et al. (1998) considered 50 m as a conservative estimate of the depth of the coniferous forest edge environment.

3.4.7. Selected References for Further Reading

Bender, D.J., T.A. Contreras, and L. Fahrig. 1998. Habitat loss and population decline: A meta-analysis of the patch size effect. *Ecology* 79(2): 517–533.

McGarigal, K. and W.C. McComb. 1995. Relationships between landscape structure and breeding birds in the Oregon Coast Range. *Ecological Monographs* 65(3): 235–260.

Sorrell, J.P. 1997. Using geographic information systems to evaluate forest fragmentation and identify wildlife corridor opportunities in the Cataraqui Watershed. Ontario: York University Faculty of Environmental Studies.

Van Dorp, D. and P.F.M. Opdam. 1987. Effects of patch size, isolation and regional abundance on forest bird communities. *Landscape Ecology* 1(1): 59–73.

Bennett, A. F. 1999. Linkages in the landscape: The role of corridors and connectivity in wildlife conservation. Gland, Switzerland and Cambridge, UK: IUCN.

Dramstad, W.E., J.D. Olson, and R.T.T. Forman. 1996. Landscape ecology principles in landscape architecture and land-use planning. Washington, D.C.: Island Press.

MacArthur, R.H. and E.O. Wilson. 1967. *The theory of island biogeography*. Princeton, N.J.: Princeton University Press.

Opdam, P. 1991. Metapopulation theory and habitat fragmentation: A review of holarctic breeding bird studies. *Landscape Ecology* 5(2): 93–106.

Saunders, D.A., R. Hobbs, and C.R. Margules. 1991. Biological consequences of ecosystem fragmentation: A review. *Conservation Biology* 5(1): 18–32.

3.5. Shape (SHAPE)

3.5.1. Concept

SHAPE is a measure of the geometric complexity of a patch. SHAPE is a measure of *landscape configuration*; it deals explicitly with the spatial

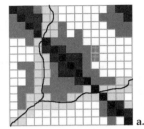 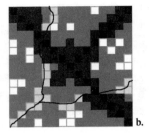

Figure 3.16. Contrasting example landscapes. The landscape is composed of seven land cover types: road (black), urban (dark gray), agriculture (medium gray), riparian (light gray), forest (white), meadow (cross hatch), and wetland (stipple).

character of patches and is expressed as the ratio of the patch perimeter to the perimeter of the most simply-shaped patch with the same area. In contrast to the raw perimeter-to-area ratio, which varies with the size of the patch (i.e., increases in patch size cause a decrease in the perimeter-area ratio), SHAPE and related indices are size independent; patches with widely different areas can be compared in a valid manner (Iverson 1988; Hulshoff 1995). SHAPE can also be categorized as a *compactness* index based on the fact that a circle or square contains a maximum interior area with the least amount of perimeter (i.e., maximum compaction). Compact, simple-shaped patches have SHAPE values close to 1.0, while geometrically more complex patches have values greater than 1.0.

The shape of land cover patches is an important factor in determining how they affect the ecological characteristics of the landscape. Simple patch shapes like circles, squares and rectangles have different implications for human use and ecological function than more complex patches with highly convoluted edges. Figure 3.16 shows two contrasting landscapes. Landscape (a) has larger irregularly shaped patches of forest (white grid cells) as compared to landscape (b). The forest patches in landscape (b) are more compact, and share proportionally less edge with the surrounding landscape.

3.5.2. *Metric Equation and Calculation*

SHAPE is given as the ratio of actual patch perimeter to the perimeter of the theoretically most compact patch. It is smallest for circular (vector data) or square patches (raster or grid data), and increases as patches become increasingly irregular. The smallest value obtainable for a circle (vector) or a square (raster or grid) is 1.0, and as the shape becomes increasingly complex, the value of the index increases without limit.

$$SHAPE = \frac{p_{ij}}{\min p_{ij}}$$

p_{ij} = perimeter of patch ij

$\min p_{ij}$ = minimum perimeter of patch ij in terms of number of cell edges.

SHAPE equals the patch perimeter in number of grid cell sides, divided by the minimum perimeter (given in number of cell sides) possible for a maximally compact patch (in a square raster format) of the corresponding area. If a_{ij} is the area of patch ij (in terms of number of grid cells) and n is the side of a largest integer square number smaller than a_{ij} and $m = a_{ij} - n^2$, then the minimum perimeter of patch ij, $\min p_{ij}$ will take one of the three forms (Milne 1988; Bogaert et al. 2000).

$\min p_{ii} = 4n$, when m = 0, or
$\min p_{ii} = 4n+2$, when $n^2 < a_{ij} \le n(1+n)$, or
$\min p_{ii} = 4n + 4$, when $a_{ij} > n(1+n)$

Units: None
Range of values: 1, without limit

SHAPE corrects for the size problem (as previously described) of the perimeter-area ratio by adjusting for a square (or almost square) standard patch of the same size, and as a result is the simplest and perhaps most straightforward measure of overall shape complexity. Note that the minimum perimeter for an aggregate of like-valued square pixels (a_{ij}) is calculated as above. For large patches, say $a_{ij} > 100$ pixels, the minimum perimeter asymptotically approaches 4, a_{ij}, the perimeter of a square of size a_{ij}.

Figure 3.17 illustrates two patches with the same area (nine cells). Patch (a) is a square while patch (b) is more complex. SHAPE is calculated for each as follows:

Patch (a) SHAPE is calculated as:

$p_{ii} = 12$
$a_{ii} = 9$
$n = 3$
$m = a_{ij} - n^2$ or $9 - (3)^2 = 0$
$\min p_{ii} = 4n$ when m = 0
(See equation explanation above)

Therefore min p_{ii} = 4 (3) = 12

$$SHAPE = \frac{p_{ij}}{\min p_{ij}}$$

$$SHAPE = \frac{12}{12} = 1.0$$

Patch (b) SHAPE is calculated as:

p_{ii} = 20
a_{ii} = 9
n = 3
$m = a_{ij} - n^2$ or $9 - (3)^2 = 0$

min p_{ii} = 4n when m = 0
(See equation explanation above)

Therefore min p_{ii} = 4 (3) = 12

$$SHAPE = \frac{p_{ij}}{\min p_{ij}}$$

$$SHAPE = \frac{20}{12} = 1.67$$

The SHAPE metric equation and examples presented thus far have shown how SHAPE is measured when using gridded or raster format data. In this case the standard compact shape is the square, or near square, when dealing with a non-square number of grid cells. An alternative form for measuring SHAPE is used when the data is in a polygon or vector format. In this case, the ratio is between the actual length of the patch perimeter and the circumference of a circle of the same area (i.e., the most compact patch in vector form). Because of the inherent differences in the representation of

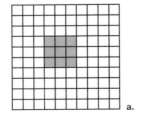 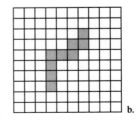

a.   b.

Figure 3.17. Two simple patch examples for illustrating how SHAPE is calculated.

patch perimeters between raster and vector data forms, one should not assume that measurements using the raster and vector forms are directly comparable.

SHAPE is measured at the patch level, and it can be summarized at the class and landscape levels. At the class level, SHAPE typically takes the form of the mean or area-weighted mean SHAPE value for patches of a particular class or LCT. In this case, it describes the average complexity of patch shape for a particular LCT. At the landscape level SHAPE measures the mean or area-weighted mean SHAPE for all patches of all LCTs within a landscape. In this case, it describes the overall complexity of patch shape for the entire landscape mosaic.

Area-weighted mean SHAPE index (SHAPE_AM) is a useful form of the SHAPE metric. With SHAPE_AM, the SHAPE of each patch is weighted by its area relative to the area of the corresponding LCT. Consequently, large patches are weighted more heavily than small patches. This reflects the fact that large patches often play a dominant role in landscape function. SHAPE_AM can be particularly useful in landscapes where one or more large native ecosystem patch dominates. Any effects of patch shape (e.g., edge effects) associated with these patches may therefore have more of an impact upon the ecological functioning of the landscape than those associated with very small patches (e.g., small patches having less habitat value for fewer species).

Class-level calculation of SHAPE_MN:

$$SHAPE\_MN = \frac{\sum_{j=1}^{n} \dfrac{p_{ij}}{\min p_{ij}}}{n_i}$$

n_i = number of patches of the ith LCT.

SHAPE_MN (mean) at the class level equals the sum, across all patches of the corresponding patch type (or LCT), of the SHAPE value for each patch, divided by the number of patches of the same type. Units and range are the same as for SHAPE.

Class-level calculation of SHAPE_AM:

$$SHAPE\_AM = \sum_{j=1}^{n} \left[\frac{p_{ij}}{\min p_{ij}} \left(\frac{a_{ij}}{\sum_{j=1}^{n} a_{ij}} \right) \right]$$

The SHAPE_AM (area-weighted mean) at the class level equals the sum, across all patches of the corresponding patch type (or LCT), of the

SHAPE value for each patch multiplied by the proportional abundance of the patch (patch area divided by the sum of all patch areas). Units and range are the same as for SHAPE.

Landscape-level calculation of SHAPE_MN:

$$SHAPE\_MN = \frac{\sum\limits_{i=1}^{m}\sum\limits_{j=1}^{n}\dfrac{p_{ij}}{\min p_{ij}}}{N}$$

SHAPE_MN (mean) at the landscape level equals the sum, across all patches in the landscape, of the SHAPE value for each patch, divided by the total number of patches. Units and range are the same as for SHAPE.

Landscape-level calculation of SHAPE_AM:

$$SHAPE\_AM = \sum\limits_{i=1}^{m}\sum\limits_{j=1}^{n}\left[\frac{p_{ij}}{\min p_{ij}}\left(\frac{a_{ij}}{\sum\limits_{i=1}^{m}\sum\limits_{j=1}^{n}a_{ij}}\right)\right]$$

SHAPE_AM (area-weighted mean) at the landscape level equals the sum, across all patches in the landscape, of the SHAPE value for each patch multiplied by the proportional abundance of the patch (patch area divided by the sum of all patch areas). Note that the proportional abundance of each patch is determined from the sum of patch areas rather than the total landscape area, because the latter may include internal background area not associated with any patch. Units and range are the same as for SHAPE.

3.5.3. *Applications*

Patch shape strongly influences the magnitude and nature of the interaction of a patch with its surrounding neighborhood, principally via edge effects and cross-boundary processes. Edge effects refer to changes in microclimate, disturbance, and demographic processes that alter vegetation composition and structure, and animal occurrence, abundance, and fitness at the edge or boundary between adjacent patches. In general, patch shape influences the magnitude and nature of edge effects because, as shape complexity increases, the proportional abundance of edge-influenced habitat increases as well. It is important to recognize that edge effects have both positive and negative ecological consequences. For example, early wildlife management efforts were focused on maximizing edge habitat because it was believed that most species favored habitat conditions created by edges and that the juxtaposition of different habitats would increase species diversity (Leopold 1933). Indeed, it has been shown that some species appear to respond positively to edge effects (Kremsater and Bunnell 2000; Carlson and Hartman 2001; Laurance et al. 2001). Recent studies, however, have suggested that changes in microclimate, vegetation, invertebrate populations, predation, brood parasitism, and competition along forest edges has resulted in the population declines of several vertebrate species dependent upon forest interior conditions (e.g., Strelke and Dickson 1980; Kroodsma 1982; Brittingham and Temple 1983; Wilcove 1985; Temple 1986; Noss 1988; Yahner and Scott 1988; Robbins et al. 1989; Hoover et al. 1995; Laurence et al. 2002). In fact, many of the adverse effects of forest fragmentation on organisms seem to be directly or indirectly related to these so-called negative edge effects. Ultimately, the ecological consequences of edges will depend on the details of how patterns of habitat and resource availability in the landscape interact with the ecological requirements and capabilities of individual species.

Patch shape also influences a variety of cross-boundary ecological processes (i.e., the movement of energy, materials, and organisms across patch boundaries). For example, a study in northern New Mexico on wildlife movement in relation to edges between pinyon-juniper woodland and grassland patches demonstrated that herbivore movement *along* patch boundaries decreased with curvilinearity, and that movement *across* patch boundaries increased with curvilinearity (Forman 1995, 106–107). Similarly, in a study of natural succession on reclaimed open-cast mine sites, concave boundaries (such as those found with complex patch shapes) were found to have 2.5 times the density of colonizing trees compared to convex or straight boundaries (Hardt and Forman 1989), indicating that seed dispersal across patch boundaries increased with curvilinearity.

Lastly, patch shape and spatial orientation may play an important role in the movement of plants and animals across the landscape. For example, an elongated patch oriented broadside to the prevailing winds is more likely to intercept plant seeds than a compact circular patch in the same location. Likewise, an elongated patch oriented broadside to the general migratory pathways of certain animals is more likely to be encountered by them than a more compact patch (Gutzwiller and Anderson 1992).

Figure 3.18 depicts a globally common sequence of landscape changes in which a forested landscape is gradually transformed via clearing for agriculture and urban development. The physical change in the structure of the landscape occurring during this transformation process has significant impacts on landscape function. As the proportions of the different LCTs within the landscape change so do the shapes of the patches.

The graph in figure 3.19 illustrates these changes. Initially, the com-

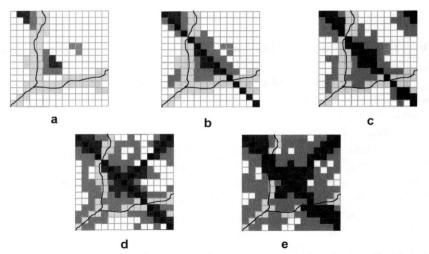

Figure 3.18. Hypothetical landscape transformation associated with agricultural and urban development. The landscape is composed of seven land cover types: road (black), urban (dark gray), agriculture (medium gray), riparian (light gray), forest (white), meadow (cross hatch), and wetland (stipple). The sequence illustrates a typical transformation in which the landscape changes from a forested landscape (a) to an agricultural/urban landscape (e).

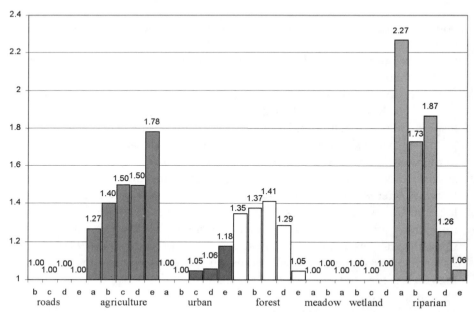

Figure 3.19. Graph depicting the changes in area-weighted SHAPE_AM values for the various LCTs within the landscape depicted in figure 3.18. Note, in particular, the contrasting trends of the agricultural and riparian LCTs, as well as the initial increase and then decline in SHAPE_AM complexity of forest patches.

Table 3.3. If one considers the implications of patch shape complexity for movement of plants and animals through the landscape and its relationship to patch core area, the following characteristics might be expected to occur as patch shape complexity increases and subsequent core area decreases.

Increasing	Decreasing
Numbers and populations of invasive species within remnant forest patches	Occurrence rates for rare plant species that require specific forest patch interior conditions
Predation within remnant forest patches from species adaptive to edge conditions, and domesticated predators such as house cats	Populations of ground-nesting songbirds due to increased predation pressure
Rates of evapo-transpiration along forest edges exposed to sunlight and wind, and over agricultural fields	Stormwater storage in remnant forest patches due to smaller simpler shapes intercepting less surface runoff
Levels of sub-population isolation for plants and animals less gene exchange	Movement of plants and animals across the landscape
	Opportunities for recreational movement by humans along native LCT corridors

plexity of forest patches increases as development progresses, but drops dramatically as the landscape (d and e) progresses through the later stages of development where forest patches are reduced significantly in area. As agriculture and urban land uses come to occupy most of the land once covered with forest and riparian areas, they also assume a greater shape complexity.

3.5.4. *Limitations*

SHAPE has important limitations related to data formats and patch morphology. First, raster and vector datasets may yield different SHAPE values for a given patch, class of patches, or entire landscape because the absolute value of perimeter and area measurements differ between vector and raster data models. In particular, edge lengths, and therefore SHAPE complexity, will be biased upward in raster models due to the stair-step outline of patches. The magnitude of this bias will vary with the resolution of the raster data.

Second, as an index of patch shape, SHAPE is relatively insensitive to differences in patch morphology. Differently shaped patches will have identical SHAPE values as long as the perimeter and area remain the same. For this reason, SHAPE is not useful as a measure of patch morphology, rather it is best considered a measure of overall patch shape complexity.

Lastly, the mean SHAPE index and the area-weighted mean SHAPE index are subject to the limitations of first-order statistics. Neither of these mean values will be very meaningful if the distribution of patch shapes is skewed or complex (McGarigal and Marks 1995).

3.5.5. *Recommendations*

SHAPE provides important information about the geometry of patches that can have important consequences for how a landscape may function. However, as is the case with many other landscape pattern metrics, SHAPE is most meaningful when used in a comparative fashion, when coupled with other related metrics, and when coupled with other data of interest from the landscape. Given the advantages and the limitations of the SHAPE metric described above, we offer the following recommendations for its use:

- SHAPE can function well as a comparative metric, however, basic guidelines should be followed closely. When making comparisons between different datasets, first ensure that the datasets are comparable. The original data should be of the same or very similar spatial resolution. Simply having the same grid cell size does not guarantee that the original datasets are of the same spatial resolution. In addition, because SHAPE is computed differently between vector and raster datasets, only use datasets of the same format when comparing SHAPE values.

- Analysts should also be cautious about the spatial resolution of the dataset relative to the size of the patches—particularly when dealing with raster datasets. If a landscape has many very small patches that are close to or exactly the same area as the grid cell size or minimum mapping unit of the dataset, then the values for SHAPE will be downwardly biased, because a single grid cell will always yield a SHAPE value of 1.0. If a landscape has many small patches, it may be advisable to seek out a dataset that has a spatial resolution that is significantly smaller than these patch areas.

- Patch Area (AREA) and Edge Contrast (ECON) are two metrics that may provide the best complement to SHAPE. AREA provides information that is particularly complementary with SHAPE when considering the total potential *core area* of a patch, i.e., the portion of the patch that is not affected by the edges of the patch. ECON can be useful in comparisons with SHAPE, as ECON also involves examining the length of a patch's perimeter.

- Finally, analysts should always bear in mind that shape complexity is not synonymous with patch morphology. SHAPE can be used effectively to compare relative patch shape complexity within and between different landscapes. But, it cannot tell the analyst, for example, if two patches have similarly shaped "peninsulas" that project into surrounding LCTs. In the end, when this level of information is needed, the data should be plotted in map form for visual analysis and comparison.

3.5.6. *Related Metrics*

Another shape index based on perimeter-area relationships is the fractal dimension index. In landscape ecological research, patch shapes are frequently characterized by their *fractal dimension* (Krummel et al. 1987; Milne 1988; Turner and Ruscher 1988; Iverson 1988; Ripple et al. 1991). The appeal of fractal analysis is that it can be applied to spatial features over a wide variety of scales. Mandelbrot (1977; 1982) introduced the concept of fractals, a geometric form that exhibits structure at all spatial scales, and proposed a perimeter-area method to calculate the fractal dimension of natural planar shapes. The perimeter-area method quantifies the degree of complexity of the planar shapes. The degree of complexity of a polygon is characterized by the fractal dimension (D), such that the perimeter (P) of a patch is related to the area (A) of the same patch by $P \approx \sqrt{A}^{D}$ (i.e., $\log P \approx \frac{1}{2}D \log A$). For simple Euclidean shapes (such as circles and rectangles), $P = \sqrt{A}$ and D = 1 (the dimension of a line). As the polygons become more complex, the perimeter becomes increasingly plane-filling and $P \approx A$ with D = 2. Although fractal analysis typically has not been used to characterize individual patches in landscape ecological research, we can use this relationship to calculate the fractal dimension of each patch separately. Note that the value of the fractal dimension calculated in this manner is dependent upon patch size and/or the units used (Rogers 1993). Moreover, because this fractal measure is based on perimeter and area measurements, it is subject to the same limitations as SHAPE.

Another method of assessing patch shape is based on the ratio of patch area to the area of the smallest circumscribing circle (Baker and Cai 1992). The smallest circumscribing circle provides a measure of overall patch elongation. A narrow (i.e., linear) but highly convoluted patch will have a low circumscribing circle index due to the relative compactness of the patch. Conversely, a narrow but elongated patch will have a high circumscribing circle index. Thus, this index may be particularly useful for distinguishing patches that are both linear (narrow) and elongated.

3.5.7. *Selected References for Further Reading*

Baker, W. L. and Y. Cai. 1992. The r.le programs for multiscale analysis of landscape structure using the GRASS geographical information system. *Landscape Ecology* 7: 291–302.

Forman, R.T.T. 1997. *Land Mosaics: The ecology of landscapes and regions*. New York: Cambridge University Press.

Hulschoff, R.M. 1995. Landscape indices describing a Dutch landscape. *Landscape Ecology* 10(2): 101–111.

Verson, L. R. 1989. Land use changes in Illinois, USA: The influence of landscape attributes on current and historic land use. *Landscape Ecology* 2: 45–61.

Krummel, J. R., R. H. Gardner, G. Sugihara, R. V. O'Neill, and P. R. Coleman. 1987. Landscape patterns in a disturbed environment. *Oikos* 48: 321–324.

Mandelbrot, B.B. 1977. *Fractals, form, chance and dimension*. New York: W.H. Freeman.

Mandelbrot, B.B. 1982. *The fractal geometry of nature*. New York: W.H. Freeman.

McGarigal, K., S. A. Cushman, M. C. Neel, and E. Ene. 2002. FRAGSTATS: Spatial pattern analysis program for categorical maps. Computer software program produced by the authors at the University of Massachusetts, Amherst. Available online at: www.umass.edu/landeco/research/fragstats/fragstats.htm.

McGarigal, K. and B.J. Marks. 1995. FRAGSTATS: Spatial pattern analysis program for quantifying landscape structure. *Gen. Tech. Rep.* PNW-GTR-351. Portland, OR: U.S. Dept. of Agriculture, Forest Service, Pacific Northwest Research Station.

Milne, B. T. 1988. Measuring the fractal geometry of landscapes. *Applied Mathematics and Computation* 27: 67–79.

Rogers, C. A. 1993. *Describing landscapes: Indices of structure*. [M.S. Thesis] Burnaby, British Columbia: Simon Fraser University.

Turner, M. G. and C. L. Ruscher. 1988. Changes in landscape patterns in Georgia, USA. *Landscape Ecology* 1: 241–251.

3.6. Radius of Gyration (GYRATE)

3.6.1. *Concept*

Radius of Gyration (GYRATE) is the mean distance (in meters) between each cell in a cluster of contiguous cells (i.e., a patch) and the patch centroid (which is the average *x* and *y* coordinates for all the cells in the patch). GYRATE is a measure of *landscape configuration* that deals explicitly with the spatial character of patches. GYRATE provides a useful measure of patch extensiveness, i.e., how far across the landscape a patch extends. All other things equal, the larger the patch, the greater the radius of gyration. Similarly, holding area constant, the more elongated or far-reaching the patch, the greater the radius of gyration. GYRATE can be affected by patch shape (e.g., elongated patch shapes have higher GYRATE than compact patch shapes of the same size), but it is not an explicit measure of patch shape. Other metrics have been developed to measure patch shape complexity (e.g., SHAPE fractal dimension and perimeter-to-area ratio). GYRATE can be interpreted as a measure of the average distance an organism can move across the landscape while remaining within the focal

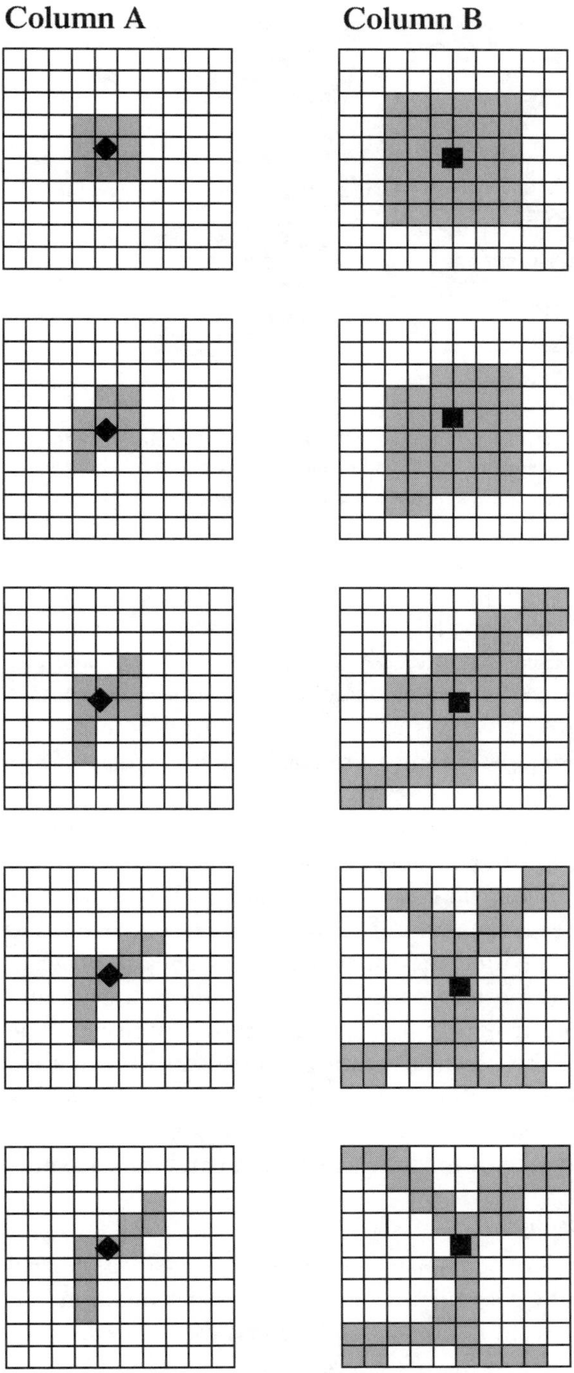

Column A

Column B

Figure 3.20. Example landscapes with different-sized patches (column A has 9-cell patches while column B has 36-cell patches). The square and diamond indicate the location of the patch centroid in the 36- and 9-cell patches, respectively.

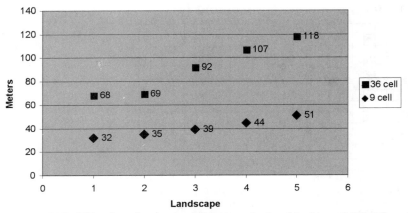

Figure 3.21. GYRATE values for the ten landscapes depicted in figure 3.20. Note the overall difference in values between the 9-cell and the 36-cell patches and the greater increase in values for the 36-cell patch as it becomes more irregular and extensive.

patch from a random starting point in that patch. When GYRATE is aggregated at the class or landscape level (known as correlation length), it provides a measure of landscape connectivity that represents the average traversability of the landscape for an organism that is confined to remain within a single patch. GYRATE retains actual distance measurement units, and therefore is easily related to other measured data, such as species home range size and dispersal distance.

To illustrate GYRATE, consider the landscapes depicted in figure 3.20. Column A contains five hypothetical landscapes, each containing a single small patch (area = nine grid cells), while Column B contains five hypothetical landscapes, each containing a single larger patch (area = thirty-six grid cells). Both the nine and thirty-six cell patches start out in a square configuration, the most compact shape possible in a grid, and become progressively more irregular in shape and more extensive. The GYRATE value for all of the patches within column B are larger than those for the patches within column A, and the differences become greater as the patch size increases (Figure 3.21). As these differences indicate, patch size is a limiting factor for how extensive a patch can become.

3.6.2. *Metric Equation and Calculation*

GYRATE is most easily calculated in a grid representation, since the grid cells provide explicit x and y coordinates for centroid determination and measurement of distances to the centroid. GYRATE is the mean distance between each cell in a patch and the patch's centroid.

$$GYRATE = \sum_{r=1}^{z'} \left(\frac{b_{ijr}}{z} \right)$$

b_{ijr} = distance (m) between cell ijr (located within patch ij) and the centroid of patch ij (the average location), based on cell-center-to-cell-center distance.

z = number of cells in patch ij.

Units: distance units of the dataset (typically meters)
Range of values: ≥ 0, without limit.

GYRATE = 0 when the patch consists of a single cell and increases without limit as the patch increases in extent. GYRATE achieves its maximum value when the patch comprises the entire landscape. GYRATE is calculated for individual patches and can be summarized at the class and landscape levels. The most common summary is the Area-Weighted Mean Radius of Gyration (GYRATE_AM).

GYRATE_AM (area-weighted mean) at the class level equals the sum, across all patches of the corresponding patch type, of the radius of gyration (GYRATE) multiplied by the proportional abundance of the patch (i.e., patch area divided by the sum of all patch areas of the corresponding patch type). Units and range are the same as for GYRATE.

Class-level calculation of GYRATE_AM:

$$GYRATE\_AM = \sum_{j=1}^{n} \left[\sum_{r=1}^{z'} \left(\frac{b_{ijr}}{z} \right) \left(\frac{a_{ij}}{\sum_{j=1}^{n} a_{ij}} \right) \right]$$

GYRATE_AM provides the analyst with a measurement of connectivity known as *correlation length*. Correlation length is the average distance one might traverse across the map while remaining within a patch from a random starting point and moving in a random direction. In other words, correlation length is the expected traversability of the map (Keitt et al. 1997). Large values of GYRATE_AM indicate more connected (less subdivided) landscapes.

Landscape-level calculation of GYRATE_AM (correction length):

$$GYRATE\_AM = \sum_{i=1}^{m} \sum_{j=1}^{n} \left[\sum_{r=1}^{z'} \left(\frac{b_{ijr}}{z} \right) \left(\frac{a_{ij}}{\sum_{i=1}^{m} \sum_{j=1}^{n} a_{ij}} \right) \right]$$

GYRATE_AM (area-weighted mean) at the landscape level equals the sum, across all patches in the landscape, of the GYRATE value multiplied by the proportional abundance of the patch (i.e., patch area divided by the sum of patch areas). Note that the proportional abundance of each patch is determined from the sum of patch areas rather than the total landscape area, because the latter may include internal background area that is not associated with any patch. Units and range are the same as for GYRATE.

3.6.3. *Applications*

GYRATE at the patch level is a measure of the extensiveness of the patch. Elongated patches will have higher GYRATE values than compact patches. If one has comparably sized patches, the GYRATE measurement could be used as a measure of patch shape complexity. Two patches with the same area but different GYRATE values indicate that one patch is more complex in shape (has longer "tendrils"). This application of GYRATE was proposed by Pickover (1990), but is infrequently seen in ecological applications (Gustafson 1998).

More recent and popular applications of GYRATE involve its use as a

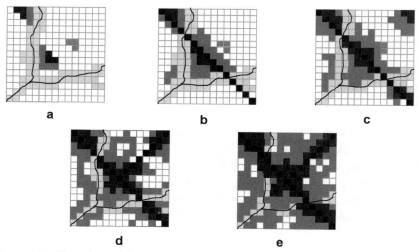

Figure 3.22. Hypothetical landscape transformation associated with agricultural and urban development. The landscape is composed of seven land cover types: road (black), urban (dark gray), agriculture (medium gray), riparian (light gray), forest (white), meadow (cross hatch), and wetland (stipple). The sequence illustrates a typical transformation in which the landscape changes from a forested landscape (a) to an agricultural/urban landscape (e).

measure of landscape connectivity, and detection of the different spatial scales at which landscape connectivity occurs (Keitt et al. 1997). This application of GYRATE involves computing the area-weighted mean of GYRATE (GYRATE_AM). GYRATE_AM allows the analyst to examine how much of the landscape can be traversed without leaving a particular patch, on average. At the landscape level, GYRATE_AM provides the analyst with an overall characterization of the level of subdivision of the landscape.

To better illustrate the use and interpretation of GYRATE, consider the landscape transformation process depicted in figure 3.22. The landscapes depicted here illustrate a common process in which the landscape is developed for agriculture, urban, and transportation uses. The landscape changes from a forested matrix towards dominance of agriculture and urban uses. Two major trends can be observed. First, the extensiveness of forest and riparian cover types decrease as the landscape moves through the transformation stages. Second, the extensiveness of agriculture roughly doubles as the landscape transforms. The road network and urban cover show little or no variability throughout the entire process.

The changes in GYRATE have direct implications for the movement of organisms across the landscape. For example, landscape (a) contains the most extensive distribution of forest and riparian land cover of all of the landscapes, and this is exhibited in the high GYRATE_AM values at the class (Figure 3.23) and landscape levels (Figure 3.24). Organisms and

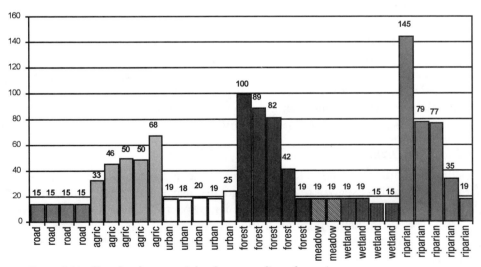

Figure 3.23. Class-level area-weighted mean radius of gyration.

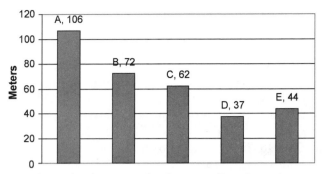

Figure 3.24. Landscape-level area-weighted mean radius of gyration.

landscape processes that are dependent upon forest cover and native riparian cover would be expected to function more naturally and be less impaired in landscape (a). Conversely, the species and processes dependent upon more extensive agricultural land may function better in landscape (e).

Also of note are the sizable drops in GYRATE_AM values between landscape (c) and (d) for both forest and riparian LCTs. This behavior could suggest to the analyst that some critical threshold in landscape structure has been passed. Strategic planning for preservation of forest and riparian LCTs in specific locations might avert a drastic drop in extensiveness and connectivity. In other words, there may be key locations where preservation of a small corridor could have maximal impact upon the connectedness of the landscape.

It should be stressed that this information must be interpreted in light of actual spatial and movement requirements for processes and species that are of interest to the analyst (e.g., dispersal distance, foraging range, or distance residents will walk to neighborhood parks). The scale of extensiveness for a given landscape only has meaning when coupled with actual spatial requirements and characteristics of species and ecological processes (see more on limitations below).

3.6.4. *Limitations*

The main limitation of GYRATE relates to the quality of the source landscape data. The spatial resolution and extensiveness of the landscape dataset will set the lower and upper limits, respectively, for the landscape analysis that can be performed. If the resolution and extensiveness of the landscape data do not match the spatial characteristics of the particular landscape processes or species being studied, then no amount of analysis for GYRATE will provide the insight desired.

In addition, GYRATE does not distinguish between larger patches that are, by definition, more extensive, and smaller patches that may possess an extensive shape (i.e., with convoluted perimeters). GYRATE represents patch extensiveness, independent of patch area, although in real landscapes the two properties are often strongly correlated.

As with many metrics, GYRATE does not directly quantify patch features that could be important to ecological function or visual quality. For example, large values of GYRATE_AM may indicate that large portions of the landscape can be traversed, but these values do not indicate the difficulty or risk associated with the movement, whether it involves a lot of high-risk movement through narrow corridors or comparatively safer movement within larger patch interiors. Likewise, for linear features of the landscape, GYRATE_AM provides no indication of the variable width that these corridors may possess, which may hold significance for the quality of their function as riparian buffers and wildlife movement routes.

Finally, GYRATE is typically used to infer connectivity of the class or landscape. It is important to note that GYRATE is a structural metric that measures the physical structure of the patch mosaic, independent of the organism or process under consideration. In other words, GYRATE does not allow the analyst to functionalize the metric so that the values have explicit meaning in relation to the organism or process under consideration. This is left to the separate and subsequent step of interpretation.

3.6.5. Recommendations

GYRATE provides a means of quantifying patch extent and connectivity that retains actual measurement units (meters). Those investigations that are specifically concerned with spatial scale of landscape function may find GYRATE to be an invaluable tool.

GYRATE is most appropriate as a measure of structural connectivity when the categorical patch mosaic is clearly an appropriate model for the landscape. If the patch mosaic is arbitrary or incorrectly specified, then the values of GYRATE will be of little meaning.

GYRATE can be used effectively in combination with a wide range of other metrics and landscape data. For example:

• Examining a landscape's values for GYRATE and GYRATE_AM in combination with Mean Patch Size (AREA_MN) allows the user to assess the relative quality of patches found within the landscape. Are they extensive *but* lack the critical area to support the desired functions or populations?

• Edge Contrast (ECON) in combination with GYRATE can provide the analyst with an indication of how strong the edge effects may be in the landscape. More extensive patches in a landscape with high edge contrast indicates the potential for greater edge effects.

GYRATE is most meaningful when the source landscape data is appropriate to the phenomenon being studied and the non-landscape data being used possesses explicit scale dependencies:

- The analyst should have some information on the scale of the phenomenon under investigation, be it cultural or ecological. Ideally, no spatial analysis should occur without first documenting these scales.
- The landscape data being analyzed should be appropriately scaled to the actual landscape. For example, there should not be an overabundance of patches in the dataset represented by a single grid cell. Conditions such as these should suggest to the analyst that they are using data with a spatial resolution too coarse for accurate analysis.

3.6.6. *Related Metrics*

GYRATE and its common derivative, GYRATE_AM, are relatively unique among landscape metrics. While other shape metrics measure the geometric complexity of patches, none address extensiveness per se. In addition, while GYRATE is often positively correlated with patch size (AREA), a strong relationship is not inherent in theory, since patches can be quite extensive yet occupy very little area (e.g., linear patches). Similarly, at the class and/or landscape levels, correlation length (GYRATE_AM) is often empirically correlated with class area proportion (CAP), and area-weighted mean patch size (AREA_AM), since an increase in class area usually, though not necessarily, involves an increase in average patch size and extensiveness. Overall, however, at least on a theoretical basis, GYRATE and its derivatives have no closely related landscape metrics.

3.6.7. *Selected References for Further Reading*

Gustafson, E. J. 1998. Quantifying landscape spatial pattern: What is the state of the art? *Ecosystems* 143–156.

Keitt, H., D.L. Urban, and B.T. Milne. 1997. Detecting critical scales in fragmented landscapes. *Conservation Ecology* 1(1): 4. Available online: www.consecol.org/vol1/iss1/art4.

McGarigal, K., S. A. Cushman, M. C. Neel, and E. Ene. 2002. FRAGSTATS: Spatial pattern analysis program for categorical maps. Computer software program produced by the authors at the University of Massachusetts, Amherst. Available online at: www.umass.edu/landeco/research/fragstats/fragstats.html.

Pickover, C. A. 1990. *Computers, pattern, chaos and beauty: Graphics from an unseen world.* New York: St. Martin's Press.

3.7. Contagion (CONTAG)

3.7.1. *Concept*

Contagion (CONTAG) quantifies the degree to which land cover types (LCTs) occur in clumped distributions as opposed to being dispersed in many smaller fragments. Contagion refers to the tendency of LCTs to be spatially aggregated; that is, to occur in large, aggregated or "contagious" distributions. Contagion is a measure of *landscape configuration* because it deals explicitly with the spatial distribution of LCTs. It is computed only at the landscape level and therefore considers all LCTs simultaneously. Contagion quantifies the "clumping" aspect of landscape pattern by computing the number and type of LCT grid cell adjacencies within a gridded dataset. If a landscape's LCTs are increasingly aggregated into a few large clusters of grid cells, the number of like adjacencies (i.e., adjacent cells of the same LCT) will increase, while the number of co-adjacencies (i.e., adjacent cells of different LCTs) will decrease, and the value of contagion will increase. For example, a forested landscape with a few smaller clusters of cells of other LCTs will have a high value of contagion as compared to a landscape with the same number of LCTs but with many patches of similar sizes (Figure 3.25), because the former landscape will have proportionately more like adjacencies. The Midwestern U.S. agricultural landscape provides a good example of a clumped landscape with high contagion because it is typically dominated by a single crop type (corn for example) in one continuous cluster of cells (or patches). It is a highly ordered landscape with very low spatial diversity.

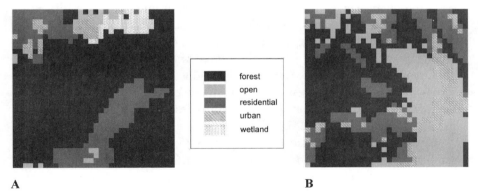

A   B

Figure 3.25. Two sample landscapes drawn from a broader regional landscape in western Massachusetts with differing levels of contagion. Landscape A has a less diverse arrangement of land cover, and a contagion value of 85% while landscape B has a more diverse arrangement of land cover, and a contagion value of 24%.

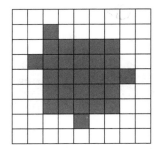

Adjacency Matrix

		k		
		white	dark gray	total
i	white	144	29	173
	dark gray	29	88	117

Figure 3.26. Example calculation for a binary landscape with a contagion value of 25%. Note the number of dark gray and white cells, the total number of cells, and the total number of shared cell edges. Note also that equivalent adjacencies (e.g., dark gray—white, and white—dark gray) are counted twice, as different adjacencies, and that the total number of shared cell edges is also counted twice (144 + 56 + 88 = 288) (see Table 3.4).

An <u>adjacency matrix</u> is simply a way of tabulating and presenting this type of information about the degree of "clumpiness" of a landscape (Figure 3.26). Individual LCTs are listed along the *x* and *y* axes and the number of cell adjacencies is recorded for each possible pairing of LCTs. For a landscape with a large number of LCTs, the matrix can be difficult to calculate and to interpret. The contagion metric takes the adjacency matrix one step further by computing a single value that summarizes the proportional distribution of adjacencies among all possible pairings, including like adjacencies. The greater the concentration of adjacencies along the diagonal (representing like adjacencies), and the lower the equitability of adjacencies among co-adjacencies, the greater the degree of "clumpiness." This makes contagion a useful metric to rapidly and broadly characterize landscape pattern with a single value. As such, contagion can be used effectively to describe differences between landscapes or to describe changes in landscape pattern over time that have significant implications for ecosystem function.

Consider the two landscapes in figure 3.25 from western Massachusetts, which contain the same complement of LCTs. Both landscapes have large areas of forest cover and residential land use. The most significant differences between the two landscapes are the spatial arrangement and proportions of LCTs, which can be summarized by their differences in contagion.

Landscape (a) is arranged in a clumped pattern that is 85% of the maximum aggregation or "clumpiness" of LCTs. Within landscape (a), the movement of organisms dependent upon forest cover (dark gray) would be expected to be fairly uninhibited. In addition, the role of forest cover in the types and rate of nutrient cycling would likely be significant. Landscape (b), on the other hand, has only 24% of the maximum aggregation. In other words, landscape (a) is 3.5 times more clumped than landscape (b). Landscape (b), with a lower contagion value, is spatially more diverse, primarily due to the spatial arrangement of its LCTs. Note that both landscapes have the same complement of LCTs. The LCTs in landscape (b) occur in many smaller patches than in landscape (a). There is also a greater degree of inter-digitation between contrasting LCTs in landscape (b). With smaller patches, particularly forest patches, it is unlikely that landscape (b) could support the same-sized populations of forest-dependent organisms as landscape (a). More complex edges (increased inter-digitation) also mean that the number of shared edges between contrasting LCTs is increased. Edges are often responsible for increased predation, invasion of exotic plant species and, in many cases, serve as barriers to movement for both plants and animals. In sum, landscape (b) would be expected to have fewer forest interior species (plant and animal), smaller populations of these species, and groups of these organisms (i.e., local population) would be relatively isolated from one another. In addition, forest and other native cover types would play a smaller role in nutrient cycling and storage. Given the important role of LCT pattern in these characteristics, and since both landscapes have the same complement of LCTs and comparable areas of forest and residential land cover, it is important to find a means of quantifying the spatial pattern differences between the landscapes. Contagion provides an objective means for quantifying this comparison.

3.7.2. *Metric Equation and Calculation*

Contagion describes the diversity of shared edges between different land cover types (LCTs) in a rasterized, or gridded dataset. At the landscape level, contagion sums, for all LCTs, the product of two distinct proportions for each LCT (McGarigal and Marks 1995). The first proportion is that of the landscape occupied by a particular cover type i represented by the term P_i (this is equivalent to class area proportion; see section 3.2). The second is the proportion of LCT adjacencies that involve any two LCTs, including like and different LCTs. For example, LCT i and LCT k are represented by the term P_{ik}. The equation is shown below. P_{ik} can be easily computed from an adjacency matrix (see Figure 3.26).

$$CONTAG = \left(1 + \frac{\sum_{i=1}^{m}\sum_{k=1}^{n}[(P_i)(P_{ik})]\circ\ln[(P_i)(P_{ik})]}{C\max}\right)\circ 100$$

Table 3.4. Calculating partial values for the numerator of the Contagion equation using the landscape and values from Figure 3.26. Values in the last column on the right will be used in the Contagion equation below in the text. Note that although P_i values are expressed as a decimal value and CAP as a percentage, they are similar.

i	k	P_i (or CAP)	P_{ik}	$(P_i)(P_{ik})$	$\ln[(P_i)(P_{ik})]$	$(P_i)(P_{ik})\ln(P_i)(P_{ik})$
white	dark gray	$\frac{52}{81}=0.64$	$\frac{28}{172}=0.16$	0.10	$\ln(0.10)=-2.3$	$(0.10)(-2.3)=-0.23$
dark gray	white	$\frac{29}{81}=0.36$	$\frac{29}{116}=0.25$	0.09	$\ln(0.09)=-2.4$	$(0.09)(-2.4)=-0.22$
white	white	$\frac{52}{81}=0.64$	$\frac{144}{172}=0.84$	0.54	$\ln(0.54)=-0.6$	$(0.54)(-0.6)=-0.32$
dark gray	dark gray	$\frac{29}{81}=0.36$	$\frac{88}{116}=0.76$	0.27	$\ln(0.27)=-1.3$	$(0.27)(-1.3)=-0.35$

Contagion equals one minus the sum of the proportional abundance of each patch type multiplied by the proportion of adjacencies between cells of that patch type and another patch type, multiplied by the logarithm of the same quantity, summed over each unique adjacency type and each patch type, divided by two times the logarithm of the number of patch types, multiplied by 100 (to convert to a percentage). In other words, the observed contagion over the maximum possible contagion for the given number of patch types, m, given as $C_{max} = 2\ln(m)$.

Units = Percent
Range of values = 0 < CONTAG < 100

Contagion approaches zero when the patch types are maximally disaggregated (i.e., every cell is a different patch type) and interspersed (i.e., equal proportions of all pairwise adjacencies). Contagion approaches 100 when all patch types are maximally aggregated.

The dataset in figure 3.26 illustrates how contagion is calculated for a nine by nine cell binary landscape (two LCTs).

The numerator portion of the equation has several components, as listed and calculated in table 3.4. Essentially the numerator is quantifying the amount of spatial diversity of LCTs. This is affected by the number of LCTs and the spatial arrangement of the different LCT grid cells. Some readers may recognize the Shannon and Weaver diversity index in the numerator (Shannon and Weaver 1949).

$$\sum_{i=1}^{m}\sum_{k=1}^{m}\left[(P_i)(P_{ik})\right]\circ\ln\left[(P_i)(P_{ik})\right]$$

Lastly the denominator of the equation, C_{max}, must be calculated. This is the maximum possible value for contagion given m number of LCTs. Since the landscape example has two LCTs, m = 2, therefore:

$$C_{max} = 2 \ln (m) = 2 \ln (2) = 1.386$$

At this point all the component values of the equation are known, and can be entered into the contagion equation:

$$CONTAG = 1 + \left(\frac{(-0.21) + (-0.24) + (-0.32) + (-0.35)}{1.386}\right) \times 100$$

$$CONTAG = (1 - 0.81) \times 100 = \mathbf{19\%}$$

As the variety of shared edges between LCTs increases, the value of the contagion numerator increases. As the landscape becomes more fragmented, the fractional part of the contagion equation approaches the value of -1, and the entire value of contagion approaches zero. On the other hand, if the LCTs are clumped, and have low spatial diversity, the fractional part of the contagion equation approaches a value of zero, and the total value for contagion approaches one.

Contagion is reported as a percentage by multiplying by 100, thus, values can range from zero to 100%. A landscape with a high value of contagion, by definition, has low spatial diversity. The land cover is likely to be more clumped than fragmented. The denominator C_{max} represents the maximum contagion value for shared edges between LCTs, for example, the maximum variety of shared LCT edges. Dividing the actual value of shared edge variety by the maximum possible value *normalizes* the metric, removing the effect of the number of LCTs on the metric value, thus allowing accurate comparisons of landscapes with differing numbers of LCTs (Gergel and Turner 2003, 88).

As can be observed in the example calculation, a very simple landscape that appears to be very clumped in spatial arrangement actually yields quite a low value for contagion. While this simplified example serves to illustrate how the metric is calculated, it also highlights a potential pitfall and limitation of the contagion metric that is explained in section 3.7.4 on limitations.

It is important to recognize that the contagion metric is based on grid cell adjacencies, not on "patch" adjacencies; therefore it ignores patches *per se* and measures the extent to which cells of the same LCT are aggregated (McGarigal et al. 2002). In addition, contagion is a landscape-level measurement; it is calculated for the entire landscape under analysis and combines information about all of the LCTs within the landscape. Other related measurements may be calculated at the individual class level (individual LCTs), such as CLUMPY and Edge Density (see section 3.7.6 Related Metrics).

3.7.3. *Applications*

The contagion metric has been widely used in landscape ecology and shows promise for landscape planning because it provides a succinct description of landscape texture; specifically, the clumpiness or aggregation of LCTs. With contagion, landscapes with differing numbers of LCTs can be easily compared, and can be compared with other data from the landscape such as composition and frequency of plant and animal communities, visual landscape preferences, and historic landscape events (e.g., fire, flooding, development). Contagion can also be used to compare a landscape at different time periods, to quantify how the degree of clumpiness has changed over time as urbanization has progressed, for example.

Contagion provides information that can be useful in an initial characterization of a landscape. High or low values of contagion may suggest to the planner what the most useful subsequent measures might be. For instance, low values for contagion can be an indirect indicator of a landscape with high levels of shared edge between different ecosystems or land use types. Subsequent measurements on this landscape might be more effective if they focus on describing and quantifying the types of edges occurring within the landscape. High values of contagion likely indicate that several LCTs are clustered in large patches. Confronted with this result, the planner might ask: what types of land cover are aggregated into large patches, and why do they occur in this fashion? How does the aggregation of particular LCTs affect the functioning of the landscape—both ecologically and in terms of human activity?

Early applications of contagion examined the probability of organisms locating food within the landscape and how this probability was correlated with the degree of contagion (O'Neill et al. 1988; Turner et al. 1997). As the mathematical behavior and limitations of the metric are now clearer to researchers, there is an opportunity for broader application in planning. For example, as the European agricultural market is liberalized, increasing areas of land are being abandoned and allowed to return to forest with significant aesthetic implications. In a study of landscape abandonment, reforestation, and landscape aesthetics in Austria, Hunziker and Kienast (1999) found contagion to be a useful metric to index visual landscape complexity. The investigators employed a two-step process. First, the public's reactions to increasing levels of reforestation were assessed. The investigators found that a medium degree of reforestation was considered most aesthetically desirable. Second, the investigators examined the relationship between perceived scenic beauty and measures of landscape pattern. They found a clear linear relationship between perceived scenic beauty and the complexity of the landscape. Contagion was among those metrics of landscape pattern found to relate well with landscape complexity. These findings are in accordance with the theoretical models of Kaplan et al. (1972; 1989, cited in Hunziker and Kienast 1999, 172), which also claim a linear relationship between complexity and landscape preference. Given the significant positive correlation between contagion and landscape preference values, maps of the landscape that indicate likely areas of high scenic value were made for planning purposes without exhaustive public visual surveys.

In figure 3.27, we observe the behavior of contagion in our standard example of a landscape undergoing urban and agricultural development. Early in the landscape transformation process the landscape remains dominated by forest and riparian LCTs. As people begin to use the landscape intensively, the number of LCTs increases and the spatial arrangement of LCTs becomes more fragmented, causing the level of connectivity across the landscape to decline. In the final stages of transformation, human-made LCTs such as agriculture, urban uses, and transportation begin to coalesce into larger patches (and corridors) and thus become a dominant component of the landscape.

The landscape depicted in figure 3.27 is undergoing significant changes in the levels of fragmentation, connectivity, and potentially, human visual appeal. The initial LCTs are relatively undisturbed and maintain their connectivity, particularly the riparian corridors, and the landscape has a moderate level of contagion (55%). Some naturally rare LCTs (meadow and wetlands) occur in isolation and remain undisturbed. As the anthropogenic LCTs are introduced, the connectivity of the riparian corridors is disrupted and the amount of forest decreases. Accordingly, the landscape exhibits decreasing levels of contagion, dropping from 40% to 29%. Dispersal of plants and animals may be inhibited in landscapes (b) and (c), and the riparian zone may be functioning near its limits as a buffer for stormwater runoff. As the transformation process continues, contagion reaches its lowest level of 24%. Forest and riparian zone LCTs are reduced and further fragmented, thus eliminating their habitat value for specialists and their utility for attenuating and filtering stormwater runoff. In the final stage (e), as the agricultural areas begin to coalesce into larger interconnected areas, the contagion value begins to rise again to a value of 25%. As can be seen in figures 3.27 and 3.28, contagion is an integral aspect of landscape pattern directly related to the level of habitat

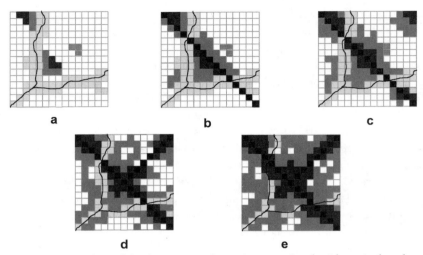

a   b   c

d   e

Figure 3.27. Hypothetical landscape transformation associated with agricultural and urban development. The landscape is composed of seven land cover types: road (black), urban (dark gray), agriculture (medium gray), riparian (light gray), forest (white), meadow (cross hatch), and wetland (stipple). The sequence illustrates a typical transformation in which the landscape changes from a forested landscape (a) to an agricultural/urban landscape (e).

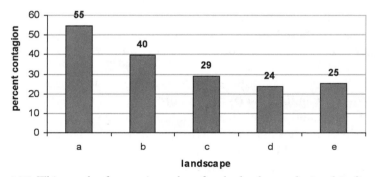

Figure 3.28. This graph of contagion values for the landscape depicted in figure 3.27 shows a clear decline in contagion values that parallels the landscape transformation process. Note the slight increase in contagion from landscape (d) to landscape (e), which corresponds with agricultural land use coalescing into larger patches.

fragmentation. As habitat fragmentation proceeds, contagion decreases, and with it, certain ecological functions are impaired (Saunders et al. 1991).

Given the consistent behavior of contagion in relation to the progressive transformation of the landscape and visual landscape preferences (Hunziker and Kienast 1999), it follows that contagion may prove useful in other applications that involve landscape or regional-scale analyses. Contagion can be used when a large region or regions must be assessed quickly in terms of a landscape characteristic that is not easily mapped in the conventional sense. If a clear statistical relationship can be established between the characteristics of concern and contagion, then contagion may be useful as a surrogate, which can be easily calculated and mapped over large areas.

3.7.4. *Limitations*

CONTAG has five principal limitations. First, CONTAG aggregates a great deal of information about the dispersion (a class-level phenomenon) and interspersion (involving multiple classes of LCTs) of all the LCTs present in the landscape. This feature is both a strength and limitation. Because contagion integrates so much information, the complex patterning of a landscape can be quantified quickly and collapsed into a single numeric value. However, precisely because it aggregates a great deal of information, it is difficult to interpret the full meaning of the metric value without it being accompanied by information about what kinds of LCTs are present in the landscape, or about the relative proportion of those LCTs in the landscape.

Second, CONTAG, as with many other measurements based on quantifying diversity, has no intrinsic meaning in terms of ecology, economics, or natural resources. CONTAG must be used in conjunction with other landscape data, or as a comparative measure to compare different landscapes or to compare alternative plans for a landscape. The primary function of CONTAG is to describe the degree to which LCTs are clumped together. The analyst should understand that landscape patterns similar in terms of CONTAG may be very different in terms of function due to differences in composition. For example, clustering of urban land cover could generate contagion values similar to large contiguous expanses of forest, but the implications of each of these patterns are very different.

Third, CONTAG measures the clumping of LCTs at the level of the grid cell. It is important to recognize that this does not represent the clustering of patches of LCTs (or to put it in other terms, the clustering of clusters of grid cells). Contagion describes, over the entire landscape and across all LCTs, the degree to which grid cells of the same LCT are clumped together (touching one another) (Hargis 1998). Thus, in contrast to most other landscape metrics described in this book, CONTAG is not a patch-based metric, i.e., it is not derived explicitly from the patch mosaic structure.

Fourth, CONTAG can only be calculated on data in a grid format and not on polygonal landscape data. CONTAG measurements can be made on data that was originally produced in polygonal form, but this requires conversion of the polygonal data to a grid format, and caution must be taken when selecting the cell size during the rasterization process, since it can affect the value of CONTAG (see Recommendations).

Finally, CONTAG is affected by two other characteristics of a gridded/raster dataset: the relative amount of outer or landscape boundary cell edges relative to the interior grid cell edges, and the total number of LCTs within the landscape. If the spatial extent of the dataset is very limited (as in the example calculation of section 3.7.2) or has very few LCTs (say, fewer than four), then the values calculated for contagion will appear to be lower than expected. Precautions should be taken, such that the landscapes being examined have an ample spatial extent (landscape boundary cell edges being significantly less than twenty-five percent of the total shared cell edges within the landscape) and that the total number of LCTs is at least greater than four. These precautions are particularly important if comparisons are to be made between different landscapes. Each landscape in the comparison should have spatial extents that are reasonably close to one another (not more than a 25% difference), and likewise have a similar number of LCTs. It would not be advisable, for instance, to compare a landscape such as the one illustrated in section 3.7.2 (9 x 9 grid with two LCTs) with a landscape represented with a 500 x 500 grid and twelve different LCTs.

3.7.5. *Recommendations*

CONTAG is a tool that can only be used for broad overall characterizations of landscape pattern and for comparisons between landscapes. Given the amount of information that is aggregated into CONTAG and the lack of land cover specificity, the best use of CONTAG is in the early or initial stages of landscape analysis. The planner should use CONTAG as a means of comparing similar landscapes, to compare the same landscape at different points in time, or to compare different areas within the same landscape with each other. With these considerations in mind we offer the following recommendations:

- Preparatory work should be done before using CONTAG. The an should start by looking at CAP values—the proportion of the landsc comprised of each LCT. Be advised that landscapes that are highly dominated by one cover type or are highly fragmented may yield values for CONTAG that do not provide much new information.

- Use CONTAG in conjunction with other measurements of landscape composition and configuration, particularly those that provide some information about individual LCTs. Measurements of the number and size of patches and the density of edge helps to explain the observed value of CONTAG.

3.7.6. *Related Metrics*

Edge Density (ED), Clumpiness Index (CLUMPY), and Aggregation Index (AI) are three metrics related to contagion in that they measure aspects of the same phenomenon, but from slightly different perspectives.

ED is a metric that measures the density of edges within a landscape. It can be calculated at the class level for a particular LCT, or it can be calculated at the landscape level across all LCTs in the landscape. The calculation of ED at the landscape level is most closely related to CONTAG as it considers all LCTs within the landscape. The metric value is the number of units of edge per unit area of landscape (for example meters of edge per hectare of landscape). Low ED across all LCTs would correspond to a high value of contagion for that landscape (McGarigal et al. 2002).

CLUMPY compares the proportion of cell adjacencies that are of the same LCT to the proportion of adjacencies of the same LCT that would be expected under a spatially random distribution of LCTs. In other words, is the clumpiness of a particular LCT greater than what would be expected within a random arrangement of this particular LCT? CLUMPY is computed at the class level rather than the entire complement of LCTs within the landscape (McGarigal et al. 2002).

AI measures the proportional aggregation of all LCTs within a landscape. For each LCT the number of like cell adjacencies is totaled and divided by the maximum possible value given the total number of cells of that LCT. This value is then multiplied (weighted) by the proportion of the landscape comprised of that particular LCT. The resulting values for each LCT are summed and the total value is multiplied by 100 to provide a percentage value. As described previously, this metric characterizes all LCTs within the landscape. The value for AI could also be calculated for an individual LCT without the need to weight the value according to the LCT's landscape proportion (McGarigal et al. 2002). AI is similar to contagion in that it aggregates information across all of the LCTs within the landscape, but differs from contagion because it only considers like adjacencies, whereas contagion considers both like and unlike adjacencies. Thus, AI deals with only dispersion, but contagion deals with both dispersion and interspersion

An important commonality of these metrics (CONTAG, ED, CLUMPY, AI) is that they utilize information about the adjacency of LCTs—whether this information is recorded in an adjacency matrix or recorded as lengths of edge or patch perimeters. Adjacencies of cells of LCTs, whether they are of the same type or different, are at the crux of what these metrics measure. Because adjacency of same type LCTs within a grid is computationally easier to handle than adjacency within a polygonal model (polygonal topology doesn't allow for the like adjacencies to be calculated), all of these metrics, with the exception of ED, are presented with the assumption that the calculation will be performed on a rasterized landscape dataset. It is important to remember that all measures based on a grid data model are strongly affected by the grain size or resolution of the grid. Given a particular distribution of clusters of like value cells (patches), a smaller grain size will result in a proportional increase in like adjacencies. Given this scale dependency, these metrics are best used if the scale is held constant.

3.7.7. Selected References for Further Reading

Graham, R.L., C.T. Hunsaker, R.V. O'Neill, and B. Jackson. 1991. Ecological risk assessment at the regional scale. *Ecological Applications* 1: 196–206.

Gustafson, E.J. and G.R. Parker. 1992. Relationships between land cover proportion and indices of landscape spatial pattern. *Landscape Ecology* 7: 101–110.

Hargis, C.D., J.A. Bissonette, and J.L. David. 1998. The behaviour of landscape metrics commonly used in the study of habitat fragmentation. *Landscape Ecology* 13: 167–186.

Hunziker, M. and F. Kienast. 1999. Potential impacts of changing agricultural activities on scenic beauty: A prototypical technique for automated rapid assessment. *Landscape Ecology* 14 (2): 161–176.

Li, H. and J.F. Reynolds. 1993. A new contagion index to quantify spatial patterns of landscapes. *Landscape Ecology* 8: 155–162.

Miller, J.N., R.P Brooks, and M.J. Croonquist. 1997. Effects of landscape pattern on biotic communities. *Landscape Ecology* 12: 137–153.

O'Neill, R.V., J.R. Krummel, R.H. Gardner, G. Sugihara, B. Jackson, D.L. DeAngelis, B.T. Milne, M.G. Turner, B. Zygmunt, S.W. Christensen, V.H. Dale, and R.L. Graham. 1988a. Indices of landscape pattern. *Landscape Ecology* 1: 153–162.

O'Neill, R.V., B.T. Milne, M.G. Turner, and R.H. Gardner. 1988b. Resource utilization scales and landscape pattern. *Landscape Ecology* 2: 63–69.

Saunders, D.A., R. Hobbs, and C.R. Margules. 1991. Biological consequences of ecosystem fragmentation: A review. *Conservation Biology* 5: 18–32.

Turner, M.G. 1990. Landscape changes in nine rural counties of Georgia. *Photogrammetric Engineering and Remote Sensing* 56: 379–386.

Turner, M.G., S.M. Pearson, W.H. Romme, and L.L. Wallace. 1997. Landscape heterogeneity and ungulate dynamics: What spatial scales are important? In *Wildlife and Landscape Ecology*, ed. J.A. Bissonette, 331–348. New York: Springer-Verlag.

3.8. Edge Contrast (ECON) ✳

3.8.1. *Concept*

Edge Contrast (ECON) is a basic measure of the amount of contrast between adjacent land cover patches, where contrast must be defined for each application based on one or more attributes of interest (e.g., floristics, vegetation structure, hydrography). High edge contrast, such as a forest adjacent to an urban land cover patch, suggests that the ecological effects of a shared patch edge may be significant. Conversely, similar adjacent patches will likely create an edge with minimal ecological effects, for example adjacent patches of forest and wetland. ECON is a measure of *landscape configuration* because it deals explicitly with the spatial arrangement and juxtaposition of LCTs. Figure 3.29 below compares landscapes with high and low amounts of edge contrast.

In essence, ECON is a measurement of *functional* edge based on predetermined contrast weights assigned to specific pairwise comparisons of

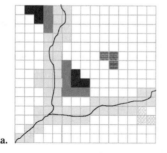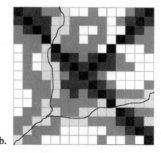

Figure 3.29. A comparison of landscapes with high (a) and low edge contrast (b). The two landscapes have a mixture of seven land cover types: roads (black), urban (dark gray), agriculture (medium gray), riparian (light gray), forest (white), meadow (cross hatch), and wetland (stipple). The landscape on the left possesses a low edge contrast value for forest (23.8%), while the landscape on the right has a relatively high forest edge contrast value of 66.33%.

LCTs. ECON is usually represented as a percentage of total edge calculated by means of a set of contrast weights applied to segments of the perimeter of a patch.

Patch edges play a recognized and important ecological role in the movement of plants, animals, people, and nutrients across landscapes. Forman (1995) defines five potential functions of edges as: barrier, filter, source, sink, and conduit. Edges are fairly easily observed in most mapped data, however it is difficult to make explicit measurements or comparisons between landscapes, or to compare a particular landscape at multiple times. ECON offers a means for the analyst to mathematically quantify and define the quality of edge based on a particular phenomena or process of concern.

The two landscapes depicted in figure 3.29 help illustrate the implications of differing levels of edge contrast for humans or wildlife. The largely forested landscape (a) shows little edge contrast. Therefore, the movement of plants, animals, and nutrients would be expected to be relatively uninhibited by edge impediments. Landscape (b), on the other hand, exhibits a greater number of contrasting land cover types (LCTs), thus, it has a higher edge contrast. In this landscape, there are urban areas adjacent to forest and farmland, and highways adjacent to riparian and wetland LCTs. Edges with high contrast may have significant implications for movement within a landscape. While automobiles may traverse landscape (b) easily, other entities such as pedestrians and wildlife may find it difficult or even impossible to cross certain types of high-contrast edges (e.g., forest–highway edges). High contrast edges can also hold important implications for landscape use or safety. Consider two situations likely to occur in landscape (b):

1. *Urban/highway corridor cutting through a forest*: One species of songbird may flourish in the edge environment created by the highway corridor, using it as a source of nesting materials and food (insects and berries). A ground nesting songbird species adjacent to the very same corridor may suffer increased nest predation from animals such as domestic cats that use the corridor as a pathway and hunting ground (Yahner 1988; Gates, 1991).

2. *Urban park edge versus abandoned lots adjacent to forest*: There is a high level of contrast between a forested urban park and a surrounding urban streetscape. Within the same urban area, however, the contrast in edge between abandoned city lots and an adjacent forested area may be less, because the lots are likely to be in succession with weeds and small trees present. In the former situation, people may feel secure by virtue of the well-defined and maintained edge between the

two environments, while in the latter situation the sense of safety may
be less, owing to the unkempt appearance of the abandoned lots. In
terms of wildlife preferences, the exact opposite may be true, with various forms of wildlife avoiding the highly contrasted edge of the
forested park in favor of the abandoned lots that possess food sources
and hiding places.

A skilled analyst can calibrate the edge contrast weights to the relative
sensitivities of any species of interest or segment of human society, and
thereby measure edge contrast in a meaningful way for their particular
application. The key to using the edge contrast metric is to have a clear
understanding of the specific ecological, physical, and/or social factors or
processes that are of interest to the investigator, and how these factors are
affected by the various conditions created by different adjacent patch types
(McGarigal and Marks 1995). The same type of edge may have different
effects on different wildlife species, ecological processes, and on the quality
of life for people. Understanding these potential differences is crucial since
the ECON metric requires that the investigator weight or rate the degree
of contrast between the different LCTs. This weighting scheme forms the
basis of the edge contrast calculation, and it must be explicitly connected to
the landscape phenomena being examined. Without a good understanding
of how different land cover types are from one another, the chances for calculating meaningful results are slim (McGarigal and Marks 1995).

3.8.2. *Metric Equation and Calculation*

The measurement of ECON has two basic parts. The first part is the contrast weight, between zero and one, which is assigned to all possible com-
binations of LCTs based upon their contrast with each other relative to a
specified process or relationship. The second part of the measurement is
the amount of each particular type of edge present. Each segment of the
patch perimeter is multiplied by the contrast weight that is assigned to
that type of shared edge. Therefore, some segments of a perimeter of a
patch may represent edges of very high contrast, while other segments of
the perimeter of the patch may represent very low contrast edges. In
either case, high or low contrast, the product is represented as a percentage of the actual length of the perimeter segment. It is larger if there is
more contrast (i.e., approaching the actual perimeter length) and smaller
if there is less contrast (i.e., approaching zero).

$$ECON = \frac{\sum_{k=1}^{m'} (p_{ijk} \cdot d_{ik})}{p_{ij}} (100)$$

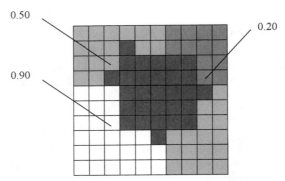

Figure 3.30. Example patch (dark gray) for single patch edge contrast calculation.

ECON equals the sum of the patch perimeter segment lengths multiplied by their corresponding contrast weights, divided by the total perimeter of the patch p_{ij}. The resulting value is multiplied by 100 to convert it to a percentage value (McGarigal and Marks 1995).

> Units = percentage
> Range of values = $0 \le EC \le 100$

To illustrate the calculation of ECON, consider the patch mosaic in figure 3.30. In this example, the patch perimeter can be subdivided into segments corresponding to the number of cell sides. In this case, let's assume that cells are ten meters in length. If one perimeter grid cell is adjacent to a cover type that is contrast weighted at 0.10, then the edge contrast length for that segment is 10 × 0.10 contrast = 1. This means there is the equivalent of only one meter of maximum-contrast edge associated with that segment. The dark gray patch in the middle of the diagram has a perimeter of 280 m in length. Assume the following contrast weights for the various patch types surrounding the patch.

To determine ECON, first examine the neighboring patches and tally up how many meters of edge are shared with them. Then the following equation is applied to the "example" dark gray patch in figure 3.30.

Table 3.5. Contrast weights for example land cover types depicted in Figure 3.30.

	CONTRAST WEIGHTS		
	White	*Medium Gray*	*Light Gray*
Dark Gray Patch	0.90	0.20	0.50

Table 3.6. Amount of shared edge between LCTs in Figure 3.30.

Dark Gray and White edge: (80) x (0.90) =	72
Dark Gray and Light Gray edge: (150) x (0.50) =	75
Dark Gray and Medium Gray edge: (40) x (0.20) =	8
TOTAL	155

The numerator portion of the equation is calculated as shown in table 3.6. Next we divide the 155 by the total perimeter length (280) and multiply the quotient by 100 to produce the edge contrast percentage value:

$155 \div 280 = 0.554$
$0.554 \times 100 = 55.4$ percent

Contrast can range between zero and 100%. If the dark gray patch had possessed maximum contrast edges around its entire perimeter (every segment having an edge contrast of one), then the value for ECON would be 100%. Conversely, if the dark gray patch had only a minimal edge contrast for all of its perimeter segments, then the value for ECON would be very close to zero percent.

Edge contrast can be measured at the patch, class, or landscape level. The calculation for an individual patch is described above. At the class and landscape levels, ECON can be calculated as the Mean Edge Contrast Index (ECON_MN) or MECI, Area-weighted Mean Edge Contrast Index (ECON_AM), and Total Edge Contrast Index (TECI). ECON-MN is calculated as the mean of the individual patch ECON values. At the class level, the result is the average edge contrast index for all the patches of a particular LCT within the landscape.

Class-level calculation of mean edge contrast index (ECON_MN):

$$ECON\_MN = \frac{\sum_{j=1}^{n} \left[\frac{\sum_{k=1}^{m'} (p_{ik} \cdot d_{ik})}{p_{ij}} \right]}{n_j}(100)$$

ECON_MN (mean) at the class level equals the sum of all the patch perimeter segment lengths (m) involving the corresponding patch type multiplied by their corresponding contrast weights, divided by the total patch perimeter, summed across all patches of the corresponding type, divided by the number of patches of the same type, multiplied by 100 (McGarigal and Marks 1995). Units and range are the same as for ECON.

Class-level calculation of area-weighted mean edge contrast (ECON_ AM):

$$ECON\_AM = \sum_{j=1}^{n} \left(\left[\frac{\sum_{k=1}^{m'} (p_{ik} \cdot d_{ik})}{p_{ij}} \right] \left[\frac{a_{ij}}{\sum_{j=1}^{n} } \right] \right) (100)$$

ECON_AM (area-weighted mean) at the class level equals the sum of the segment lengths (m) of the perimeter of each patch multiplied by its corresponding contrast weights, divided by total patch perimeter, multiplied by patch area divided by the sum of patch areas, summed across all patches of the corresponding patch type with the product multiplied by 100. Units and range are the same as for ECON.

With this measurement, large patches are weighted more heavily than small patches in recognition of the fact that large patches often play a dominant role in how a landscape functions. This metric can be particularly useful in situations where one or more large patches of native ecosystem may be dominant within the landscape. Any edge effects associated with these patches may therefore have more of an impact upon the ecology of the landscape than edge effects associated with very small patches (small patches having less habitat value for fewer species).

An alternative to the patch-based metrics (ECON, ECON_MN, and ECON_AM) is TECI. This metric enables the investigator to examine all the edges of a particular LCT (class level), or over the entire landscape (landscape level), based solely upon the characteristics of each edge segment, independent of its patch affiliation.

Class-level calculation of total edge contrast index (TECI):

$$TECI = \frac{\sum_{k=1}^{m'} (e_{ik} \cdot d_{ik})}{\sum_{k=1}^{m'} e'_{ik}} (100)$$

e_{ik} = total length (m) of edge in landscape between patch types (classes) i and k; includes landscape boundary segments involving patch type i.

e'_{ik} = total length (m) of edge in landscape between patch types (classes) i and k; includes the entire landscape boundary and all background edge segments, regardless of whether they represent edge or not.

d_{ik} = edge contrast weight between patch types i and k.

TECI (Total Edge Contrast Index) at the class level equals the sum of the lengths (m) of each edge segment involving the corresponding patch type multiplied by the corresponding contrast weight, divided by the sum of the lengths (m) of all edge segments involving the same type, multiplied by 100 (McGarigal and Marks 1995). Units and range are the same as for ECON.

Each of the class-level metrics just described are adapted for measurement at the landscape level, which considers the edges of all patches of all types within the landscape.

Landscape-level calculation of mean edge contrast ECON_MN:

$$ECON\_MN = \frac{\displaystyle\sum_{i=1}^{m}\sum_{j=1}^{n}\left[\frac{\displaystyle\sum_{k=1}^{m'}(p_{ik}\cdot d_{ik})}{p_{ij}}\right]}{N}(100)$$

Edge contrast calculations are performed for each patch in the landscape (across all patch types) and then summed. This total is divided by the total number of patches N in the landscape. The resulting quotient is multiplied by 100 to generate a percentage value. Units and range are the same as for ECON.

Landscape-level calculation of area-weighted mean edge contrast ECON_AM:

$$ECON\_AM = \sum_{i=1}^{m}\sum_{j=1}^{n}\left(\left[\frac{\displaystyle\sum_{k=1}^{m'}(p_{ik}\cdot d_{ik})}{p_{ij}}\right]\left[\frac{a_{ij}}{A}\right]\right)(100)$$

ECON_AM (area-weighted mean edge contrast) at the landscape level equals the sum, across all patches in the landscape, of the value of ECON, multiplied by the proportional abundance of the patch (i.e., patch area divided by the sum of all patch areas in the landscape). Note that the proportional abundance of each patch is determined from the sum of patch areas rather than the total landscape area, because the latter may include internal background area not associated with any patch. Units and range are the same as for ECON.

ECON_AM at the landscape level is particularly helpful in landscapes that exhibit a wide range of patch sizes across different patch types. By weighting the contrast values by patch area the investigator can control the disproportionate effect that many small patches might exert in the calculation of edge contrast. TECI is adapted for landscape-level measurement in a fashion similar to ECON_MN and ECON_AM, with the mean being based upon all edges across all LCTs in the landscape:

Landscape-level calculation of total edge contrast index (TECI):

$$TECI = \frac{\sum_{i=1}^{m'} \sum_{k=1}^{m'} (e_{ik} \cdot d_{ik})}{E'} (100)$$

e_{ik} = total length (*m*) of edge in landscape between patch types (classes) *i* and *k*; includes landscape boundary segments involving patch type *i*.

E' = total length (*m*) of edge in landscape; includes entire landscape boundary and background edge segments regardless of whether they represent edge or not.

d_{ik} = dissimilarity (edge contrast weight) between patch types *i* and *k*.

TECI at the landscape level equals the sum of the lengths (m) of each edge segment in the landscape multiplied by the corresponding contrast weight, divided by the total length (m) of edge in the landscape, multiplied by 100 (to convert to a percentage). Edge segments along the landscape boundary are treated like background. Units and range are the same as for ECON.

3.8.3. *Applications*

While edges within the landscape are not inherently positive or negative features, they are an important component of landscape structure and function. For this reason, metrics of landscape edge conditions are useful for landscape planning. ECON can provide an indication of how important a role edge may be playing in a landscape. ECON provides a useful analysis on categorical land cover data. It allows the analyst to depict edge in a way that aids comparison among landscapes and, via contrast weights, can be based upon factors that are relevant to the phenomenon(s) under primary consideration (i.e., human perception, or landscape resistance to species movement). Several general observations can be made regarding the ecological effects of edges:

- High-contrast edges may collect a greater variety of plants, thus concentrating biodiversity in certain areas of the landscape.

- Movement of animals and dispersal of plant seeds may be inhibited by high-contrast edges.

- Landscapes with a moderate amount of edge contrast may hold the most visual interest and aesthetic value for humans.

- Landscapes with little edge and/or little edge contrast may allow greater movement of plants and animals, thus reducing the isolation of separate plant and animal populations. However, a landscape with little edge contrast might lack effective barriers to the spread of catastrophic disturbance such as wildfire or insect infestation.

In landscapes being intensively managed by people, the amount of edge contrast may correlate well with differing rates of land development or urbanization. Areas of varying amounts of edge contrast can be identified by mapping ECON values over the entire landscape, and the resulting maps can be used as a means for identifying specific portions of the landscape that require a particular type of management. Once an area of high-edge contrast has been identified, for instance, the types of edge at the level of the individual patches can be examined to determine the most appropriate management practice for those edges. This type of targeted edge management could be useful in planning further urban and suburban development as well as in habitat management (Schonewald-Cox and Buechner 1990; Schonewald-Cox and Bayless 1986).

Figure 3.31 depicts a common land transformation sequence in which a forested landscape is sequentially developed for agriculture, urban, and transportation uses. During the transformation process, the variety of LCTs changes, with an overall decrease in the total number of LCTs (a reduction of one LCT). The more rare native cover types, wetlands and meadows, are reduced throughout the transformation, and are entirely absent from the fully developed landscape (e). In general, for native cover types there is an increase in ECON, while for human-made cover types there is either a reduction in ECON or very little change in ECON.

As can be seen in figure 3.32, ECON increases for most of the native land cover types as the landscape is transformed from forest to agriculture and urban uses. (Note that forest contrast ranges from 23.8% initially to

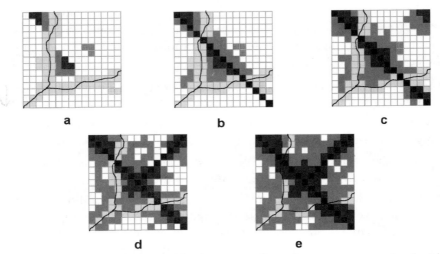

Figure 3.31. Prototypical forested landscape transformation sequence associated with agricultural and urban development. The landscape is composed of seven land cover types: road (black), urban (dark gray), agriculture (medium gray), riparian (light gray), forest (white), meadow (cross hatch), and wetland (stipple). The sequence illustrates a typical transformation in which the landscape changes from a forested landscape (a) to an agricultural/urban landscape (e).

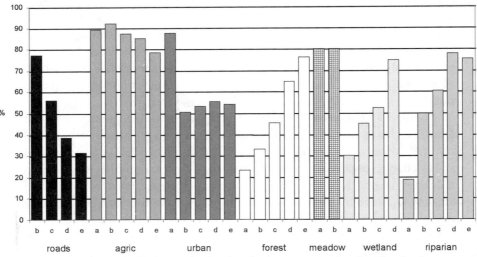

Figure 3.32. This graph shows the levels of edge contrast for the five landscapes depicted in figure 3.31. Note the changes in edge contrast for each land cover type as the landscape changes.

Table 3.7. Contrast levels used in calculating the five landscapes in Figure 3.31.

	Forest	*Urban*	*Agriculture*	*Riparian*	*Road*	*Wetland*	*Meadow*
Forest	0	1	0.9	0.1	1	0.4	0.8
Urban	1	0	1	1	0.2	1	1
Agriculture	0.9	1	0	0.9	1	1	1
Riparian	0.1	1	0.9	0	1	0.2	0.8
Road	1	0.2	1	1	0	1	1
Wetland	0.4	1	1	0.2	1	0	0.7
Meadow	0.8	1	1	0.8	1	0.7	0

77.8% in the fully developed landscape, wetlands contrast ranges from 30% to 75%, and riparian contrast ranges from 18.6% to 73% in the developed landscape.) Conversely, some of the human-made cover types show a progressive decrease in contrast (road ECON changes from 77% to 31%) or a stepwise drop in contrast (urban ECON drops initially from 87.5% to 53.75%, and then remains near 55%). Table 3.7 indicates the contrast levels that were used in calculating EC for the five landscapes in Figure 3.31. These assigned contrast values directly influence the calculations, and therefore should be based on as much scientific information as possible.

For native land cover types (e.g., forest, wetland) there is a clear progression towards a higher ECON condition in the later stages of the sequence. One would expect that these LCTs would become progressively more difficult for non-flying wildlife species to reach. For manmade LCTs, particularly agriculture, the relatively constant level of contrast would probably have little impact on production, while for less tangible qualities such as scenic beauty, the landscape stages that show a moderate level of contrast for native cover types may also offer the most scenic appeal to people.

Landscape planners and managers deal with present and future landscape patterns to consider multiple values and perspectives. Private economic values are considered as well as the natural resources that are part of the public trust. In general, ECON allows the analyst to explicitly understand how edges are changing on an individual LCT basis. One potential planning application would be to examine the ECON of build-out landscapes—those patterns that would result with the full realization of land use based upon current zoning, similar to landscape (e) in figure 3.31. If potential conflicts became apparent with this analysis of the build-out landscapes, then planners might simulate, with alternative future scenarios, how ECON would change with a different spatial arrangement of permitted land uses.

Additionally, the planner might explore future landscape pattern scenarios in which corridor features such as recreational greenways and riparian corridors are employed as buffers to reduce a detrimental ECON between ecosystem patches. These future scenarios could be quantitatively evaluated and "fine tuned" with ECON analysis as one of the guiding tools.

3.8.4. *Limitations*

ECON measurements have three basic limitations. First, quantification of the amount of ECON present in the landscape should not be confused with the quantification of edge effect. At best, the quantification of ECON can suggest whether or not edge effect is probable and predict its likely magnitude. This type of measurement is best used as a tool to guide field work but not to be a substitute for it. The metric is explicitly limited by the investigator's knowledge of the characteristics of the land cover being measured. If a weighting factor is misjudged or misapplied, all subsequent results are called into question.

Second, the contrast weights assigned are one dimensional. What may be very high contrast for one valued species (including humans) could be only a moderate contrast for another species. Perhaps the most prudent approach in using the metric is the selection of multiple contrast weights, with each being assigned according to a specific valued wildlife species or landscape management goal. With more than one set of contrast weights the investigator is able to evaluate the degree of ECON of a landscape from different perspectives and for the purposes of achieving different goals.

Third, measurements of ECON aggregate information and thus obscure other types of spatial information. While the investigator gains information about the quality of edges, they do not gain information about the total amount of edge or the specific spatial arrangement of edge types relative to one another. Are all the high-contrast edge types clustered in one area of the landscape or are they evenly distributed? Are edges clustered such that similar kinds of edges occur near one another or does the distribution of edge types appear random? These questions cannot be answered by the edge contrast metric alone. Application of edge contrast measurements may best be accomplished by mapping the measured values, with patches keyed according to amount and type of edge, thus making the spatial arrangement of edge types more obvious.

3.8.5. *Recommendations*

Measurements of edge contrast must be interpreted in light of the specific context of their application—no single generalization will hold value for all landscapes. Conversely, no single landscape pattern metric will suffice for all landscapes. The most powerful insights are gained by using multiple landscape metrics in concert. Consequently we offer the following recommendations when using ECON and its derivatives:

• *Understand what kinds of land cover and ecosystems are within the landscape being analyzed.* The greatest gain in knowledge and information will occur when the analyst has an informed understanding of the different types of land cover occurring within the study landscape. Field-based information and knowledge of the various ecosystems within the landscape are crucial complements to ECON measurements. There is no substitute for field work such as sampling vegetation, conducting field visits, and monitoring conditions over time. Without an adequate knowledge of the types of land cover present in the landscape there is no basis for assigning realistic edge contrast weights. Accurate contrast weights are fundamental to the successful use of the ECON metric.

• *Determine that there is a good reason for measuring ECON.* Does the analyst suspect that the amount of ECON within the landscape is playing a major role in the form or function of the landscape? Is ECON inhibiting the movement of plants, animals, or people? Is there the possibility of a significant correlation between varying amounts of ECON and the degree of visual preference given to particular landscapes by people? These are all relevant questions. The best results from measuring ECON will most likely come about when an organized series of questions are formulated beforehand.

• *Plan in advance the types of analytical comparisons that will be made.* A single measurement of total ECON (e.g., TECI) for a single landscape is of limited value because there is nothing to compare with the ECON measurements. Good comparisons should be planned in advance of taking any ECON measurements, in much the same fashion as formulating basic research questions. Good comparisons may be in the form of the change in landscape structure over time measured from historical land cover data. Comparisons could also be arranged to assess the correlation between changes in ECON with changes in plant and animal communities within the landscape, or with changes in the visual quality assigned to the landscape over time by its human inhabitants. In many of these applications, the mapping of ECON values may provide more useful information than simply examining the numerical results with no explicit reference to spatial arrangement.

3.8.6. *Related Metrics*

Contrast-Weighted Edge Density (CWED) standardizes edge to a per unit area basis that supports comparison between landscapes of varying size. As with ECON, this index reduces the length of each edge segment proportionate to the degree of edge contrast. Thus, 100 m/ha of maximum-contrast edge (weight = 1) is unaffected, but 100 m/ha of edge with a contrast weight of 0.2 is reduced by 80% to 20 m/ha of contrast-weighted edge. This index measures the equivalent maximum-contrast edge density. For example, an edge density of 100 means that there is 100 m of edge per hectare in the landscape. A contrast-weighted edge density of 80 m for the same landscape means that there are the equivalent of 80 m of maximum contrast edge per hectare in the landscape. A landscape with 100 m/ha of edge and an average contrast weight of 0.8 would have twice the contrast-weighted edge density (80 m/ha) as a landscape with only 50 m/ha of edge but with the same average contrast weight (40 m/ha). Thus, both edge density and edge contrast are reflected in this index. For many ecological phenomena, edge types function differently. Consequently, comparing total edge density among landscapes may be misleading because of differences in edge types. This contrast-weighted edge density index attempts to quantify edge from the perspective of its functional significance. Thus, landscapes with the same contrast-weighted edge density are presumed to have the same total magnitude of edge effects from a functional perspective (McGarigal and Marks 1995).

3.8.7. *Selected References for Further Reading*

Bennett, A.F. 1990. Habitat corridors: Their role in wildlife management and conservation. Victoria, Australia: Department of Conservation and Environment.

Forman, R.T.T. 1995. *Land mosaics. The ecology of landscapes and regions, Second Edition*. New York: Cambridge University Press.

Galli, A.E., C.F. Leck, and R.T.T. Forman. 1976. Avian distribution patterns in forest islands of different sizes in central New Jersey. *Auk* 93: 356–64.

Gates, J.E. 1991. Powerline corridors, edge effects, and wildlife in forested landscapes of the central Appalachians. In *Wildlife and habitats in managed landscapes*, J.E. Rodiek and E.G. Bolen, eds. Washington, D.C.: Island Press.

Hansen, A. and F. di Castri, eds. 1992. *Landscape boundaries*. New York: Springer-Verlag.

Lynch, J.F. and D.F. Whigham. 1984. Effects of forest fragmentation on breeding bird communities in Maryland, USA. *Biological Conservation* 28: 287–324.

McGarigal, K. and B.J. Marks. 1995. FRAGSTATS: Spatial pattern analysis program for quantifying landscape structure. Corvallis, OR: Oregon State University Forest Science Department.

Wiens, J.A., C.S. Crawford, and J.R. Gosz. 1985. Boundary dynamics: A conceptual framework for studying landscape ecosystems. *Oikos* 45: 421–427.

Yahner, R.H. 1988. Changes in wildlife communities near edges. *Conservation Biology* 2: 333–9.

3.9. Euclidean Nearest Neighbor Distance (ENN)

3.9.1. *Concept*

The Euclidean Nearest Neighbor Distance (ENN) is the shortest Euclidean distance from one patch to another patch of the same land cover type (LCT) (McGarigal and Marks 1995). ENN is a measure of *landscape configuration* because it deals explicitly with the relative locations and arrangements of patches. ENN is useful for characterizing the spatial distribution of patches of a particular type. For example, are the patches close to each other or far apart, and how do the actual distances between patches relate to ecological factors such as the dispersal distance of a particular wildlife species?

Figure 3.33 depicts two landscapes drawn from western New England,

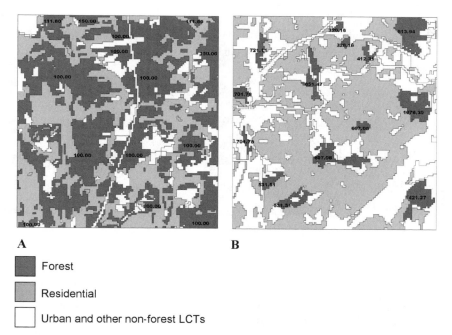

A   B

■ Forest

▨ Residential

☐ Urban and other non-forest LCTs

Figure 3.33. Landscape A has forest patches (dark gray) with a lower nearest neighbor distance than landscape B (ENN) values are noted in the patch.

USA, that serve to illustrate contrasting ENN values for forest patches. Landscape (a) clearly has more forest cover than landscape (b), and the forest occurs in much larger patches, many of which appear to be of similar size. Note that the ENN values for forest in landscape (a) are quite even, all of them being at or near 100, while the ENN distances for forest in landscape (b) range from just over 300 to nearly 1,500 (see table 3.8). In landscape (b), forest patches are smaller and more separated from other forest patches (greater ENN). Plant and animal species that depend on large tracts of forest may not survive in any one of the remnant patches in landscape (b), and the increased distance between patches further reduces the probability of interpatch dispersal, migration, and colonization.

3.9.2. *Metric Equation and Calculation*

ENN is a patch-level measurement of the shortest Euclidean distance from a focal patch to another patch of the same LCT. Thus, every patch in a landscape has a value for ENN unless it is the only patch of a particular LCT, in which case ENN is undefined.

$$NEAR = h_{ij}$$

Where h_{ij} equals the distance to the nearest neighboring patch of the same type i for the specific patch j, based on the shortest distance between patch edges (McGarigal and Marks 1995).

Units = standard distance units such as meters or feet
Range of values = > 0, without limit

ENN is calculated at the patch level and can be summarized at the class and landscape levels. One of the most basic characterizations of ENN at the class level is the average or mean value of ENN across all patches of the same LCT:

$$ENN\_MN = \frac{\sum_{j=1}^{n'} h_{ij}}{n'_i}$$

Where ENN_MN (mean) equals the sum, across all patches of the corresponding patch type, of the distance to the nearest neighboring patch of the same type, based on patch edge to patch edge distance, divided by the number of patches of the corresponding LCT (McGarigal and Marks 1995). Units and range are the same as ENN.

Table 3.8. Nearest neighbor distances for
ENN_MN of sample landscape B in Figure 3.33

Patch Number	Nearest Neighbor Distance (meters)
1	320.16
2	320.16
3	701.78
4	667.08
5	412.31
6	701.78
7	531.51
8	721.11
9	531.51
10	851.47
11	667.08
12	1421.27
13	1079.35
14	813.94
SUM	9740.51
ENN_MN	(9740.51/14) = 695.75 meters

The following is an example of how ENN_MN is calculated for forest patches in landscape (b) in figure 3.33 (Table 3.8).

One of the potentially more useful forms of ENN is the area-weighted mean nearest neighbor distance (ENN_AM).

Class-level calculation of area-weighted mean nearest neighbor distance:

$$ENN\_AM = \sum_{j=1}^{n} \left[b_{ij} \left(\frac{a_{ij}}{\sum_{j=1}^{n} a_{ij}} \right) \right]$$

ENN_AM (area-weighted mean) equals the sum, across all patches of the corresponding patch type, of the nearest neighbor distance of each patch multiplied by the proportional abundance of the patch (i.e., patch area divided by the sum of patch areas of the corresponding patch type). Units and range are the same as for ENN.

As noted previously for other patch-based metrics, the area-weighted mean gives greater weight to larger patches in recognition that larger patches often play a more important role in the functioning of the landscape and therefore may warrant a disproportionate emphasis in the metric.

ENN can also be summarized at the landscape level using the simple arithmetic mean or area-weighted mean by considering all patches of all LCTs, as follows.

Landscape-level calculation of mean nearest neighbor distance (ENN_MN):

$$ENN\_MN = \frac{\sum\limits_{i=1}^{m}\sum\limits_{j=1}^{n} h_{ij}}{N}$$

ENN_MN (mean) equals the sum, across all patches in the landscape, of the nearest neighbor distance, divided by the total number of patches of all LCTs. Units and range are the same as for ENN.

Landscape-level calculation of area-weighted nearest neighbor distance:

$$ENN\_AM = \sum\limits_{i=1}^{m}\sum\limits_{j=1}^{n}\left[h_{ij}\left(\frac{a_{ij}}{\sum\limits_{i=1}^{m}\sum\limits_{j=1}^{n} a_{ij}} \right) \right]$$

ENN_AM (area-weighted mean) equals the sum, across all patches in the landscape, of the nearest neighbor distance of each patch multiplied by the proportional abundance of the patch (i.e., patch area divided by the sum of patch areas). Note that the proportional abundance of each patch is determined from the sum of patch areas rather than the total landscape area, because the latter may include internal background area not associated with any patch. Units and range are the same as for ENN.

3.9.3. *Applications*

ENN and its derivatives provide a means for an analyst to mathematically describe the distribution of LCTs across a landscape. Since people, agriculture, and some wildlife species use the entire landscape rather than single patches, ENN can aid in assessing how a particular landscape may function with regard to the movement of people and wildlife, the spread of disease and crop pests, or any phenomenon or process of interest that involves movement between patches of the same LCT.

The distance between neighboring patches of habitat has long been recognized as an important ecological factor. For instance, patch isolation, which is partially a function of the distances between neighboring patches, has been offered as an explanatory factor for the smaller populations (and diversity) of bird species observed in fragmented habitats (Dickman 1987; Forman et al. 1976; Hayden et al. 1985; Helliwell 1976; Moore and Hooper 1975; Whitcomb et al. 1981). Distances between the nearest neighbors of the same LCT are a central consideration in island biogeography and metapopulation theories (MacArthur and Wilson 1967; Gilpin and Hanski 1991; Levins 1970). For fragmented populations, the distance that must be traveled in order to find another patch of habitat becomes an extremely important factor influencing the persistence or viability of the population.

While ENN originated within conservation biology, and most applications of ENN to date have focused on this arena, ENN can be used to study nearly any phenomena in which the distance between patches is important. For instance, planners may wish to compare ENN for recreational parkland within different portions of the landscape as a means of characterizing the relative accessibility of parks to the community. Areas with high ENN values may be considered candidates for adding new parks. Planners or developers may wish to examine the ENN of a specific type of retail complex or specific department stores to evaluate and compare potential sites for new facilities.

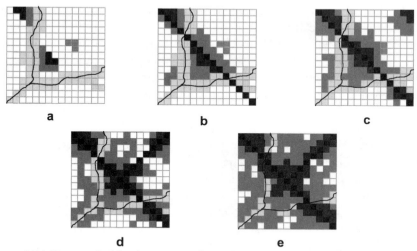

Figure 3.34. Prototypical landscape transformation sequence associated with agricultural and urban development. The landscape is composed of seven land cover types: road (black), urban (dark gray), agriculture (medium gray), riparian (light gray), forest (white), meadow (cross hatch), and wetland (stipple). The sequence illustrates a typical transformation in which the landscape changes from a forested landscape (a) to an agricultural/urban landscape (e).

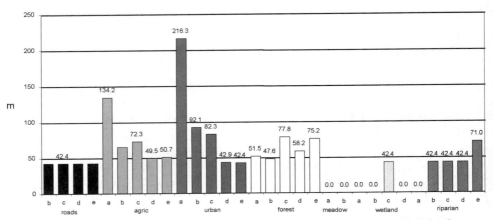

Figure 3.35. Area-weighted mean nearest neighbor distances (ENN_AM) for the five landscapes depicted in figure 3.34. Note the changes in average nearest-neighbor distance for each land cover type as the landscape changes.

Figures 3.34 and 3.35 illustrate a common process whereby a forested landscape is developed incrementally for intensive human uses (urban, transportation, agriculture). Figure 3.34 provides a graphic depiction of changing values of ENN at each stage of the transformation process.

At the beginning of the land transformation sequence (a), human-made patches are relatively far apart from one another (high ENN_AM), and conversely native LCT patches are relatively close to one another (low ENN_AM). As the landscape is subdivided, ENN_AM is temporarily lowered for forest patches due to the creation of "new" patches of forest by road construction (note lower right corner of [b]). As the transformation process continues, the size of native LCT patches continues to decrease, thereby increasing the distance between them. The exact opposite is occurring with the human use patches. They continue to enlarge and actually "grow" closer together to the point where the shortest ENN occurs just before they coalesce into a single large patch.

Each of these changes holds implications for both the forest and agricultural ecosystems within the landscape. As the forest becomes more sparsely distributed, the distances between patches may become too great for particular plants and animals to traverse, thus resulting in isolation of sub-populations. At the same time, as the agricultural ecosystems grow closer together, the opportunity for movement across the landscape increases for species of plants and animals that coexist with crop plants or livestock. Additionally, certain crop plants may more easily disperse over the landscape spreading pests or weeds, or cross-pollinate with neighboring genetically related crop plants, which is a potential concern with the advent of genetically modified crop plants.

3.9.4. *Limitations*

The limitations inherent with ENN are not complex. But nearest neighbor distance metrics do have a few important limitations.

First, ENN only measures the Euclidean distance between patches and their nearest neighbors. While the straight-line, or Euclidean, distance is useful information, there may be other factors of greater importance that contribute to a patch's functional degree of spatial isolation. For instance, while a patch surrounded by major highway corridors may have the same nearest neighbor distance as a patch that is not surrounded by highways, the actual level of isolation is not the same since the highway may represent a complete barrier to species movement. In addition, while the Euclidean distance between two patches may be short, the natural route for plants and animals flowing between patches might be somewhat longer depending on the character of the intervening landscape. In other words, the shortest distance may not represent the true functional distance between patches from the perspective of the organism or process under consideration. Thus it is recommended not to unequivocally equate nearest neighbor distance with isolation.

Second, only a single aspect of the patch neighborhood is being considered—the distance to the nearest neighboring patch of the same type. Other neighboring patches of different LCTs may be important as well, but are not considered because they are of a different type. Other attributes of the neighboring patches are not characterized, such as the area or shape of those patches. For example, the nearest neighboring patch of the same type may be miniscule in area, but the second nearest neighboring patch may be very large, but not characterized.

Third, the analyst should remember that, while ENN is useful, mean values do not provide the best measure of central tendency when the distribution of metric values is non-normal. For example, there may be one area of the landscape where most of the patches are clumped together with a few other patches scattered throughout the rest of the landscape. The mean value for ENN does not provide an adequate characterization of the *spatial distribution* of patches in this case. A landscape with all of the patches clumped in one location can generate the same mean value for ENN as a landscape with widely dispersed pairs of patches (Rogers 1993). For this reason it is important to closely examine the data and use maps of the patches as an accompaniment to the values for ENN. Think critically about the values that are produced by the metric and what may be influencing them.

3.9.5. *Recommendations*

There are three basic guidelines for ENN in planning, design and management:

- ENN should be used when it is important or useful to understand the distances between patches.
- Place the measurement values for ENN within a meaningful context. Understand how these values relate to other phenomena of interest within the landscape. As with measurements of any kind, ENN becomes substantially more useful when the analyst understands why the measurement is being taken. Is the distance from one patch to its nearest neighbor an important factor in describing or explaining the phenomenon of interest? As with most of the metrics in this handbook, ENN cannot stand alone.
- Whenever feasible, use the area-weighted mean as a complementary form of ENN, as this incorporates patch area information that may be important to assessing landscape function.

3.9.6. *Related Metrics*

Other metrics that quantify similar aspects of the landscape pattern include contagion and proximity. Like ENN, contagion (CONTAG) and proximity (PROX) both deal with the aggregation or clumping of LCTs, but do so in a very different manner. CONTAG considers the aggregation or clumping of cells of all LCTs present in the landscape and thus ignores the arrangement of patches per se. In addition, CONTAG considers the degree of aggregation among all LCTs and thus is a landscape-level metric only, whereas ENN is computed at the patch level and then summarized at the class and landscape levels.

PROX characterizes the degree of spatial isolation of patches from other patches of the same LCT, but, in contrast to ENN, it takes into account all neighboring patches of the same LCT that occur within a specified search radius, not simply the nearest neighbor. In addition, PROX factors in the size of the neighboring patches. Large patches that are also near the focal patch will be weighted more heavily in the proximity index value. Thus, PROX provides a more comprehensive measure of patch isolation than does ENN.

3.9.7. *Selected References for Further Reading*

Burkey, T.V. 1989. Extinction in nature reserves: The effect of fragmentation and the importance of migration between reserve fragments. *Oikos* 55: 75–81.

Dickman, C.R. 1987. Habitat fragmentation and vertebrate species richness in an urban environment. *Journal of Applied Ecology* 24: 337–351.

Forman, R.T.T., A.E. Galli, and C.F. Leck. 1976. Forest size and avian diversity in New Jersey woodlots with some land use implications. *Oecologia* 26: 1–8.

Gilpin, M.E. and I. Handki, eds. 1991. Metapopulation dynamics: Empirical and theoretical investigations. San Diego: Academic Press.

Hayden, I.J., J. Faaborg, and R.L. Clawson. 1985. Estimates of minimum area requirements for Missouri forest birds. Maryville, MO: Missouri Academy of Science 19: 11–22.

Helliwell, D.R. 1976. The effects of size and isolation on the conservation value of wooded sites in Britain. *Journal of Biogeography* 3: 407–416.

Lamberson, R.H., R. McKelvey, B.R. Noon, and C. Voss. 1992. A dynamic analysis of northern spotted owl viability in a fragmented forest landscape. *Conservation Biology* 6(4): 1–8.

Levins, R. 1970. Extinctions. In *Some mathematical questions in biology. Vol.2: Lectures on mathematics in the life sciences.* M. Gertebhaber, ed., 77–107. Providence, R.I.: American Mathematical Society.

MacArthur, R.H. and E.O. Wilson. 1967. *The theory of island biogeography*. Princeton, N.J.: Princeton University Press.

McGarigal, K. and B.J. Marks. 1995. FRAGSTATS: Spatial pattern analysis program for quantifying landscape structure. Gen. Tech. Rep. PNW-GTR-351. Portland, OR: U.S. Department of Agriculture, Forest Service, Pacific Northwest Research Station.

McKelvey, K., B.R. Noon, and R. Lamberson. 1992. Conservation planning for species occupying fragmented landscapes: The case of the northern spotted owl. In *Biotic interactions and global change*. J. Kingsolver, P. Kareiva, and R. Hyey, eds., 338–357. Sunderland, MA: Sinauer Associates.

Moore, N.W. and M.D. Hooper. 1975. On the number of bird species in British woods. *Biological Conservation* 8: 239–250.

Rogers, C.A. 1993. *Describing landscapes: Indices of structure.* [Master's Thesis] Burnaby, B.C.: Simon Fraser University.

Whitcomb, R.F., C.S. Robbins, and J.F. Lynch, et al. 1981. Effects of forest fragmentation on avifauna of the eastern deciduous forest. In *Forest island dynamics in man-dominated landscapes*. R.L. Burgess and D.M. Sharpe, eds., 125–205. New York: Springer-Verlag.

3.10. Proximity (PROX)

3.10.1. *Concept*

The Proximity Index (PROX) is a unitless measure of patch isolation that integrates information on the size and distance of like patches from a specified "focal patch" within a defined search radius. PROX is a measure of *landscape configuration* that deals explicitly with the spatial arrangement of patches. PROX examines the spatial characteristics within a specified "search radius" centered on a focal patch. The distance to patches of the same type as the focal patch and the area of these patches are analyzed to calculate a composite PROX value. Large patches that are close to the focal patch contribute significantly to the PROX value, while small patches that are distant from the focal patch contribute less.

PROX provides the analyst with a means of quantifying the spatial distribution of specific patch types across a landscape. In other words, PROX allows the analyst to examine how resources, represented as LCT patches, are distributed over a landscape relative to one another, and relative to a user-specified "focal patch." A search radius or "neighborhood" for each focal patch related to the particular organism or ecological process of interest is set by the analyst. In this way, the arrangement of LCT patches can be quantified in a manner that is relevant to processes and issues of interest, for example, the spread distance of plant propagules, or the walking distance of people to neighborhood parks.

Figure 3.36 shows two contrasting landscapes. Landscape (a) is dominated by forest LCT while landscape (b) possesses a relatively even mixture of LCTs. In this example, each grid cell is 30 m², and the PROX search radius is 300 m or ten grid cells. Figure 3.37 lists the individual PROX values for patches of forest and agriculture.

The most obvious distinction between landscapes is the number of patches of forest and agriculture. Landscape (a) contains fewer forest patches than landscape (b), but they are much larger on average than in landscape (b), where forest has been converted to other land uses and fragmented into small patches in the process. Consequently, the forest patches in landscape (a) each contain a few very large neighboring forest patches within the specified neighborhood, which results in relatively large values of PROX. Conversely, the forest patches in landscape (b) each contain several small neighboring forest patches, but the cumulative area of forest patches within the specified distance is still relatively small, which results in relatively small values of PROX. Similarly, landscape (a) contains only two small agricultural patches, which results in very small values of PROX. Landscape (b), on the other hand, contains several larger agricultural patches and they are closer together, which results in larger values of PROX. In terms of resource distribution, any forest-dependent organisms that are able to move among forest patches should function better in landscape (a) than in landscape (b). Conversely, organisms

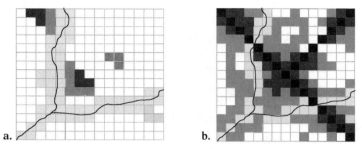

a. b.

Figure 3.36. Two contrasting landscapes. Each landscape is composed of some or all of seven land cover types: road (black), urban (dark gray), agriculture (medium gray), riparian (light gray), forest (white), meadow (cross hatch), and wetland (stipple).

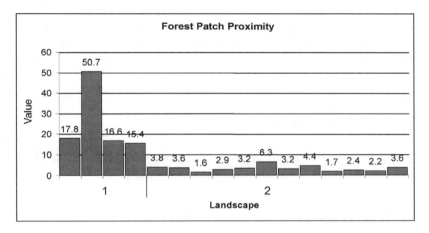

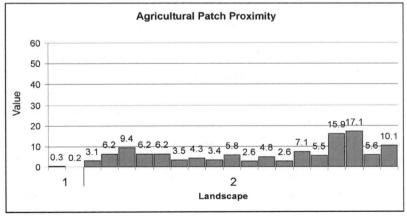

Figure 3.37. Proximity values for forest patches and agricultural patches within the two landscapes depicted in Figure 3.36.

dependent upon agricultural ecosystems (including farmers) will likely function better in landscape (b), as these patches are more proximal to one another than they are in landscape (a).

3.10.2. *Metric Equation and Calculation*

PROX is calculated for each patch by summing the area of each neighboring patch of the same LCT that lies within a specified neighborhood distance from the focal patch, after weighting the area of each neighboring patch by its distance from the focal patch.

$$PROX = \sum_{s=1}^{n} \frac{a_{ijs}}{h_{ijs}^2}$$

Where a_{ijs} = the area of the sth? patch within the specified search radius of patch ij and h_{ijs} = the distance from patch ij to the sth? neighboring patch of the same type, based upon edge-to-edge distance.

Units = dimensionless
Range of values > 0, without limit

Figure 3.38 below illustrates the calculation of PROX for a focal patch within a landscape (represented by a fifty-cell square grid).

$$PROX = \sum_{s=1}^{n} \frac{a_{ijs}}{h_{ijs}^2} = \frac{9}{3^2} + \frac{46}{5^2} + \frac{50}{5.83^2} + \frac{5}{10^2} + \frac{1}{5.83^2} + \frac{1}{2^2} + \frac{107}{3^2} = 16.529$$

This example illustrates the application of PROX to raster landscape data. It is also possible to apply PROX to polygonal landscape data with similar computational results, however it is easier to analyze raster data, due to the inherent spatial indexing (row and column) of raster datasets.

PROX results are dimensionless and can range upwards from zero with no limit. Larger values of PROX indicate that neighboring patches of the same LCT are larger and closer together, i.e., that patches are less isolated. Small values indicate that patches are further apart and may be smaller in area, i.e., that patches are more isolated. If a patch is the only one of its type within a landscape, the value for PROX is zero because it does not have any other patches of the same type that are proximate to it.

PROX is calculated at the patch level and can be summarized at the

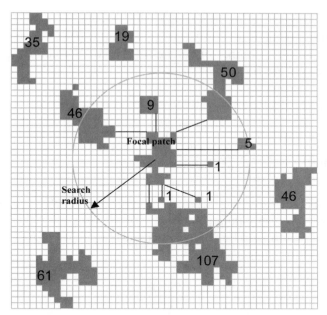

Figure 3.38. Focal patch located in the center of the search radius. Area in this example is measured as the number of grid cells per patch. Distance is measured solely from the focal patch as the number of grid cells between patches. By definition, no distances are measured from the focal patch to patches outside of the search radius.

class and landscape levels. The mean value of PROX can be calculated at the class and landscape levels. At the class level, the mean PROX value (PROX_MN) measures the degree of isolation (and fragmentation) for all patches of a particular LCT, while at the landscape level the PROX value is averaged across all LCTs, thus providing a measure of overall landscape structural complexity (McGarigal and Marks 1995). As described in chapter one, area-weighted means are a very useful form of many patch-based metrics because they incorporate information about the relative importance of each patch as judged by patch size. Patch size is a significant controlling factor in the composition, configuration, and functioning of the landscape. Therefore, the area-weighted mean proximity (PROX_AM) is the recommended form of the PROX metric for most applications.

Class-level calculation of PROX_MN:

$$PROX\_MN = \frac{\sum\limits_{j=1}^{n} \sum\limits_{i=1}^{n} \dfrac{a_{ijs}}{b_{ijs}^{2}}}{n_i}$$

PROX_MN (mean) at the class level equals the sum, across all patches of corresponding patch types, of the proximity index (PROX) of each patch divided by the total number of patches of the corresponding patch type. Units and range are the same as for PROX.

Class-level calculation of PROX_AM:

$$PROX\_MN = \sum_{j=1}^{n} \left[\left(\sum_{i=1}^{n} \frac{a_{ijs}}{h_{ijs}^{2}} \right) \left(\frac{a_{ij}}{\sum_{j=1}^{n} a_{ij}} \right) \right]$$

PROX_AM (area-weighted mean) at the class level equals the sum, across all patches of corresponding patch types, of the proximity index (PROX) of each patch multiplied by the proportional abundance of patches. Units and range are the same as for PROX.

Landscape-level calculation of PROX_MN:

$$PROX\_MN = \frac{\sum_{i=1}^{m} \sum_{j=1}^{n} \sum_{i=1}^{n} \frac{a_{ijs}}{h_{ijs}^{2}}}{N}$$

PROX_MN (mean) at the landscape level equals the sum, across all patches in the landscape, of the proximity index (PROX) of each patch, divided by the total number of patches. Units and range are the same as for PROX.

Landscape-level calculation of PROX_AM:

$$PROX\_AM = \sum_{i=1}^{m} \sum_{j=1}^{n} \left[\left(\sum_{i=1}^{n} \frac{a_{ijs}}{h_{ijs}^{2}} \right) \left(\frac{a_{ij}}{\sum_{i=1}^{m} \sum_{j=1}^{n} a_{ij}} \right) \right]$$

PROX_AM (area-weighted mean) at the landscape level equals the sum, across all patches in the landscape, of the proximity index (PROX) of each patch multiplied by the proportional abundance of the patch (i.e., patch area divided by the sum of patch areas). Note, the proportional abundance of each patch is determined from the sum of all patch areas within the landscape. Units and range are the same as for PROX.

3.10.3. *Applications*

Since PROX generates a unitless value, its main use is in comparative analysis between different patches within a landscape or in comparing the spatial configuration of patches in different landscapes.

A potentially useful application of PROX is to prioritize the acquisition of wildlife conservation reserves. By setting the search radius to match the scale of a home range of a species and then calculating the proximity value for each habitat patch in the landscape, one can gain a better understanding of the relative proximity of habitat patches for a particular species (Figure 3.39).

The proximity values for all patches in a landscape can be sorted into ranges to depict the relative PROX of habitat patches across the landscape. In this fashion proximal clusters of habitat patches beneficial to wildlife movement can be identified for protection (Figure 3.40).

The example below shows a landscape undergoing urban and agricultural development (Figure 3.41 and 3.42). Early in the landscape transformation process the landscape remains dominated by forest and riparian LCTs. As people begin to use the landscape intensively, the number of LCTs increases, the spatial arrangement of LCTs becomes more fragmented, and the level of connectivity across the landscape declines. In the final stages of land transformation, human-made LCTs such as agriculture, urban uses, and transportation begin to coalesce into larger patches and corridors to become a dominant component of the landscape.

In ecological terms, the assortment of LCTs within the landscapes of

Figure 3.39. Simplified map of a landscape containing habitat patches. Each habitat patch will have its proximity value calculated using a search radius that matches the target species' movement scale. Here just one of the patches is shown with the search radius applied. *Figure concept adapted from Gustafson and Parker 1994.*

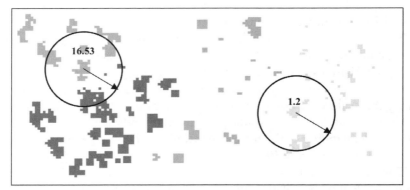

Figure 3.40. Map of habitat patches that have been measured for proximity. Dark gray patches are most proximal and lighter shades of gray represent progressively more isolated patches.

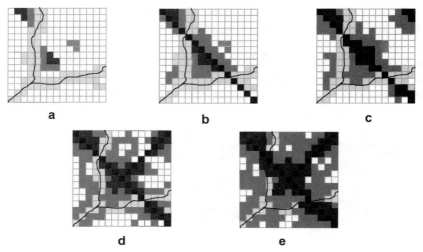

Figure 3.41. Hypothetical landscape transformation associated with agricultural and urban development. The landscape is composed of seven land cover types: road (black), urban (dark gray), agriculture (medium gray), riparian (light gray), forest (white), meadow (cross hatch), and wetland (stipple). The sequence illustrates a typical transformation in which the landscape changes from a forested landscape (a) to an agricultural/urban landscape (e).

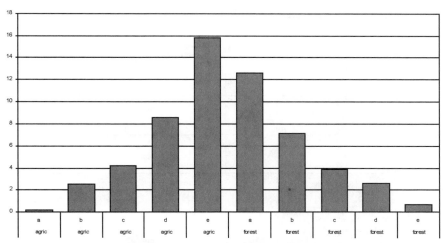

Figure 3.42. Area-weighted mean proximity values (PROX_AM) for agricultural and forest patches within the landscape transformation scenario illustrated in figure 3.41.

figure 3.41 are becoming more diverse. There is an increase in the total number of LCTs and their distribution by area becomes more even. Ultimately, no single LCT dominates the landscape in terms of area, as there are many small patches of the various LCTs. An expected consequence of this transformation would be the decline in numbers of specialist species that require large contiguous tracts of specific LCTs. Additionally, specialist species would not survive well in landscapes (d) and (e) because movement between fragmented habitats would be difficult.

The structural change in the landscapes is reflected in the change in PROX_AM for two of the prominent LCTs (Figure 3.42). Forest patches become progressively more isolated even as they increase in number. This is due to the fragmentation of the forest into smaller individual patches. Agricultural patches increase in number and become less isolated as the landscape is transformed. Agricultural patches begin to coalesce into larger patches that are also less proximal to one another than the assortment of smaller agricultural patches in landscape (d).

Because PROX is a unitless, comparative metric, its application value lies in comparing the direction and magnitude of change over the transformation process rather than the absolute PROX value. In terms of habitat conservation, a critical transition occurs between landscape (b) and (c) (Figure 3.43). The landscape changes from a situation in which four out of six patches have a PROX value greater than ten to one in which there are five patches total, and in all of them PROX is less than ten. The

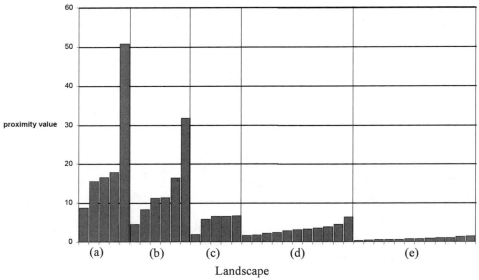

Figure 3.43. Proximity values for individual forest patches within the landscape transformation process depicted in Figure 3.41.

transition between (b) and (c) may represent a critical threshold. Strategic planning may be warranted in order to lessen the ecological impact of this transition, for example to establish and protect wildlife corridor linkages between isolated patches. This type of threshold or sharpness in transition is not limited to wildlife habitat. It may be observed in any kind of LCT. In a planning application, where multiple land use scenarios are being examined, one could compare alternative future patterns of LCTs in terms of PROX. If sharp transitions or contrasts are apparent, this may indicate the need to alleviate the apparent isolation of particular LCTs.

3.10.4. *Limitations*

The major limitation of PROX as a measure of patch isolation has to do with the use of Euclidean distances. Only straight line distances between patches are quantified without regard to the intervening LCTs that may actually play a larger role in effective isolation (by being hostile to wildlife attempting to move between patches for example). This fact underscores the importance of understanding the rationale for measuring PROX. There may be biological or ecological factors (i.e., habitat preference, dispersal distance, or home range size) or sociological factors that exert more control over isolation and proximity than distance alone.

Second, PROX is a unitless measure and therefore its absolute value does not have a straightforward and intuitive interpretation. However, PROX can be used as a comparative index. Comparisons between landscapes or of the same landscape through time using the same LCT classification, search radius, and data resolution, can reveal important contrasts or changes. The magnitude of these contrasts and changes should be examined as an aid in prioritizing landscape planning goals.

Third, the user of PROX must specify a search radius in order for patches to be selected for inclusion in the proximity calculation. This radius must be selected with care in order that it is relevant to the application at hand. For instance, one would not choose the same search radius for human hiking distance that one might choose for songbird dispersal. Likewise, one could not legitimately compare PROX values for the same target organism or process if the search radii were different.

Fourth, there are multiple factors that contribute to PROX values. The distance between patches, the area of the neighboring patches, and the number of patches all have an effect on the proximity index. Understanding these relative effects is important for the analyst who is attempting to interpret observed PROX changes or contrasts in a landscape, or between landscapes. Once a change or contrast has been measured, the next important question is: what factors are likely responsible for this observed change? Only when this question is clearly understood and satisfactorily answered can possible planning remedies be considered.

3.10.5. *Recommendations*

PROX can offer the analyst important insights into the spatial arrangement of patches relative to other patches of the same type. This kind of information and insight can have a wide range of applications. However, there are important limitations as well, as discussed above. With these advantages and limitations in mind we offer the following recommendations for the use of PROX:

- Because PROX is a unitless geometric metric, it is most useful in a comparative mode—to detect changes or differences between landscapes or different landscape conditions.

- PROX is best used in conjunction with other metrics that describe the factors that affect PROX. Class area proportion, patch size, number of patches, and nearest neighbor distance are all metrics that can provide additional explanatory power when used in combination with PROX.

- Because PROX is a comparative metric, it is vitally important that all data used is equivalent in terms of spatial resolution, spatial extent,

LCT classification, and search radius. PROX conditions can be evaluated across different species for example, but the analyst must never assume that a PROX value of twenty for species x is equivalent to a PROX value of twenty for species y. The utility of PROX should be for detecting change and contrast.

3.10.6. *Related Metrics*

The Euclidean Nearest Neighbor Distance (ENN) is related to PROX (see ENN section) as they are both measures of patch isolation. In practice, ENN is most useful when its variation is examined (mean, median, standard deviation, and coefficient of variation). Like PROX, ENN also measures straight line distance from one patch to another. However, ENN considers only the nearest neighboring patch, while PROX considers all patches within a given search radius. One advantage of ENN is that the measurement remains in actual distance units, while PROX composites patch area and distance into a unitless result.

3.10.7. *Selected References for Further Reading*

Gustafson, E.J. and G.R. Parker. 1992. Relationship between landcover proportion and indices of landscape spatial pattern. *Landscape Ecology* 7: 101–10.

Gustafson, E.J. and G.R. Parker. 1994. Using an index of habitat patch proximity for landscape design. *Landscape and Urban Planning* 29: 117–30.

McGarigal, K. and B.J. Marks. 1995. FRAGSTATS: Spatial pattern analysis program for quantifying landscape structure. *Gen.Tech.Rep.* PNW-GTR-351. Portland, OR: U.S. Dept. of Agriculture, Forest Service, Pacific Northwest Research Station.

Whitcomb, R.F., C.S. Robbins, and J.F. Lynch et al. 1981. Effects of forest fragmentation on avifauna of the eastern deciduous forest. In *Forest Island Dynamics in Man-dominated Landscapes*, eds. R.L. Burgess, D.M. Sharpe, eds., 125–205. New York: Springer-Verlag.

4

Applications of Landscape Metrics in Planning and Management

4.1. Introduction

This chapter explores the usefulness of landscape metrics applied to an integrated planning application. In previous chapters, specific metrics have been explained and discussed independently. However, since all landscape components interact with one another, ecological processes are seldom best explained by a single variable (or perspective). To better understand the relationships established between landscape resources, a more integrated approach involving multiple landscape metrics is recommended.

The form of a landscape is influenced by many factors, such as climate, geology, hydrology, biota, and people. These factors operate independently and interactively to form landscapes and to affect change. By using several landscape metrics in conjunction we can gain new insights on the interactions of landscape ecological features and processes (Botequilha Leitão and Ahern 2002).

In this chapter, we first introduce the study area, Amherst, a watershed located in western Massachusetts, USA (Section 4.2). This is followed by a brief introduction to data and methods (Section 4.3). In Section 4.4 we describe the existing watershed (time step 0 or T0). Then we define two alternative future scenarios: *Trend, TR* and *Smart Growth, SG.* For each scenario, we compute landscape metrics for four time steps (T1, T2, T3, and T4). We structure our planning exercise according to the five planning phases of the sustainable land planning framework (see section 2.3). The goal of this chapter is to demonstrate the utility of a suite of metrics used in conjunction to describe and support several planning tasks at different stages in the planning process.

4.2. The Study Area

To illustrate the application to planning of landscape ecology principles and metrics, we adopted a rural watershed (223 km²) (hereafter referred to as Amherst) in western Massachusetts as a study area. Amherst is composed of two adjacent watersheds that constitute a single planning unit. As a watershed, the study area is well suited to analyze the ecological processes related to water resources.

The Pioneer Valley region where Amherst is located was dominated by a forest matrix until the eighteenth century (Figure 4.1). The region was transformed incrementally for agriculture, which was initially focused on the valley bottom, and later extended into the hills. In the nineteenth century, agriculture was largely abandoned and the forest returned through succession.

The present land use trend in Amherst is similar to the urban sprawl

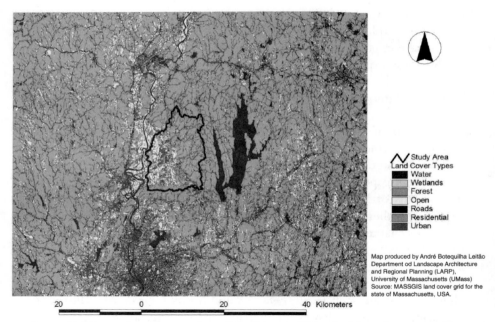

Figure 4.1. The study area, a section of the Pioneer Valley in Massachusetts, and its regional context. The Connecticut River flows from north to south across the left center of the map. The city of Springfield, MA forms a large red "blob" located at the lower center of this map. The Amherst watersheds (center), located between the Quabbin reservoir (large blue patch, center right) and the Connecticut, will serve as the study area for the example planning exercise. *Map produced by André Botequilha Leitão.*

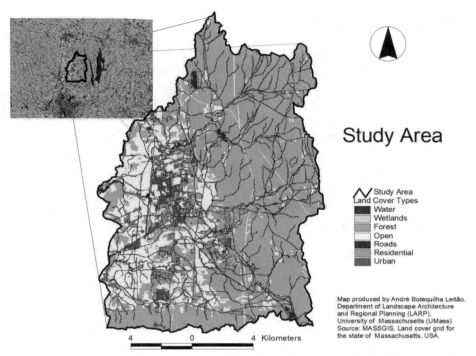

Study Area

Study Area
Land Cover Types
■ Water
  Wetlands
  Forest
  Open
■ Roads
  Residential
■ Urban

Map produced by André Botequilha Leitão.
Department of Landscape Architecture
and Regional Planning (LARP),
University of Massachusetts (UMass)
Source: MASSGIS. Land cover grid for
the state of Massachusetts, USA.

4   0   4 Kilometers

Figure 4.2. Present land cover situation (T0) for Amherst watersheds. The town of Amherst (Pioneer Valley, MA) is located at the left center; urban denotes the center of this town, surrounded by residential and open fields. *Map produced by André Botequilha Leitão.*

happening in other parts of North America and elsewhere in the world. People increasingly want to live near forest and nature, away from large city centers and urban conurbations. A typical trend for sprawl is for development to align and concentrate along major transportation corridors forming strips of development, and eventually edge cities. Although we address a specific watershed as an example in this chapter, these land use changes are considered to be representative of urbanizing landscape dynamics worldwide.

Two distinct subareas can be observed in Amherst: (1) a central area corresponding to the lower part of the valley near the Connecticut River, which is dominated by a mix of housing and agricultural fields; and (2) a forested area in the headwaters and middle reaches of the watershed (Figure 4.2). In the forested portion housing is located along the roads, with a particular concentration around crossroads. Small patches of open land are often found in association with dwellings.

4.3. Data and Methods

This application is based on the abiotic-biotic-cultural resource model (ABC) planning framework and landscape ecological planning guidelines presented earlier (see chapter two). The data model is a raster/grid map with the 30-m cell size of the original data preserved. This map was extracted from a land cover map for the state of Massachusetts produced by MassGIS, the state of Massachusetts Geographic Information Systems agency.

We condensed the original land cover type classes into seven LCTs: Water, Wetlands, Forest, Open, Roads, Residential, and Urban (Figure 4.2). The LCT classification, based on the ABC resource model, is explained in more detail below.

1. Abiotic Resources:

   Water (LCT 1): includes water bodies, such as lakes and ponds, and streams.

   Wetlands (LCT 2): includes forested and non-forested wetlands.

2. Biotic Resources:

   Forest (LCT 3): includes deciduous, coniferous, and mixed forest.

3. Cultural Resources:

   Agriculture and Recreation (in housing settings):

   Open (LCT 4): includes croplands, pastures, orchards, nurseries, abandoned fields, herbaceous or shrubby vegetation, participatory recreation, urban open areas, and cemeteries.

   Infrastructure:

   Roads (LCT 5): includes all types of roads, from unpaved roads to highways, and railroads.

   Housing:

   Residential (LCT 6): includes housing land use with a density of less than four units per acre, and where the average density is one unit per two acres (rural is broadly defined as one unit per two to three acres, or one unit per hectare).

   Urban (LCT 7): includes any industrial land use (including mining and waste disposal), transportation facilities, commercial land use, spectator and water-based recreation, and housing land use with more than four units per acre.

We adopted two important rules to construct the base map and the alternative scenarios: (1) Roads supersede all other LCTs. Since Roads will

expand to support development, this means that all other LCTs are fragmented by Roads both in the present situation and in every time step in
which Roads are expanding (not all time steps), and (2) Water is the second prevailing LCT, superseding all other LCTs except Roads, so that,
for example, Forest is fragmented by Water.

These rules have significant effects on the simulation results (i.e., landscape metrics). For example, when a new road crosses a large patch of
Forest, the patch is bisected, altering patch size, shape, and many other
landscape metrics.

Patch richness (PR) was the only one of our core metrics that was not
used in this application. The small number of LCTs (7) in our data did not
allow for significant variations of PR throughout the time steps. For the
proximity index (PROX) we defined an ecological neighborhood of 500 m.
To calculate edge contrast metrics (ECON) we constructed a weight matrix
(Table A4.1, available online at www.islandpress.org/measuringlandscapes).

A caveat is worth noting regarding the behavior of some landscape
metrics when considering the growth or expansion (estimated for each
scenario) of prevailing LCTs such as Roads and Water. Prevailing LCTs
will never be segmented by expansion of other LCTs. However, when
prevailing LCTs such as Roads expand, it often results in the segmenta-
tion of other LCTs, including Water, which will have an effect on patch
number/density (PN/PD), patch size (AREA), radius of gyration
(GYRATE) and Euclidean nearest neighbor distance (ENN). For example, a stream that is crossed by a road will be segmented into two smaller
and less extensive stream patches. In addition, the stream patches derived
from the fragmenting road crossing will have a short ENN because the
disjunction between patches is due to a narrow road crossing. Consequently, ENN for the fragmented class (Water, in this case) may actually
decrease as result of the fragmentation.

We analyzed and diagnosed the watershed and explored two alternatives for future development: (1) *Trend Scenario, TR*: what if future development continues to follow established trends?, and (2) *Smart Growth
Scenario, SG*: what if we could implement the overall spatial strategy syn-
thesized under the spatial concept of the ecological backbone, a *green*
structure that supports the ecological functioning of the landscape? We
applied a creative approach to conceive the spatial concept as an important complement to the quantitative approach using landscape metrics.

Based on the Present Situation (T0) and a set of assumptions, we mod-
eled four time steps (T1, T2, T3, and T4) for each of the two alternative
futures (for a total of eight scenarios). Importantly, the *TR* and *SG* scenarios have equivalent amounts of development in each time step, thus the

differences between scenarios result from the spatial strategy selected for development allocation and resource protection. The hypothesis to be tested was that a different spatial solution can make a significant difference for the protection of landscape resources (Forman and Collinge 1997).

4.4. Applications of Landscape Metrics

Landscape metrics can help gauge how a landscape functions under different spatial planning and design solutions. In this planning example we focus on those ABC resources and processes found to be most relevant to the issue of sustainability. Since planning resources are always scarce, and landscape issues are, by definition, complex, landscape metrics can provide indicators to indirectly evaluate ecological performance based on the landscape's spatial structure. In turn, spatial structure is associated with ecological function. The landscape metrics that are most relevant for our exercise will be those that provide insights on the key ecological components and processes of species habitat, wildlife movement, hydrological flows, and urbanization patterns. As stated before, landscape metrics are of the greatest value when used in conjunction with one another, and for certain planning phases and landscape phenomena, not for all.

This application of landscape metrics focuses on the ABC resources (Section 2.2) addressed by three major planning sectors: watershed planning and management, conservation planning, and urban and recreation planning. To provide some simple guidelines for sustainable planning, we used Forman's (1995) indispensable spatial patterns as a guideline:

1. Maintain large patches of native vegetation

2. Maintain wide riparian corridors

3. Maintain connectivity between important resource patches

4. Maintain heterogeneous bits of nature throughout human-developed areas

We structured the planning application according to five planning phases: focus, analysis, diagnosis, prognosis, and sinteresis (Botequilha Leitão 2001; Botequilha Leitão and Ahern 2002). Figure 4.3 shows how these phases represent a cyclical, continuous, and evolving process (see also figure 2.2).

This planning application is driven by planning goals representing alternative resolutions of the fundamental tension between supply

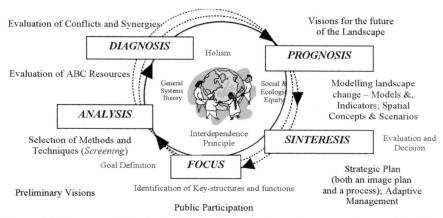

Evaluation of Conflicts and Synergies

DIAGNOSIS   Holism

Evaluation of ABC Resources

General
Systems
Theory

ANALYSIS

Selection of Methods and
Techniques (*Screening*)

Goal Definition   FOCUS

Preliminary Visions   Identification of Key-structures and functions

Public Participation

Visions for the future
of the Landscape

PROGNOSIS

Social &
Ecologic
Equity

Modelling landscape
change – Models &,
Indicators; Spatial
Concepts & Scenarios

Interdependence
Principle   SINTERESIS   Evaluation and
Decision

Strategic Plan
(both an image plan
and a process); Adaptive
Management

Figure 4.3. The sustainable land planning framework applied to Amherst with its five planning phases: focus, analysis, diagnosis, prognosis, and sinteresis, represented as a cyclical, continuous and evolving process. This figure is a simplified diagram of figure 2.2 (Section 2.3).

(resource base) and demand (needs of society). From this perspective, abi-otic and biotic resources represent the supply side, while cultural resources represent demand. Additionally, when planning holistically it is important to move up and down the scale of observation; specifically, to consider a coarse-scale view representing broad groups of resources (e.g., ABC), as well as a finer-scale view representing more resource-specific information (e.g., LCTs). Moving down (to a finer scale) provides more detailed information on a specific site or phenomenon. It is also useful to move up in scale (to a coarser scale) to place detailed observations into the broader context, thus establishing relationships with other sites and phenomena.

In this application, land cover types (LCTs) are grouped under the ABC resource framework and as the natural resource base (A+B) and development resource base (C). As noted above, at a general level we can observe two main parts of Amherst: (a) the headwaters and mid-reaches, and (b) the valley bottom. In these two parts, ABC resources are unevenly concentrated. Cultural resources (Residential, Urban and Open) are more concentrated in the valley bottom, and biotic resources (Forest) in the headwaters and mid-reaches, while abiotic resources (Water and Wetlands) are more evenly distributed across the watershed. Therefore, in this application resources are grouped accordingly, but LCTs are also analyzed separately.

4.4.1. *Landscape Focus*

The landscape focus phase begins by defining goals, which are typically revisited and refined throughout the planning cycle. An important result

of this phase is a preliminary landscape vision that encapsulates and summarizes the goals (see section 2.3). Landscape focus includes scoping, a
preliminary identification of the key issues to address in the plan and
identification of the principal structures and functions of the landscape.
In this case, the key issues involve protecting landscape structures that
adequately support key landscape functions, and provide alternative spatial solutions for those that do not. Landscape focus applies a preliminary
analysis and diagnosis, integrating both rational and intuitive thinking.
These tasks are revised in a more explicit manner later in the formal
analysis and diagnosis planning phases.

Amherst clearly shows segregation of ABC resources and LCTs (Figure 4.4a). In the headwaters, the forested matrix supports functions associated with the hydrological cycle, semi-natural vegetation, and wildlife
habitat. Forests located in the headwaters protect abiotic resources by
promoting infiltration of precipitation, which supports groundwater and
streamflows and protects soils from erosion. In addition to providing
important habitat for flora and fauna, Forest provides cultural functions,
including timber and scenic resources. However, all these functions can
be impaired by development, as in the lower reaches of the watershed
(Figure 4.2). Here Forest is fragmented into isolated woodlots within a
matrix of Residential and Agriculture/Open.

In the landscape focus phase trends are identified with CONTAG and
CAP. The value for CONTAG is 49.5%, an intermediate value that
describes the overall aggregation of LCTs across the watershed. Recall
the CONTAG values in figure 3.25 representing two landscapes: a high
(85%) and a low value (24%), respectively, represented by landscapes (a)
and (b). Over one half of Amherst is Forest (biotic resources); the rest is
a mix of Open/Residential and Urban (cultural resources). With the dominance of a few LCTs one might expect higher CONTAG values, however it is intermediate due to the relative intermixing of LCTs in the central part of the watershed. Recall that CONTAG is a pixel-based metric
that quantifies the "clumping" of LCTs by computing the co-adjacency of
LCT grid cells (Section 3.7.1). Roads and streams that bisect and segment
patches introduce adjacencies of different LCTs, which seem to decrease
the value of CONTAG.

By evaluating CAP, we can confirm that Amherst has a Forest matrix.
Forest occupies more than half of the watershed area ($CAP_{Forest} = 56.6\%$).
Open is the second dominant LCT, concentrated in the lower part of the
watershed. Together these LCTs cover about 75% of the watershed.
These are followed by Residential and Roads (Table 4.1).

The overall goal defined in this phase of the planning application is to
promote an integration of LCTs (Figure 4.4b). A preliminary landscape

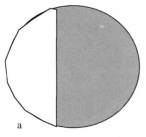 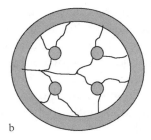

a   b

Figure 4.4. Two preliminary spatial concepts for Amherst. The hatched pattern represents the ecological (blue and green) infrastructure; white represents landscape cultural components (the *gray infrastructure*: housing, transportation, production, recreation, etc). The diagram on the left (a) represents the present landscape (see also Figure 4.2) and, in a way, the fundamental dichotomy between man and nature; the concept on the right (b) represents a preliminary vision for Amherst, and a possible and desirable future, where nature and culture are integrated as a networked system.

vision for Amherst that articulates this overall goal is expressed as a simplified spatial concept (Figure 4.4b). The concept is a network of abiotic and biotic patches connected by linear features such as streams. This spatial concept identifies blue, green, and gray infrastructures, each having essential functions to assure that development is balanced and sustainable. The blue infrastructure includes the hydrological network as well as aquatic ecosystems, such as ponds, lakes, and wetlands. The green infrastructure includes terrestrial semi-natural ecosystems linked with linear features, including riparian corridors. These ecological infrastructures are

Table 4.1. Class area (CA) in hectares (ha) and class area proportion (CAP) as a percentage of all seven land cover types (LCTs) presently found in Amherst (T0). The dominant LCT (the landscape matrix) is bold.

	PRESENT SITUATION (T0)	
LCTs	*CA (Ha)*	*CAP (%)*
1. Water	1295	5.8
2. Wetlands	90	0.4
3. **Forest**	**12636**	**56.6**
4. Open	4134	18.5
5. Roads	1651	7.4
6. Residential	2039	9.1
7. Urban	495	2.2
Total	22340	100

manifest as interconnected patches and linear features that function to help provide stability for hydrological processes, provide wildlife habitat, and facilitate wildlife movement across the landscape. They also provide for human use and enjoyment of the landscape. This ecological infrastructure supports the gray infrastructure, represented by Residential-Urban development and Roads, and other more dynamic uses and functions associated with human activities, including commercial and institutional uses.

4.4.2. *Landscape Analysis*

Landscape Analysis focuses on the characterization of the study area and its landscape context in several dimensions—ecological, economic, and social. In this planning exercise we focus on the ecological, with indirect attention to the economic and social. In the analysis phase we employ class-level metrics to explore in greater detail the issues revealed in landscape focus.

In order to analyze the landscape patterns and and infer their implications on ecological processes in Amherst (Figure 4.2), we will discuss the landscape metrics presented in table 4.2.

Water resources (Water and Wetland LCTs) are not yet at risk. The headwaters are reasonably well protected by Forest cover, and the hydrological network is highly connected across the landscape. However, Wetlands are small and isolated, and those embedded in the Forest matrix are more protected than those in the Urban-Residential center of Amherst.

Water occupies an area equivalent to Roads (the other linear LCT) and CAP_{Water} = 6%; Class Area CA_{Water} = 1,295 ha. There are a considerable number of Water patches (PN_{Water} = 271), which include streams and ponds. This is due in part to our prevailing LCT rule that dictates that whenever a stream is crossed by a road, the stream is dissected into two patches (Section 4.3). A similar result can be observed with ($GYRATE\_AM_{Water}$ = 503), which is ten times lower than GYRATE for Roads ($GYRATE\_AM_{Roads}$ = 4820). Wetlands are a relatively rare element in the watershed ($CAP_{Wetlands}$ = 0.4%; $CA_{Wetlands}$ = 90 ha) and have the smallest number of patches for any non-linear LCT ($PN_{Wetlands}$ = 140). By analyzing ECON it can be determined that Wetlands are reasonably well protected ($ECON\_AM_{Wetlands}$ = 25), which is the lowest of all ECON values in the study area. This is largely because most Wetlands are embedded in and buffered by the Forest matrix. They are also relatively more isolated from one another when compared to all other LCTs as shown by PROX_AM = 4 and ENN_AM = 278 m. These results suggest that wildlife movement from one wetland to another could be affected by the resistance of the intervening matrix lands between Wetlands. Therefore, attention

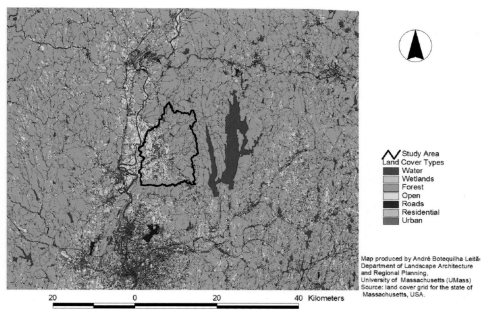

Study Area
Land Cover Types
■ Water
  Wetlands
  Forest
  Open
■ Roads
  Residential
  Urban

Map produced by André Botequilha Leitãe
Department of Landscape Architecture
and Regional Planning,
University of Massachusetts (UMass)
Source: land cover grid for the state of
Massachusetts, USA.

20   0   20   40 Kilometers

Figure 4.1. The study area, a section of the Pioneer Valley in Massachusetts, and its regional context. The Connecticut River flows from north to south across the left center of the map. The city of Springfield, M.A. forms a large red "blob" located at the lower center of this map. The Amherst watersheds (center), located between the Quabbin reservoir (large blue patch, center right) and the Connecticut will serve as the study area for the example planning exercise. *Map produced by André Botequilha Leitão.*

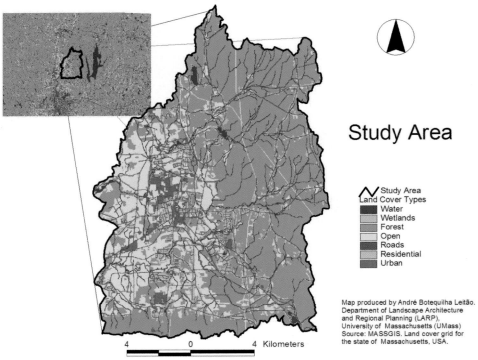

Study Area

Study Area
Land Cover Types
Water
Wetlands
Forest
Open
Roads
Residential
Urban

Map produced by André Botequilha Leitão.
Department of Landscape Architecture
and Regional Planning (LARP),
University of Massachusetts (UMass)
Source: MASSGIS. Land cover grid for
the state of Massachusetts, USA.

4   0   4 Kilometers

Figure 4.2. Present land cover situation (T0) for Amherst watersheds. The town of Amherst (Pioneer Valley, M.A.) is located at the left center; urban denotes the center of this town, surrounded by residential and open fields. *Map produced by André Botequilha Leitão.*

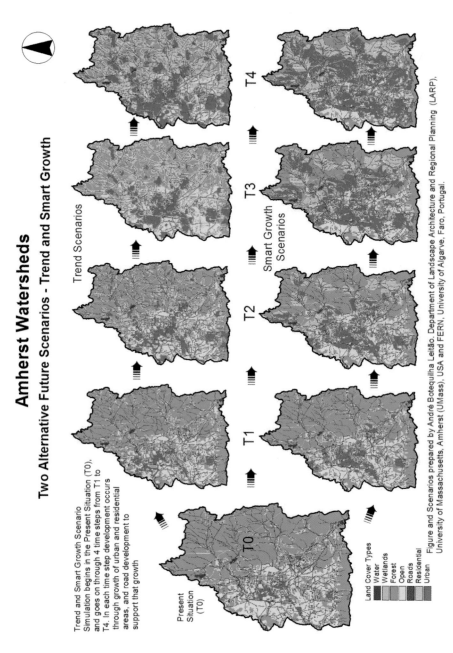

Amherst Watersheds
Two Alternative Future Scenarios - Trend and Smart Growth

Trend Scenarios

Smart Growth Scenarios

Present Situation (T0)

Trend and Smart Growth Scenario
Simulation begins in the Present Situation (T0), and goes on through 4 time steps from T1 to T4. In each time step development occurs through growth of urban and residential areas, and road development to support that growth

T0

T1 T2 T3 T4

Land Cover Types
Water
Wetlands
Forest
Open
Roads
Residential
Urban

Figure and Scenarios prepared by André Botequilha Leitão. Department of Landscape Architecture and Regional Planning (LARP), University of Massachusetts, Amherst (UMass), USA and FERN, University of Algarve, Faro, Portugal.

Figure 4.6. Two alternative future scenarios simulated for Amherst: *Trend*, and *Smart Growth*. The present situation served as a starting point (T0); four time steps were simulated based on the spatial strategies established for each scenario (T1 to T4). *Figure and scenarios prepared by André Botequilha Leitão*

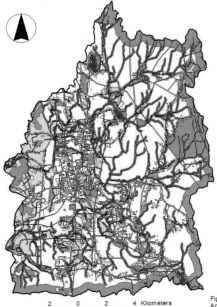

Amherst Watersheds

Smart Growth Scenario

A Spatial Concept

Notice that the Forest is designed as to maximize several criteria: large patches protecting the headwaters, forested riparian buffer as much as possible without adding new forest, 2 large patches, one patch connected with the headwaters, as much isolated as possible to development, and compact, the second one providing a large urban park at the bottom valley and near the river (also potentially absorbing floods), and last providing stepping stones across the landscape which are also connected to the riparian corridors, some of those protecting existing water features, such as lakes and wetlands. Open patches: large agricultural areas located at the flood plain where the best soils are located, but also providing stepping stones of recreational areas across the landscape; these, when possible, are adjacent to forested stepping stones.

Note: Areas represented in white are those areas where future development can take place.

Fragland Spatial Concept
- Water
- Wetlands
- Forest
- Open

2   0   2   4 Kilometers

Figure and Spatial Concept prepared by André Botequilha Leitão. Department of Landscape Architecture and Regional Planning (LARP), University of Massachusetts (UMass) USA, and FERN, University of Algarve, Faro, Portugal.

Figure 4.8. The "ecological backbone," a spatial concept used for the Amherst *Smart Growth* scenario. Forested headwaters are linked to the farmlands located in the floodplain through the hydrological network, which also provides connections for the forest stands and agricultural plots spread across the entire watershed. Farmland (Open) is, whenever possible, associated with housing development, and with forest stands, providing habitats for multi-habitat species, and scenic diversity. Finally forested riparian corridors were maintained along streams and water features. White areas represent those remaining areas where it is allowed more dynamic uses, such as housing and recreation. *Figure and spatial concept prepared by André Botequilha Leitão*

Table 4.2. Class-level metrics of all seven land cover types (LCTs) presently found in Amherst (T0): CA - class area, i.e., the area of each LCT, in hectares (ha); class area proportion (CAP) (%), patch number (PN), mean patch size (AREA_MN) (ha), and the following area-weighted metrics (_AM): mean patch size (AREA_AM) (ha), radius of gyration (GYRATE_AM) (ha), proximity index (PROX_AM), Euclidean nearest neighbor distance (ENN_AM) (meters), edge contrast (ECON_AM), and shape index (SHAPE_AM). Highest and lowest values for each metric are in bold typeface; when metrics values for LCT roads stand out as the highest, we chose to also highlight the second highest value occurring for a non-linear LCT (see text for discussion on the modeling rules and its effects on the behavior of metrics); the row with the dominant LCT (Forest) is the landscape matrix. We have included one decimal case for some of the metrics which present a small range of values and/or overall small variations—otherwise differences between LCTs would be camouflaged, i.e., for CAP, AREA_MN and SHAPE_AM.

PRESENT SITUATION (T0)

LCTs	CA (Ha)	CAP (%)	PN	Area_MN	Area_AM	Gyrate_AM	Prox_AM	ENN_AM	Econ_AM	Shape_AM
1. Water	1,295	5.8	271	4.8	20	503	60	66	36	**5.7**
2. Wetlands	**90**	**0.4**	140	**0.65**	**2**	**71**	**4**	**278**	**25**	**1.5**
3. Forest	**12,636**	**56.6**	**908**	**13.9**	**238**	**625**	1,352	**61**	44	2.7
4. Open	4,134	18.5	676	6.1	36	266	212	71	49	2.0
5. Roads	1,651	7.4	**29**	**56.9**	**1,580**	**4,820**	17	67	**50**	**61.7**
6. Residential	2,039	9.1	**1,302**	1.6	5	109	30	69	33	1.8
7. Urban	495	2.2	204	2.4	10	131	44	145	33	1.7

should be given to maintain linkages between Wetlands, preferably via riparian corridors (the blue corridors referred to in the previous section).

Forest clearly dominates the watershed and constitutes the landscape matrix. Forest is considered to be the prime representative of biotic resources, although we acknowledge that biotic resources are present in other LCTs such as Water (aquatic and amphibian biota), open Wetlands (including crops), and even in Residential and Urban (urban and suburban flora and fauna). The matrix is identified by applying the dual criterion of LCT dominance and connectivity (Forman 1995). Forest is the dominant LCT in total area in the watershed ($CAP_{Forest} \approx 57\%$; $CA = 12,636$ ha). Forest is also considered the most connected LCT in the watershed, both physically and functionally (see chapter one, section 1.3.3).

The assertion of high Forest connectivity is based on the values of three related landscape metrics: GYRATE_AM, PROX_AM, and ENN_AM. Forest has the highest values of GYRATE_AM for a non-linear LCT. Since this metric measures patch extent, it can serve as a rough surrogate for physical connection. Forest also has the highest value of PROX_AM and the lowest value of ENN_AM. Both of these metrics measure patch isolation. They could be considered as surrogates for functional connectivity, where ENN works inversely from PROX. The closer the patches are to each another (low ENN), the less isolated they are, and thus the more (functionally) connected.

Although displaying high levels of connectivity, the Forest LCT is fragmented into ≈ 900 patches (PN_{Forest}), which equals one-fourth of all patches in the landscape, with a reasonably high average size of 14 ha (AREA_MN_{Forest} = 13.9 ha). To explain this apparent contradiction, it is useful to look at AREA_MN together with the complementary metric AREA_AM. Recall that the difference between these two indices is that the weighted-mean (AM) index (for any metric) gives more importance to large patches, and less importance to small patches (because the metric value is weighted by patch area), while the unweighted version (AREA_MN) averages the size of all patches, regardless of size, from the smallest to the largest.

The large difference in values between AREA_MN_{Forest} (13.9 ha) and AREA_AM_{Forest} (238 ha) tells us that patches are, on average, quite large, but that there are also many small patches of Forest.

The discrepancy between the mean and area-weighted mean patch sizes could be detected by looking at a variability measure such as the coefficient of variation (see section 1.4.3 for a discussion). In this case, there is a large variation in patch size distribution (AREA_$CV_{Forest} \approx 400$, the second highest). The watershed, therefore, contains a wide diversity of sizes of forest habitat patches. There are extremely large patches along with patches of all different sizes (medium, small, and very small patches).

Besides the existence of large patches (AREA_AM), the additional information provided by comparing AREA_AM and AREA_MN or alternatively by looking at AREA_CV reveals a large variability of forest patch sizes. Particularly AREA_MN reveals the existence of a large number of smaller patches. This information on the diversity of Forest patch sizes could be of importance for the conservation planner when considering habitat diversity for a wide range of Forest species, e.g., large mammals to amphibians and reptiles. It could be equally important for an urban planner in order to be aware of the existence of a significant number of small Forest patches within a more urbanized environment, i.e., when considering the role of small Forest patches near the town center of Amherst.

The Open LCT is concentrated in Amherst town center, mainly in large patches, but it also exists as small patches associated with dwellings in the forested matrix. Open is the second dominant LCT after Forest, occupying almost 20% of the total study area ($CAP_{Open} \approx 19\%$; $CA_{Open} \approx$ 4,100 ha). Open is also quite fragmented ($PN_{Open} \approx 680$). In comparison with Forest, Open has three-fourths the total number of patches, but only one third of the total area. These metrics suggest that Open is more fragmented into smaller patches on average than Forest ($AREA\_MN_{Open} =$ 6.1 ha; $AREA\_MN_{Forest} = 13.9$ ha).

Roads are spread out across the landscape. Not surprisingly, Roads are the most connected LCT in the watershed, with a value of $GYRATE\_AM_{Roads} = 4,820$ m, which is by far the highest value of any LCT (the second highest value is eight times lower: $GYRATE\_AM_{Forest} =$ 625). Roads also have a complex shape ($SHAPE\_AM_{Roads} \approx 60$), which is ten times higher than any other LCT (the second highest value $SHAPE\_AM_{Water} \approx 6$). This result is not surprising considering both the inherent linear nature of Roads and the modeling rule adopted, i.e., that Roads fragment all other LCTs (see section 4.3).

The Residential LCT is distributed almost entirely along Roads. A few minor patches occur in the town center. Residential land cover is quite fragmented ($PN_{Residential} = 1,302$). Additionally, notice that $CAP_{Residential} \approx 9\%$ ($CA_{Residential} \approx 2,000$ ha). Therefore, Residential has twice the number of patches as Open and 1.5 times the number of patches as Forest, but half of the total area of Open and only 10% of the total Forest area. This means that overall Residential is very fragmented and occurs in small size patches ($AREA\_AM_{Residential} = 5.0$ ha).

Urban is concentrated almost entirely in the center of Amherst, however some Urban occurs in the more forested part of the watershed. Overall, Urban presents a more compact pattern than Residential. Thus, Urban is less fragmented than Residential ($PN_{Urban} = 204$) and patches are substantially larger ($AREA\_AM_{Urban} = 10$ ha).

4.4.3. *Landscape Diagnosis*

Landscape diagnosis builds on landscape analysis by identifying resources and processes of value as well as landscape dysfunctions and spatial conflicts. Thus, the diagnosis applies both to positive and negative situations. Additionally, it applies to both the present and the future (Section 2.3). Consequently, it is possible to distinguish four distinctive potential situations as summarized in Table 4.3.

In order to assess impacts on water resources, we used the thresholds on watershed imperviousness published by the Center for Watershed Protection (2001) (Table 4.4). According to the Center for Watershed Protection, "imperviousness is a very useful indicator with which to measure the impacts of land development on aquatic systems. Reviewed here is the scientific evidence that relates impervious cover to specific changes in the hydrology, habitat structure, water quality, and biodiversity of aquatic systems. This research, conducted in many geographic areas, concentrating on many different variables, and employing widely different methods, has yielded a surprisingly similar conclusion—stream degradation occurs at relatively low levels of imperviousness (10–20%)" (CWP 2001, 1).

Total impervious cover for Amherst at T0=14.2%, where $CAP_{Impervious}$ = CAP_{Urban} + 1/2 $CAP_{Residential}$ (assumed to be half impervious) + CAP_{Roads}. Additionally, it is reasonable to assume that at T0 most of the impervious cover is concentrated in the town center, and thus in the headwaters $CAP_{Impervious}$ is likely much less than 10%.

Table 4.3. Landscape Diagnosis. Summary of possible situations for resources or functions that can potentially occur in any given landscape.

LANDSCAPE RESOURCE OR FUNCTION

	Present	Future	Diagnostic
1	+	+	Presently the resource or function is functioning well; No foreseeable threat lies in the future as to affect it.
2	+	—	Presently the resource or function is functioning well; However a threat lies in the future as to affect it.
3	—	+	Presently the resource or function is **not** functioning well; However there are possibilities to recover in the future.
4	—	—	Presently the resource or function is **not** functioning well; Additionally there no are possibilities to recover in the future.

Table 4.4. Urban stream classification according to the percentage of impervious cover in any given watershed.

Urban Stream Classification	Stressed	Impacted	Degraded
Imperviousness	0–10%	11–25%	26–100%
Channel Stability	Stable	Unstable	Highly Unstable
Water Quality	Good	Fair	Fair-Poor
Stream Biodiversity	Good-Excellent	Fair-Poor	Poor
Planning Strategies	Identify and protect large patches of critical resources	Defend/restore riparian buffers	Urban infill, redevelopment opportunities, BMPs, e.g., Stormwater mgt.

Source: This table is partially based on the Center for Watershed Protection's Best Management Practices, 1998, 2001.

As determined during the landscape focus phase, Amherst currently has an intact, contiguous Forest matrix characterized by high connectivity, and a mix of rural land uses. However, development follows a typical spatial trend, with strip development along Roads and little to no compact development being promoted. The following is a summary of the major trends in the ABC resources.

Water and Wetlands do not appear to be significantly impaired in the current landscape, but as development progresses, these features will likely be seriously affected. The alterations will start adjacent to the town center where the Urban tissue is tighter. Then it will affect aquatic features located in the forested part of the landscape as development expands into the forested headwaters.

Forest and Open land will be substantially affected by future development, both in extent and configuration. Some large patches will be fragmented by expanding Roads and Urban/Residential, and small patches in the town center are prone to disappear altogether.

New Roads will be developed and Residential will continue to expand along the new Roads in a closely associated pattern. Roads improve accessibility to parts of the landscape once isolated, facilitating new Residential growth. Roads and Residential areas also constitute a source of disturbance to ecological systems (e.g., creation of impervious areas, water pollution, noise, littering, habitat destruction, etc.). Urban growth continues to be most concentrated entirely in the center of Amherst. However, some Urban occurs in the more forested part of the watershed.

In the diagnosis table for Amherst (Table 4.5), we identified both present

Table 4.5. Diagnosis table for Amherst refers to two distinct parts of the watershed: (1) Urban-Residential-Agricultural landscape at the valley bottom (Amherst Center), and (2) forested hills and mid-reaches (forested headwaters). The table should read from left to top, i.e., how Forest in Amherst Center is providing for biotic resources. The ecological service, be it a resource (e.g., water, clean air, timber), or a function (e.g., connectivity, water cycle regulation) presently is functioning "P+", or not functioning "P-", or not functioning "F+", or not functioning "F-" (for further explanation see Table 4.3).

	Water Resources (WR)[1]	Biotic Resources (BR)	Cultural Resources (CR)
Amherst Center			
Water: streams and wetlands[1]	Unstable channels and fair water quality (P-); Increased imperviousness and stream culverts upstream will provoke downstream increase of runoff, erosion, and channel instability (F-).	Present situation of streams biodiversity is fair to poor (P-); Shortage of water and reduced water quality due to increased development will worsen these conditions (F-).	Water quality being fair, Idem (F-), recreation opportunities are thus restricted (P-), (F-).
Forest	Small forested areas and riparian vegetation provide for flood and nutrient buffering, and for percolation of precipitation (P+); If reduced or replaced entirely by development, impacts on water (erosion and pollution) and aquatic wildlife can increase (F-); The abovementioned ecosystems should be maintained or improved (F+).	Small forested areas and riparian corridors provide for biological diversity and wildlife habitat (P+); If reduced or replaced entirely by development impacts on wildlife will increase (F-); Idem (F+).	Small forested areas and riparian corridors provide for several ecological services, such as CO_2 recycling, nutrient buffering, soil protection, recreation, scenic value, etc. (P+); if impaired these services will impact quality of urban life (F-); Idem (F+).
Open	Agricultural areas at the fluvial plain provide for flood buffering (P+); If intense agricultural activities take place pollution can be generated (F-) if these areas decrease or disappear, associated ecological services will no longer be provided (F-).	Agricultural areas provide for biological diversity and wildlife habitat (P+); impacts can happen as a consequence of large patches disappearing and/or intensive agricultural activities taking place (F-).	Urban farmland has a fundamental role by providing for food and fibers, e.g., vegetables, a pedagogic role for children, scenic resource (P+), Idem (F-), and constitutes by itself a scenic resource (P+), (F-).
Urban, Residential, and Roads	Hydrological functions may be impaired by impervious cover, reduced riparian vegetation due to narrow to inexistent stream corridors, and road culverts (P-); If development grows impacts on WR will increase, e.g., imperviousness, runoff, and pollution (F-).	Wildlife presence and movement is restrained by dominance of an Urban-Residential disturbance matrix (P-); If the current existent natural corridors (riparian, forest) are not protected there is a potential risk to even more wildlife (F-).	Amherst urban-suburban area, with urban and residential LCTs providing for human habitat, and industrial, commercial areas, and recreational facilities for needed services (P+); Residential is sprawling (F-); If concentration is promoted consolidates urban areas and minimizes input on the surrounding rural landscape (F+).

	Water Resources (WR)[1]	Biotic Resources (BR)	Cultural Resources (CR)
Headwaters and Mid-Reaches			
Water: streams and wetlands[1]	Stable channels and good water quality (P+); potentially providing for landscape connectivity (P+); If impaired by development see description for Amherst Center (F-).	Good to excellent streams biodiversity (P+), Idem (F-).	Some of these resources can provide for recreation, e.g, swimming, boating, and fishing, and for WR research (P+), Idem (F-).
Forest	Watershed headwaters are sensitive areas for water protection; additionally there are still large forest tracts, thus presenting high amounts of pervious surface (P+); these are prone to deforestation and clear-cutting for logging and development (F-).	By providing core areas, large forested areas provide for habitat for specialist and large-range species (P+); these ecological services will decrease as development replaces forest (F-).	Forest provides for timber, game, recreation grounds, and secluded sites to contemplate and enjoy nature (P+); these ecological services will decrease as development replaces forest (F-).
Open	If intense agricultural activities take place, pollution can be generated, particularly on WR (F-). If open areas are substituted by impervious LCTs infiltration will be reduced (F-).	Agricultural areas provide for biological diversity, particularly high at ecotones, and wildlife habitat, e.g, for multi-habitat species (P+)[2].	Small agricultural areas mostly adjacent to residential areas provide for food production and scenic diversity (P+); Idem (F-).
Urban, Residential, and Roads	Urban, residential and roads represent impervious areas, however presently these areas are still small (P+); when crossing with streams, roads use culverts; these hinder the movement of water and species (P-). If urban and residential increase, water infiltration will decrease and as a consequence erosion can increase (F-). Pollution will also increase, particularly if development grows in a scattered pattern, and households are not connected to town sewage (associated with the larger urban concentrations) (F-).	Wildlife presence and movement can be affected by urban-residential and road disturbances (F-), but density of these LCTs is still low (P+). Agricultural areas can also be affected by the intensity of agriculture by its substitution with other LCTs (F-). Idem (see above) (F-).	Development, mainly residential, along roads (P-); urban located at major road crossings (P+). Areas of cultural value and visual scenery of high quality (P+); high-income areas (P+). If urban and residential sprawl increase, property values will drop, particularly around high-income areas, along with quality of life (F-).

[1] These observations are based on the assumptions explained in the text about watershed impervious cover at T0, i.e. it is assumed that Amherst center has an impervious cover between 10% and 25%, and the rest of the watershed is lower than 10%. See Table 4.4.

[2] These can be affected by the intensity of agricultural uses and/or by its substitution nwith other LCTs (F-).

(P) and future (F) positive (+) and negative (-) situations (see also Table 4.3) of particular LCTs on ABC resources. The table is organized by two distinct parts of the watershed: the forested hills and headwaters/mid-reaches, and the Urban-Residential-agricultural areas in the valley bottom (Amherst Center).

4.4.4. *Landscape Prognosis*

Landscape prognosis develops possible visions for landscape change to meet the planning goals defined in earlier planning phases. These visions are based on spatial concepts, and are translated into alternative scenarios. The scenarios are evaluated to assess how well they meet the overall planning goals and whether they generate solutions to the key planning issues as diagnosed in the earlier planning phases. These alternatives inform the following planning phase (sinteresis) to generate the landscape plan. Here we will be focusing on the role of landscape metrics to evaluate planning scenarios (section 2.3.1).

In order to illustrate the application of landscape metrics in planning for the ABC resources in Amherst, two alternative landscape scenarios were made, each with four time steps. Below, the general assumptions regarding both scenarios are stated, then more specific assumptions are made for each scenario: *Trend* Scenario, and *Smart Growth* Scenario, referred to respectively as *TR* and *SG*.

In addition to maps where all LCTs are represented, we also provide a second set of maps representing only total development (Urban, Residential, and Roads) to make the development pattern clearer. Landscape metrics were computed for both scenarios in order to assess landscape changes.

SCENARIOS GENERAL ASSUMPTIONS

Rate of Development Growth

The rate of development was assumed to be 80% over a time frame of twenty-five years, based on U.S. population growth trends and projections (Alig et al. 2004). This growth rate was adopted for both scenarios for each of the time steps considered (except for T2 to T3, due to modeling considerations) and was simulated by distributing growth between Urban and Residential LCTs (Table 4.6).

The spatial strategies of each scenario were designed to reflect established trends (*TR*) and innovative planning (*SG*) (Table 4.6). Differences in the proportions of Urban and Residential occur between the *TR* and *SG* scenarios (Figure 4.5). In the *TR* scenario, total development growth

Table 4.6. Development adopted for both scenarios simulated for four time steps expressed by class area proportion (CAP) for Urban, Residential, and Roads. Note under the adopted rule for development, Residential absorbs half of the total population when compared to Urban, thus the contribution of Residential (LCT6) for total population development is LCT6/2. When looking at total development, the total area is roughly doubling except from T2 to T3 (total development doubles from T0 to T1, from T1 to T2, and from T2 to T4). T4 represents a possible future for Amherst in 75 years from the present (T0).

Development (CAP)	T0 (%)	*Trend* Scenario				*Smart Growth* Scenario			
		T1 (%)	T2 (%)	T3 (%)	T4 (%)	T1 (%)	T2 (%)	T3 (%)	T4 (%)
LCT 7 I Urban	2.2	4.6	9.1	14.0	21.0	5.7	12.8	22.0	31.6
LCT 6 I Residential	9.1	13.5	25.3	36.2	42.8	11.3	17.9	20.2	21.5
Contribution of Residential (LCT6/2)	4.6	6.8	12.7	18.1	21.4	5.7	9.0	11.1	10.8
Total Development (LCT7+[LCT6/2])	6.8	11.4	21.8	32.1	42.4	11.4	21.8	32.1	42.4
LCT 5 I Roads	7.4	8.6	9.6	10.0	10.0	7.6	7.8	8.0	8.0

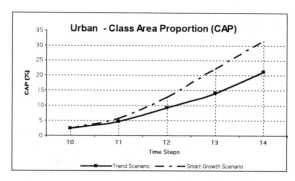

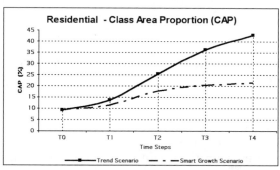

Figure 4.5. Class-level metrics and class area proportion (CAP) computed for land cover types Urban and Residential of Amherst, under both alternative future scenarios, *Trend* and *Smart Growth*, represented respectively by a solid and a dashed line. Metrics were computed with the computer software program FRAGSTATS for the Present Situation (T0), and for four time steps (T1 to T4), in a total of nine maps.

occurs at a higher proportion of Residential along Roads, thereby promoting sprawl as it occurs in reality. The *SG* applies a different spatial
strategy including: encouraging infill of existing suburban developments,
preserving the largest patches of habitat, preferably in the headwaters,
and preserving riparian corridors across the landscape (Ahern 1999;
2004). A simplified spatial concept was prepared to clearly illustrate the
spatial strategies applied in *SG*.

Other General Assumptions Applied to Both Scenarios

Besides total development growth, how and where was the *Present* landscape altered? The following additional reasonable assumptions served as
the basis for the imposed changes we simulated (see Table A4.2 available
online at www.islandpress.org/measuringlandscapes).

- Water and Wetlands are protected by law and cannot be altered.
- Proportions of Open and Forest land are likely to change. Open areas
  can be converted to Forest, Roads, Residential and Urban, whereas
  forested areas can be converted to Open, Roads, Residential and Urban.
- New Roads are needed to support the development of Urban and Residential areas.
- Significant new development will occur in roughly the same amounts in
  both scenarios. Only the spatial strategy for its allocation will differ.
- In certain contexts and time steps, Residential areas may be converted
  to Urban under an "urban infill" strategy. Here we assume that these
  converted Residential areas will absorb half of the population growth
  that new Urban would absorb.
- As a general rule, a change to Urban is not reversible. There are notable
  exceptions to this rule, for example, when a residential lot is converted
  back to forest, or when a brownfield site is restored to meadow or forest, or converted into historical—industrial landscape, a recreation
  facility, or an urban park.

Specific Assumptions Underlying the Trend and Smart Growth Scenarios

Trend Scenario *TR*

The *TR* scenario (Figures 4.6 and 4.7) is a business-as-usual (BAU) scenario (Alcamo 2001). The focus is on the established trend of development rather than on the preservation of natural or cultural resources.

This scenario serves as a baseline with which to compare the *SG* scenario (see section 2.3). Example types of actions within the *TR* scenario include:

- Natural resources strictly protected by law, including Water and Wetlands, are not directly altered as a result of new development. However, development will occur nearby, thus increasing edge contrast of both the Water and Wetland LCTs. Since it is assumed that Roads fragment all other LCTs, occasionally Water will be affected. It is assumed that road crossings of streams disrupt stream continuity and represent a permanent ecological disturbance (Forman et al. 2003).

- Development is accomplished at the expense of Open and Forest areas. The spatially dispersed pattern of new Residential and Urban areas across the landscape fragments both Open and Forest patches.

- Total housing development is more concentrated in Residential areas, however there is also growth in Urban areas.

- Housing development (mainly Residential sprawl) will not assume a compact form; rather, it will spread out in a fingered and dispersed pattern. For example, new development concentrates along major Roads. There is little or no infill of existing suburban developments.

- Urban growth is concentrated almost entirely in the center of Amherst, however some new Urban does show up here and there in the more forested part of the watershed.

- New Roads are implemented so as to support new Urban development, and serve to further fragment the landscape.

Smart Growth Scenario SG

The *SG* is a prospective scenario (Figures 4.6 and 4.7). It is focused on preservation of existing resources under the spatial concept designed for this watershed. This spatial concept (Figure 4.8) is based on the idea that a cultural landscape needs to be supported by an ecological backbone (Botequilha Leitão 2001), a *green* infrastructure that supports the ecological functioning of the landscape. This idea asserts that for sustainable human development, planning must recognize those ecological structures that are most fundamental to assure overall ecological sustainability, including abiotic, biotic, and cultural functions and processes, and to provide the capacity for the landscape to compensate for impacts caused by human uses and activities.

In the protected ecological backbone, important long-term, slowly-functioning (i.e., "low dynamic") processes are supported, including the

Amherst Watersheds
Two Alternative Future Scenarios - Trend and Smart Growth

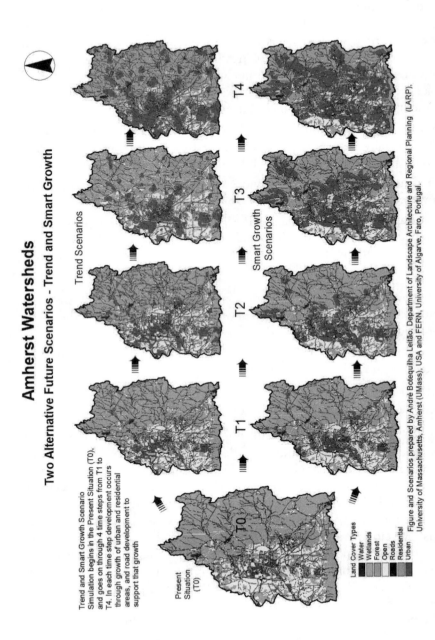

Trend and Smart Growth Scenario
Simulation begins in the Present Situation (T0), and goes on through 4 time steps from T1 to T4. In each time step development occurs through growth of urban and residential areas, and road development to support that growth

Trend Scenarios

Smart Growth Scenarios

T0 T1 T2 T3 T4

Present Situation (T0)

Land Cover Types
Water
Wetlands
Forest
Open
Roads
Residential
Urban

Figure and Scenarios prepared by André Botequilha Leitão. Department of Landscape Architecture and Regional Planning (LARP), University of Massachusetts, Amherst (UMass), USA and FERN, University of Algarve, Faro, Portugal.

Figure 4.6. Two alternative future scenarios simulated for Amherst: *Trend* and *Smart Growth*. The present situation served as a starting point (T0); four time steps were simulated based on the spatial strategies established for each scenario (T1 to T4). *Figure and scenarios prepared by André Botequilba Leitão*

180

Amherst Watersheds

Two Alternative Future Scenarios - Trend and Smart Growth
- Development Component -

Trend and Smart Growth Scenario
Simulation begins in the Present Situation (T0), and goes on through 4 time steps from T1 to T4. In each time step development occurs through growth of urban and residential areas, and road development to support that growth

Trend Scenarios

T1   T2   T3   T4

Smart Growth Scenarios

Present Situation

T0

Total Development
Roads
Residential
Urban

Figure and Scenarios prepared by André Botequilha Leitão. Department of Landscape Architecture and Regional Planning (LARP), University of Massachusetts, Amherst (UMass), USA and FERN, University of Algarve, Faro, Portugal.

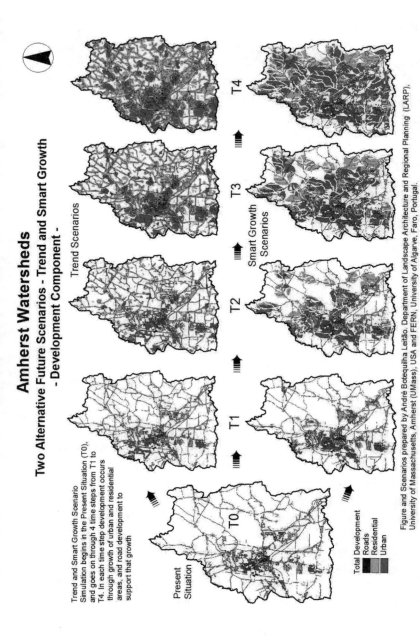

Figure 4.7. Development components (land cover types "Urban," "Residential," and "Roads") of the two alternative future scenarios simulated for Amherst, *Trend* and *Smart Growth* (see also Figure 4.6). The present situation served as a starting point (T0); four time steps were simulated based on the spatial strategies established for each scenario (T1 to T4). Notice the different spatial patterns of housing development in the two scenarios, e.g., the Residential spread along major roads in the *Trend* scenario versus the housing concentration in several nuclei in the *Smart Growth* scenario. *Figure and scenarios prepared by André Botequilha Leitão*

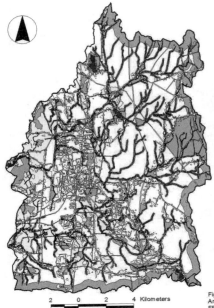

Amherst Watersheds

Smart Growth Scenario

A Spatial Concept

Notice that the Forest is designed as to maximize several criteria: large patches protecting the headwaters, forested riparian buffer as much as possible without adding new forest, 2 large patches to development, and compact, the second one providing a large urban park at the bottom valley and near the river (also potentially absorbing floods), and last providing stepping stones across the landscape which are also connected to the riparian corridors, some of those protecting existing water features, such as lakes and wetlands. Open patches: large agricultural areas located at the flood plain where the best soils are located, but also providing stepping stones of recreational areas across the landscape; these, when possible, are adjacent to forested stepping stones.

Note: Areas represented in white are those areas where future development can take place.

Fragland Spatial Concept
■ Water
■ Wetlands
■ Forest
□ Open

2   0   2   4 Kilometers

Figure and Spatial Concept prepared by André Botequilha Leitão. Department of Landscape Architecture and Regional Planning (LARP), University of Massachusetts (UMass) USA, and FERN, University of Algarve, Faro,Portugal.

Figure 4.8. The "ecological backbone," a spatial concept used for the Amherst *Smart Growth* scenario. Forested headwaters are linked to the farmlands located in the floodplain through the hydrological network, which also provides connections for the forest stands and agricultural plots spread across the entire watershed. Farmland (Open) is, whenever possible, associated with housing development, and with forest stands, providing habitats for multi-habitat species, and scenic diversity. Finally, forested riparian corridors were maintained along streams and water features. White areas represent those remaining areas where it is allowed more dynamic uses, such as housing and recreation. *Figure and spatial concept prepared by André Botequilha Leitão*

integrated ground and surface water components of the hydrological system. On the remaining areas, outside of the ecological backbone, more dynamic uses can take place, including agriculture, residential, commercial, and industrial land uses (Sijmons 2002). A similar approach was proposed under the *"casco"* or framework concept (Van Buuren and Kerkstra 1993; Ahern and Kerkstra 1994; Sijmons 2002) representing a systematic decoupling of functions, where low-dynamic functions (i.e., long-term ecological processes, such as groundwater recharge or soil formation) are combined into a coherent spatial framework, and the high-dynamic functions (i.e., production agriculture, extraction industries) are located in other spaces providing them with the essential spatial flexibility and freedom they operate under (Sijmons 2002).

This concept is discussed by the Dutch landscape architecture firm H+N+S as follows: "The issue is to find a balance between things that simply have to be planned because they are part of the inalienably collective domain, and giving space to social and natural processes which allow themselves neither to be predicted nor planned" (Sijmons 2002, 15–16). According to this perspective, different planning goals should be set for each area. The approach of differential prioritization proposed by von Haaren (2002) also addresses this issue by suggesting the following for areas with low dynamics: mandatory goals that are relevant for environmental and/or culturally valuable or sensitive areas, and for areas with high-dynamic functions desirable, often alternative objectives, which provide a minimal standard for the quality of the environment for the remaining areas.

The proposed spatial concept for the ecological backbone emphasizes the protection of the "low-dynamic" areas described above. It is spatially expressed by protecting the headwaters, river corridors connecting the headwaters to the main river that ensure buffered water flows across the entire landscape, and the largest patches of habitat linked with forested corridors when possible.

The allocation of Forest supports the spatial concept in several respects. It maximizes large patches protecting the headwaters and maintains large forested riparian buffers. A proposed uniform-width buffer around the watershed's perimeter is clearly visible in the spatial concept and is intended to provide strong and deliberate protection for the entire headwaters area. The spatial concept includes two large Forest patches: one providing core habitat connected with the headwaters and located as far as possible from the center of development, and a second providing a large urban park at the valley bottom and near the river. Additionally, stepping stones of Forest are strategically located across the landscape connected to the riparian corridors, and serve as buffers around existing Water features.

The *SG* scenario also supports cultural goals. It protects resources for food production and for recreation, and provides a better environment for Urban residents, as advocated by the New Urbanism movement in the U.S. The scenario includes patches of Open for agriculture. Large patches of farmland are integrated in the ecological backbone, the largest one located in the floodplain. The rationale is that farmland needs to be protected as it is crucial for food production, and that fertile soils require millenia to develop. The agricultural patches also have a "buffering" function through retention and infiltration of river flooding. These Open patches also serve as stepping stones for recreational activities across the landscape, and whenever possible are located adjacent to Forest stepping stones.

Other objectives in the *SG* scenario include encouraging urban infill development and discouraging sprawl along Roads, developing new Roads as little as possible to minimize fragmentation, and establishing recreation linkages between Open areas within the Urban-Residential matrix in the town center such as urban parks and gardens.

EVALUATION OF SCENARIOS

In this section, we use the selected core set of landscape metrics to evaluate and compare the two simulated scenarios. We tabulate these metrics in two tables: (1) landscape-level metrics, which include CONTAG and GYRATE (correlation length—the area-weighted mean radius of gyration computed at the landscape level) (Table 4.7), and (2) class-level metrics, which include all other core metrics (except PR) (Table 4.8). We also graphed these values to visualize and analyze spatial trends across the time steps and between scenarios (Figures 4.9 to 4.15).

Landscape-Level Metrics

CONTAG values for the present situation (T0) reflect the aggregation of LCTs in two distinct parts of the watershed: Forest in the right half of the watershed, and Urban-Open in the left part (Section 4.2 and Figure 4.4). In the *TR* scenario, CONTAG values drop from T0 to T2. This is due mainly to the development of Roads and Urban and Residential which segment other LCTs. (See table 4.7 for metric values and the graph in figure 4.9a. See also the maps in figures 4.6 and 4.7 for visualizing spatial trends.)

Recall that CONTAG is a landscape-level metric that summarizes the clumping of LCTs. The LCT that dominates the landscape (the matrix) has the strongest influence on CONTAG. By looking at the changes over time in aggregation of the dominant LCT, changes in CONTAG can be explained. Across time (T0 to T4), Forest becomes segmented into smaller patches, thus its total aggregation (and therefore CONTAG) decreases. This decrease in Forest aggregation over time is compensated for by adding new patches of development thus increasing Urban/Residential aggregation. However, at T1-T2 this is not yet valid since development initially has a dispersed or fingered pattern along Roads. From T2 onward, the stabilization (T2-T3) and increase (T3-T4) of CONTAG values reflect the increasing amounts

Table 4.7. Landscape-level metrics computed for Amherst, under both alternative future scenarios, *Trend* and *Smart Growth*. The metrics were computed for the present situation (T0), and for four time steps (T1 to T4) for both scenarios.

				Metrics Values Across Time		
Scenarios	Metrics	T0	T1	T2	T3	T4
Trend	CONTAG	49.5	44.5	38.7	38.8	41.8
Smart Growth	CONTAG		46.3	40.5	38.1	38.2
Trend	Gyrate_AM (C)	801.0	740.7	757.8	782.9	790.6
Smart Growth	Gyrate_AM (C)		804.6	768.0	752.0	740.0

and dominance of Residential, Urban, and Roads. As a result, a new matrix of Residential, Urban, and Roads development has replaced the once forested matrix.

In the *SG* scenario, the behavior of CONTAG across time is different (Table 4.7 and Figures 4.6, 4.7, and 4.9a). It drops initially from T0 to T1, but not as significantly as in the *TR* scenario. This is due to the *SG* spatial strategy, which minimizes fragmentation of the largest patches of Forest. The CONTAG values from T1 to T2 mirror the relatively higher spatial aggregation of the dominant LCT—Forest. In *SG* T2, CAP_{Forest} is 40.8% (Table 4.8), clearly dominating the watershed as compared to other LCTs. In T3 and T4, the CONTAG values stabilize, because Forest is being replaced by development (Urban, Residential, and Roads). Importantly, in the *SG* spatial strategy all LCTs are left as compact as possible, with new development occurring around existing development. And, as much as possible, large Forest patches are shrinking, but not being fragmented, or at least not as much as they are in the *TR* scenario.

At T4 the CONTAG values for the *TR* are much higher than for the *SG* because here CONTAG is influenced significantly by development, as reflected in high values of CAP (note that the sum of CAP of LCTs Urban, Residential, and Roads in T4 = circa 3/4 of the entire landscape). Not surprisingly, the *TR* scenario at T4 (Figure 4.7) resembles an Urban-Residential blob. On a final note, notice that values for CONTAG (for both scenarios) could have been even higher if Roads and Water were not treated as segmenting all other LCTs.

Here is a good example for the use of metrics in conjunction when analyzing CONTAG. The additional information provided by CAP was helpful to better understand the change of CONTAG values over time.

Table 4.8. Landscape metrics computed for all seven land cover types (LCTs) presently found in Amherst (T0), and for four time steps (T1 to T4) for both alternative future scenarios, *Trend* and *Smart Growth*.

LCTs	Metrics	*Trend* Scenario						*Smart Growth* Scenario				
		T0	T1	T2	T3	T4		T0	T1	T2	T3	T4
1. Water	CAP	5.8	5.8	5.8	5.8	5.8		5.8	5.8	5.8	5.8	5.8
	PN	271	282	295	298	297		271	271	271	271	271
	AREA_AM	20	17.4	16.6	16.4	16.4		20	20	20	20	20
	ECON_AM	36.4	41.1	47.0	57.0	67.0		36.4	36.4	36.4	36.4	36.4
2. Wetlands	CAP	0.4	0.4	0.4	0.4	0.4		0.4	0.4	0.4	0.4	0.4
	PN	140	140	140	140	140		140	140	140	140	140
	AREA_AM	2	2	2	2	2		2	2	2	2	2
	ECON_AM	25.2	25.5	29	35	39		25.2	25	25	25	25
3. Forest	CAP	56.6	51.3	37.1	24.6	14.5		56.6	52.7	40.8	31.1	22.2
	PN	908	991	1250	857	612		908	862	849	865	875
	AREA_AM	238.1	91.7	50.8	31	24.7		238.1	243	193	153	95
	GYRATE_AM	625.3	396.9	294	249.3	220.9		625.3	641	600	560	491
	PROX_AM	1352	582.7	191	98.85	60.89		1352	1255	873	544	298
	ENN_AM	61.1	63.6	68	76.16	81.16		61.1	62	62	63	64
	SHAPE_AM	2.66	2.09	1.9	1.84	1.76		2.66	2.73	2.98	3.2	3.34
4. Open	CAP	18.5	15.9	12.6	9	5.5		18.5	16.5	14.5	12.5	10.5
	PN	676	677	604	481	329		676	640	642	619	602
	AREA_AM	35.9	26.2	24.4	19.5	14.7		35.9	36	32	30	29
	GYRATE_AM	265.9	229.5	221	202	180.2		265.9	269	253	247	241

Trend Scenario

LCTs	Metrics	T0	T1	T2	T3	T4
5. Roads	CAP	7.4	8.6	9.6	10	10
	PN	29	32	35	29	29
	AREA_AM	1,580	1,868	2,101	2,194	2,194
6. Residential	CAP	9.1	13.5	25.3	36.2	42.8
	PN	1302	1390	1381	1239	1145
	AREA_AM	4.5	9.3	15.5	23.3	30.2
	GYRATE_AM	108.9	205.7	266	282.6	292.9
	PROX_AM	30.2	83.1	146	232.5	303
	ENN_AM	68.6	66.6	63	62.47	61.38
7. Urban	CAP	2.2	4.6	9.1	14	21
	PN	204	263	391	431	482
	AREA_AM	9.7	27	31.2	45.4	50
	GYRATE_AM	131	224.3	227	257.9	277.6
	PROX_AM	44	98.8	91	144.2	182.2
	ENN_AM	144.6	104.3	195	77.81	74.29

Smart Growth Scenario

LCTs	Metrics	T0	T1	T2	T3	T4
5. Roads	CAP	7.4	7.6	7.8	8	8
	PN	29	29	29	28	28
	AREA_AM	1,580	1,626	1,671	1,717	1,717
6. Residential	CAP	9.1	11.3	17.9	20.2	21.5
	PN	1302	1255	1271	1271	1276
	AREA_AM	4.5	7.4	23	28	30
	GYRATE_AM	108.9	131	203	224	236
	PROX_AM	30.2	51	115	154	174
	ENN_AM	68.6	66	67	66	66
7. Urban	CAP	2.2	5.7	12.8	22	31.6
	PN	204	322	487	668	755
	AREA_AM	9.7	17	40	60	83
	GYRATE_AM	131	173	281	342	405
	PROX_AM	44	101	116	157	277
	ENN_AM	144.6	84	81	75	70

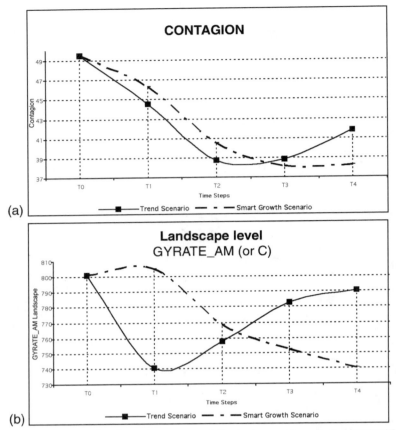

Figure 4.9. Landscape-level metrics computed for Amherst: (a) contagion (CONTAG); (b) area-weighted radius of gyration (GYRATE_AM or C). Landscape metrics were computed for the present situation (T0), and for four time steps (T1 to T4) for both alternative future scenarios, *Trend* and *Smart Growth*, represented respectively by a solid and a dashed line.

Class-Level Metrics

The following discussion will focus separately on each LCT using class-level metrics. Following the ABC resource organizational framework, we grouped LCTs by ABC resources starting with abiotic resources (Water and Wetlands), then biotic resources (Forest), and finally, cultural resources (Open, Residential, and Urban). Roads are not analyzed separately, but are analyzed and discussed in conjunction with other LCTs as appropriate. Tables 4.8 and 4.9 and the graphs in figures 4.10 to 4.15 support the analysis of class-level metric values and trends across the time steps.

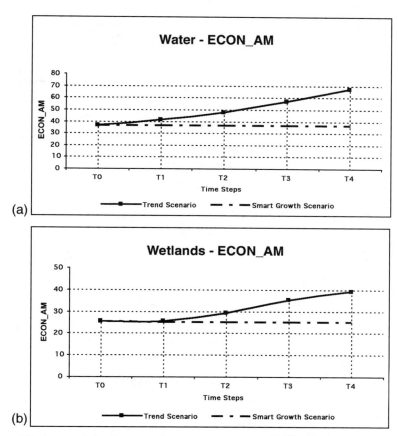

Figure 4.10. Area-weighted mean edge contrast metrics (ECON_AM) computed for land cover types: (a) Water and (b) Wetlands of Amherst. Landscape metrics were computed for the Present Situation (T0), and for four time steps (T1 to T4) for both alternative future scenarios, *Trend* and *Smart Growth*, represented respectively by a solid and a dashed line.

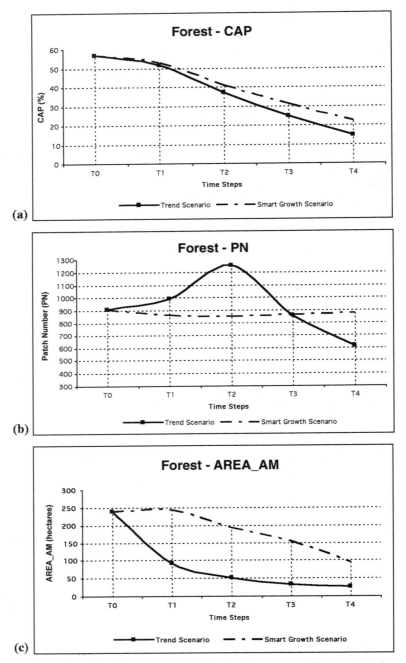

Figure 4.11. Class-level metrics computed for land cover type Forest of Amherst: (a) class area proportion (CAP); (b) patch number (PN); (c) area-weighted mean patch size (AREA_AM) (in hectares). Landscape metrics were computed for the Present Situation (T0), and for four time steps (T1 to T4) for both alternative future scenarios, *Trend* and *Smart Growth*, represented respectively by a solid and a dashed line.

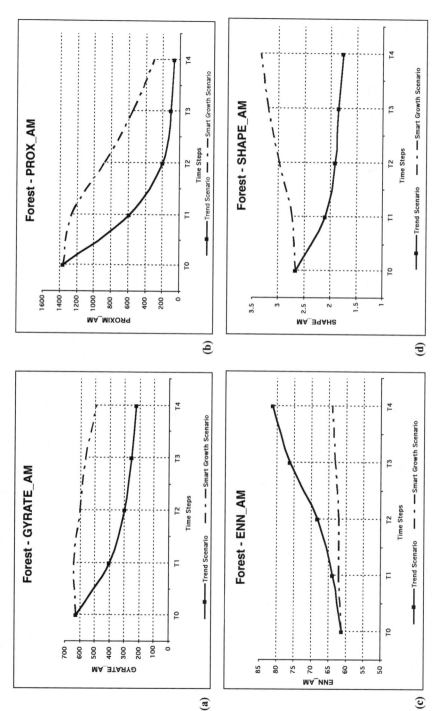

Figure 4.12. Area-weighted mean class-level metrics computed for land cover type Forest of Amherst: (a) radius of gyration (GYRATE_AM); (b) proximity index (PROX_AM); (c) Euclidean nearest neighbor distance (ENN_AM); and (d) shape index (SHAPE_AM). Landscape metrics were computed for the Present Situation (T0), and for four time steps (T1 to T4) for both alternative future scenarios, *Trend* and *Smart Growth*, represented respectively by a solid and a dashed line.

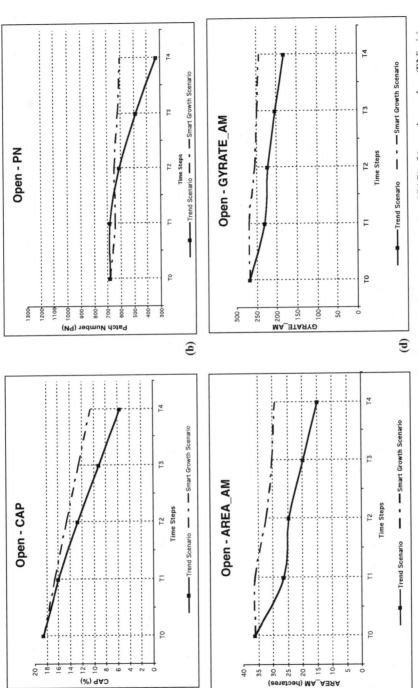

Figure 4.13. Class-level metrics computed for land cover type Open of Amherst: (a) class area proportion (CAP); (b) patch number (PN); (c) area-weighted mean patch size (AREA_AM); (d) area-weighted mean radius of Gyration (GYRATE_AM). Landscape metrics were computed for the Present Situation (T0), and for four time steps (T1 to T4) for both alternative future scenarios *Trend* and *Smart Growth*, represented by a solid and a dashed line, respectively.

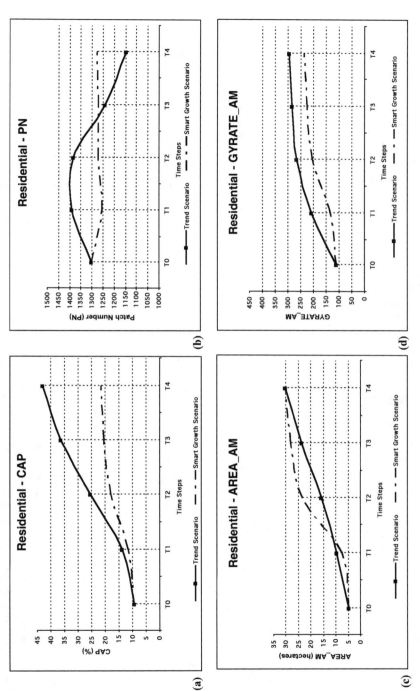

Figure 4.14. Class-level metrics computed for land cover type Residential of Amherst: (a) class area proportion (CAP); (b) patch number (PN); (c) area-weighted mean patch size (AREA_AM); and (d) area-weighted mean radius of gyration (GYRATE_AM). Landscape metrics were computed for the Present Situation (T0), and for four time steps (T1 to T4) for both alternative future scenarios, *Trend* and *Smart Growth*, represented respectively by a solid and a dashed line.

193

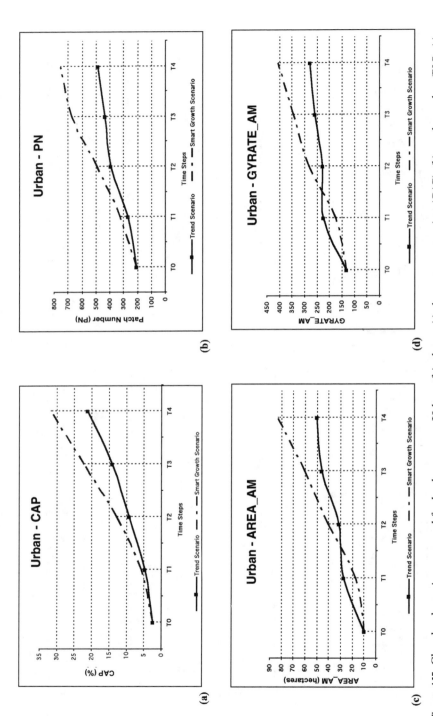

Figure 4.15. Class-level metrics computed for land cover type Urban of Amherst: (a) class area proportion (CAP); (b) patch number (PN); (c) area-weighted mean patch size (AREA_AM), and (d) area-weighted mean radius of gyration (GYRATE_AM). Landscape metrics were computed for the Present Situation (T0), and for four time steps (T1–T4) for both alternative future scenarios, *Trend* and *Smart Growth*, represented by a solid and dashed line, respectively.

Abiotic Resources

Due to the rules we defined for Water and Wetlands LCTs, they were not directly affected by development (Section 4.3). No changes were recorded in any metrics except ECON_AM, which responded at the class level to land cover changes in lands adjacent to focal patches of Water and Wetlands. For example, development in adjacent patches can cause pollution, which can decrease the overall quality of streams, lakes, ponds, wetlands and their associated habitats (see section 4.3, Data and Methods, for details on the ECON weights adopted for the scenarios simulation).

In the *SG* scenario the spatial strategy includes a buffer around all Water features within which no land use changes were allowed. For modeling purposes we initially used a 50 m buffer (vector format) around streams and water features. This buffer was later converted to a grid format to add the buffer to the *SG* raster maps. In the vector-raster conversion process a variable raster buffer resulted, ranging from a minimum width of one cell (30 m), e.g., when the streams diagonally cross the landscape, to a maximum width of two cells (60 m) in a bifurcation of two streams. Therefore the initial value for ECON_AM at T0 remained constant across all time steps for this scenario (Table 4.8 and Figure 4.10). However, the buffer was not adopted in the *TR* scenario and ECON_AM values increased from T0 to T4, which doubled the initial ECON_AM value for Water, and increased ECON_AM values for Wetlands by 60%.

When comparing the scenarios, *SG* offers stabilization of impacts on water-related features caused by adjacent LCTs. Conversely, in the *TR* scenario, the impact of other LCTs on water resources as gauged by ECON_AM is significantly increased.

This raises a "red flag" for the *TR* scenario. The ECON metric demonstrates, in comparative terms, that under the same amount of development, alternative spatial solutions can significantly reduce development impact. In fact, there is extensive literature on the benefits of riparian buffers, such as their role in decreasing inputs of agricultural pollutants to rivers and streams. The Environmental Law Institute (ELI) provides an extensive scientific literature review on riparian buffer widths applied in the USA to maintain water quality and wildlife (ELI, 2003, www.elistore.org).

It is important to realize that most landscape metrics characterize the physical structure of the landscape independent of any particular perspective or phenomenon of interest. These so-called "structural metrics" deal only with spatial pattern, and do not address the functional quality or value of any landscape element. As seen above, some landscape metrics, such as ECON, however, are "functional" in that they incorporate qualitative aspects of landscape pattern unique to a particular perspective or phenomenon, but usually in only a limited way.

Biotic Resources

Due to differences in spatial strategies for development growth adopted for the two scenarios, Forest area is higher at T4 in the *SG* scenario (CAP$_{Forest}$ = 22.2%) than the *TR* (CAP$_{Forest}$ = 14.5%) (Figure 4.11a). The higher proportion of Forest in the SG scenario demonstrates a benefit to biotic resources of the *SG* spatial strategy.

When evaluating changes over time in landscape metrics under the *TR* scenario, it is possible to distinguish two particular stages at large with Forest fragmentation (subdivision of Forest) and Forest attrition (gradual loss of Forest patches and Forest area) (Table 4.8 and Figures 4.11b and 4.11c). Specifically, the Forest is initially (T0 to T2) being fragmented into a greater number of smaller patches (PN increases from 908 to 1,250, and AREA_AM decreases from 238.1 ha to 50.8 ha). Eventually, as the loss of Forest area begins to stabilize, there is nevertheless a gradual loss or attrition of Forest patches from the landscape from T2 to T4.

It is reasonable to expect that the land transformation process occurring in the *TR* would affect forest connectivity. We can gain some insights on forest connectivity by looking at some additional area-weighted mean metrics: GYRATE_AM, PROX_AM, and ENN_AM (Table 4.8 and Figure 4.12). Note that patch extent is smaller (GYRATE_AM is smaller) and patches are more isolated from one another (PROX_AM is lower, and ENN_AM is higher). And when compared with the *SG* scenario, the largest forest patches in the *TR* are consistently less connected.

Finally, patch geometric complexity is lower under the *TR* scenario (SHAPE_AM is lower), which means that forest patch shapes are becoming less complex over time, due to being surrounded by human LCTs such as roads and housing that have more geometrically simple shapes when compared with the forest patches that buffer the hydrological network. As the landscape becomes more "humanized" it tends to become simpler geometrically, as compared to more "natural" landscapes (Forman 1995).

The changes over time in Forest under the *SG* scenario is much different (Table 4.8 and Figure 4.11). The number of patches (PN) remains relatively constant and even loses a few patches (T2 to T0: 849 – 908 = –59), and from T2 to T4 only a small number of patches were fragmented from (875 − 849 = 26). When comparing PN and AREA_AM between scenarios at T4, *SG* maintains a higher number of forest patches (875), and a larger average size (95 ha, c. half of the size as in T0) than in the *TR*.

In the preceding discussion of forest patterns and trends over time, the advantages of looking at several metrics in conjunction become clear. The following example illustrates the combined use of CAP, AREA_AM, and PN under the *SG* scenario. Note that from T0 to T1, the average size of the large patches (AREA_AM) actually increases. This might seem surprising. However it can be explained by the loss of several of the smaller forest patches (PN). Briefly, considering that no new forest is being created (and is in fact actually decreasing, i.e., CAP is decreasing) and that AREA_AM puts more weight on the largest patches, the observed increase in AREA_AM means that some of the smaller patches are disappearing, thereby increasing the average size of the remaining patches.

In the next section, we will continue to provide further examples on the combined use of metrics addressing cultural resources such as Open, Residential, and Urban.

Cultural Resources

Open

The *SG* scenario concentrates future development in the higher density urban LCT rather than in Residential. This strategy had important indirect consequences for the extent and configuration of Open areas (Figure 4.13). The *SG* spatial strategy of keeping larger patches of Open also played an important role in the patterning of Open areas. When looking at PN (Figure 4.13b) at T4 for Open, at a first glance one might conclude that the *SG* strategy resulted in a more fragmented pattern (62 patches) compared to the *TR*, which resulted in approximately half the number of patches (329). However, *SG* retained almost all Open patches, but *TR* lost almost all of them. Therefore, no fragmentation process actually occurred for *SG* as we might have concluded by comparing PN at T4 for both scenarios. Interestingly, while *SG* lost about half of the CAP of Open from T0 to T4, it retained almost all the Open patches present at T0 (90%), and the remaining larger patches suffered a reduction of 80% of average size. However, the *TR* lost half of the Open patches, and the remaining larger patches suffered a reduction of almost half of their size. As expected, these changes on spatial configuration had effects on physical connectivity, as seen in GYRATE_AM for this LCT Open (Figure 4.13d).

Urban and Residential

As stated at the beginning of this chapter, both scenarios accept the same population growth over time. However, the *SG* scenario accommodates growth in higher density Urban, while *TR* accommodates most new growth as Residential (Section 4.3). The rationale is to avoid sprawl through higher density and infill development. Thus, CAP and number of patches for Urban (PN_{Urban}) increase significantly more in the *SG* when compared with the *TR* (Figure 4.15).

The spatial consequences resulting from the contrasting spatial strategies for allocating total development cannot be understood with one single metric. When looking at the average size of the largest patches of Residential (e.g., AREA_AM at T4), both scenarios show a value of 30 ha (Figure 4.14). This is puzzling considering that at T4 Residential areas under the *TR* scenario occupy twice the area ($CAP_{Residential}$ = 43.5%) that they occupy under *SG* ($CAP_{Residential}$ = 21.5%). When comparing PN between scenarios, the situation becomes even more unusual, since at T4 the *SG* has 131 more patches than the *TR* (Figure 4.14b). One of many questions could be raised: where is the remaining $CAP_{Residential}$ in the *TR* allocated? The answer lies in the remaining, smaller patches. When comparing AREA between the scenarios focusing on small patches, those of the *TR* are twice the size as those under *SG*. This was only possible to learn by looking at an additional metric, Mean Patch Size (AREA_MN), at T4. AREA_MN in the *TR* is 8.4 ha, and in the *SG* is 3.8 ha. In this situation the area-weighted metric should be complemented with the simple (unweighted) mean. The former gives information on the largest patches only, while the latter provides information on all patches. We could also identify this counterintuitive phenomenon by looking at patchsize distribution, i.e., patch size coefficient of variation across time.

Another interesting question is: why does PN for Residential decrease in *TR* from T0 to T4? Or why does the linear development strategy of *TR*, following existing Roads, result in less fragmentation than the nuclei strategy for Residential development applied in the *SG* scenario (Table 4.9)? CAP values offer an explanation, particularly when they are large. There seems to be a scale effect, which is triggered when CAP reaches a certain threshold causing Residential patches to start coalescing. In the *SG* scenario, since CAP Residential is kept low, this phenomenon does not take place. PN in the *TR* drops down from T2 to T3 largely due to patch coalescence. In figure 4.7 the patch coalescence phenomenon can be clearly seen for T1 and T2 along the road that crosses the watershed north to south running parallel to the eastern border of the watershed.

There is a distinct jump in the *SG* Residential between T1 and T2

Table 4.9. Partial table featuring only metrics class area proportion (CAP) and patch number (PN) for Residential at T2, T3 and T4 for both alternative future scenarios, *Trend* and *Smart Growth*.

	T2		T3		T4	
	CAP	PN	CAP	PN	CAP	PN
TR	25.3	1381	36.2	1239	42.8	1145
SG	17.9	1271	20.2	1271	21.5	1276
TR-SG	7.4	110	16.0	-32	21.3	-131

where the AREA_AM value more than triples from 7.4 to 23 ha (Figure 4.14c and Table 4.8). When compared with *TR*, the *SG* spatial strategy achieves roughly the same physical connectivity of Residential patches (Figure 4.14d), with half of the CAP and a higher number of patches (Figure 4.14d). This is due to the aggregation of Residential in a deliberate pattern nuclei. This point can be observed in figure 4.7, and by comparing the Residential development pattern of the two scenarios, at T2 and T3, focusing on the north-south road mentioned above.

Connectivity in Urban and Residential LCTs translates into more walkable communities as recommended by the New Urbanism movement. This also implies a higher efficiency and lower cost to support urban infrastructures (e.g., Roads, sewage pipes, telecommunications cables). Additionally, a more compact Urban area has less perimeter, thus fewer edge effects with the surrounding landscape, in other words, less interface with contrasting LCTs (Urban/Residential and Forest). This can have two opposing results. From a wildlife perspective, it can mean less impact on forested environments, but it can also mean less human contact with more natural environments.

FUTURE TRENDS

A key question that arises from the preceding discussions is: now what? What is going to happen from T4 onward? We can extrapolate interesting and useful information from the graphs that begin to answer this question (Figures 4.9 to 4.15). If we assume that the overall trends depicted in the graphs from T0 to T4 will continue into the future, the following changes could be expected on particular resources:

• ECON for Water and Wetlands is significantly different in the two scenarios due to the *SG* strategy of keeping a buffer around major Water features (ECON_AM). Thus the impacts on Water resources observed at T4 in *TR* can be expected to continue.

- Although AREA_AM of Forest has a descending curve, PN and ENN_AM maintain relatively stable under *SG*. The trend observed in the *TR* scenario is quite different, where PN plunges and ENN_AM rises abruptly.

- Trends in SHAPE_AM of Forest, a surrogate for patch complexity, are opposite in the two scenarios: in the *SG* it rises, and in *TR* it lowers. It seems that under *TR* the watershed is less geometrically complex (i.e., less natural), where under *SG* it is more geometrically complex.

- Although CAP for Open drops in both scenarios, the changes in spatial configuration represented by AREA_AM, PN, and GYRATE_AM are quite different, being more or less stable under the *SG*. This is not the case under *TR*, where AREA_AM, PN and GYRATE_AM have negative slopes, indicating continued fragmentation.

A caveat is in order regarding scenario extrapolation. One cannot be sure if the trend depicted on the graphs for *TR* will extend into the future or if a break will occur. According to Greeuw et al. "in many long-term scenario studies, surprises and bifurcations are not taken into account; the inclusion of surprises is important since history shows us that historical trends are characterized by strong fluctuations rather than smooth curves, often triggered by unexpected changes" (Greeuw et al. 2000, 8).

4.4.5. *Landscape Sinteresis*

Landscape Sinteresis involves the development of a landscape plan based on the outputs of Prognosis, specifically the analysis and comparative evaluation of the two scenarios (see section 2.3 for further details on this phase). Here it is useful to review earlier assumptions related to the overall sustainable landscape planning process:

- The hypothesis to be tested is that a well-conceived spatial solution can make a significant difference in the sustainability of landscape resources.

- Alternative spatial solutions (e.g., *SG*) can provide equivalent amounts of development as sprawl-type development (e.g., *TR*), thus supporting a head-to-head comparison.

- Landscape ecological concepts and metrics can inform the conception and development of a sustainable landscape plan.

- Spatial strategies applied in the *SG* scenario are based on Forman's

(1995) indispensable spatial patterns: maintain large patches of native vegetation, maintain wide riparian corridors, maintain connectivity between important resource patches, and maintain heterogeneous bits of nature throughout human-developed areas.

• Landscape metrics are essential to compare and evaluate alternative scenarios informing the development of the landscape plan, and this has been discussed under Prognosis.

In this hypothetical application we have not developed a landscape plan *per se*. We note that in actual planning practice Sinteresis would be done in an iterative, public, and transdisciplinary process including: planners, scientists, government officials, and many stakeholders. However, the results of the sustainable landscape planning process, through Prognosis, are significant and provide explicit answers and general guidance for the development of a landscape plan. In particular, the application of metrics to evaluate alternative scenarios supports the following spatially explicit recommendations:

Abiotic Resources:

• The ECON metric verified that riparian corridors reduce edge contrast in the *SG* strategy. This finding lends credibility to this recommendation that is well-known in planning, but remains largely untested for its measurable effects on landscape function (i.e., water quality improvement).

Biotic Resources:

• The ecological backbone concept was proven effective to mitigate forest fragmentation and to enhance connectivity between key resource patches while accommodating equivalent levels of future development (key metrics used: PN, AREA_AM, GYRATE_AM, ENN_AM, PROX_AM).

• The nuclei and infill growth model applied and tested in the *SG* scenario also reduced fragmentation by protecting forests in the headwaters, and concentrating development in higher densities adjacent to existing developed areas and in specified new growth nuclei (key metrics used: CAP, PN, AREA_AM).

• The *SG* strategy of preserving all Open patches as much as possible is proven as well. Additionally, Open *bits of nature* which may serve as stepping stones for certain species can be maintained through a process of urbanization by applying the suite of spatial concepts featured in the *SG* scenario (key metric: PN).

Cultural Resources:

- The nuclei and infill growth model applied and tested in the *SG* scenario referred to above supports the same level of "walkability" (human connectivity) within Residential areas as *TR* in about half of the total landscape area (key metrics: CAP, GYRATE_AM, ENN_AM).

- The modeling rule adopted for Roads was partially responsible for the weak results of the expected increase of Urban compactness in the *SG* scenario. Since Roads supersede other LCTs, the modeling rule did not allow Urban patches to coalesce to one another resulting in an increase of physical compactness (key metrics: CONTAG, AREA_AM, PN, GYRATE_AM, ENN_AM).

These metric results are best understood as indicators of potential, or expected landscape structure-function relationships. While the results can reasonably be used to inform plan development, they remain to be tested and verified through implementation and monitoring.

MONITORING THE LANDSCAPE PLAN

Due to the uncertainty inherent in planning, the entire planning process should be considered a heuristic process where we learn by doing. Monitoring planning activities can play a key role in providing updated information to feed an ongoing and adaptive planning process.

Table 4.11 provides an example for a simple management framework using landscape metrics that support a suite of indicators targeting biodiversity protection in Amherst, broadly assumed to be associated with Forest, Wetlands, and Water LCTs. This framework could be applied to monitor landscape evolution over several time steps, (i.e., T0 to T4), and then onward. Landscape metrics could be used for several monitoring purposes including: (1) baseline monitoring, to describe patterns (sections 4.4.1 and 4.4.2), (2) implementation monitoring to check compliance with the suggested recommendations, (3) effectiveness monitoring to measure the effectiveness of the adopted spatial strategies in attaining the planning goals (section 4.4.4), and finally (4) validation monitoring to verify the validity of assumptions concerning structural-functional relationships, supported by functional indicators of ecological attributes including species diversity and water quality.

Therefore, in addition to monitoring of landscape structure, one should monitor ecological functions to validate original assumptions and to provide new information for landscape planners and managers on the relationships between landscape structure and specific functions.

Table 4.10. Some spatial strategies, organized under the ABC (abiotic, biotic, and cultural) resources and planning strategies. ABC resources are ordered by relative importance.

Proposed Spatial Strategies	ABC Resources	Planning Strategy
Promote large patches protecting the headwaters:		
(a) Include two or more large forest patches: some compact patches to provide for water retention and core habitat, which are connected with the headwaters, and located as far as possible from the center of development;	A, B	
		Defensive
(b) Provide urban spaces for recreation and increase the quality of urban and residential at the valley bottom and near the river (also potentially absorbing river floods).	C	
	A	
Promote forest stepping stones strategically located across the landscape connected also to the riparian corridors, some of those serving as protective buffers around existing water features, such as lakes and wetlands.	B	Defensive
	A	
Reinforce connectivity of riparian corridors at identified gaps, by restoring riparian vegetation and ecosystems.	A, B	Offensive
Establish forest corridors that connect large forest patches.	B	Offensive
Establish recreation linkages (such as greenways) between open areas such as parks and gardens within the urban-residential matrix at the Amherst Center.	C	Offensive
Develop new roads as little as possible to minimize landscape fragmentation and other road ecological effects.	C, B, A	Defensive
Encourage compact development either through urban infill development, or growth adjacent to already existent urban areas, encouraging pedestrian-friendly development; discourage sprawl along roads.	C	Defensive

For example, we hypothesized about future trends for Amherst if present development follows established trends, i.e., a business-as-usual scenario (see section 4.4.4). Some of these hypotheses address impacts on aquatic systems (Water, Wetlands), or continued fragmentation for both Open and Forest. These impacts could be monitored over time applying the suite of landscape metrics used in our planning application. In time the hypothesis about these trends could be tested, and new knowledge

Table 4.l1 . Example of a possible management framework and suite of indicators for biodiversity protection in Amherst applied across the several time steps.

Management Goals	Management Objectives	Management Actions	Components	Indicator	Metrics
A. Protect native bio-diversity at community and landscape scales	A1. Minimize habitat fragmentation	a) Maintain an approximate prescribed proportion of the forest matrix.	Habitat Patch Characteristics	• Size frequency distribution • Partition of total land cover type in an X number of patches	• AREA_AM • AREA_MN • AREA_CV • PN or PD
		b) Prevent isolation of individual patches.	Habitat Patch Characteristics	• Isolation • Clustering/connectivity	• ENN_AM and PROX_AM • CONTAG • GYRATE_AM
	A2. Minimize habitat loss	a) Monitor losses (in area) on the most critical habitat zones. Allow for an X max. Total of habitat losses, over a Y time period.	Habitat Patch Characteristics	• Size frequency distribution • Patch density • LCTs diversity (number and area representation)	• AREA_AM • AREA_MN • AREA_CV • PN or PD • PN or PD • PR and CAP
		b) Monitor habitat quality.	Habitat Patch Characteristics	• Quality of patch/degree of human impact • Convolution of patch perimeter	• ECON_AM • SHAPE_AM
B. Protect the natural processes that maintain biodiversity	B1. Maintain functioning of major natural processes that maintain biodiversity	a) Monitor natural disturbances.	Water Features	• Area of water features: streams, ponds, and wetlands • Flood area (hydrological network buffered-proportion of, and contrast with impervious LCTs)	• CAP • CAP and ECON_AM

Adapted from Botequilha Leitão 2001; originally adapted from Zorn and Upton 1997.

could be gained about how these metrics perform as indicators for the processes and functions of interest.

Subsequent to monitoring, the landscape plan should be revised accordingly in response to the new knowledge, thus reducing uncertainty of planning goals. This would be crucial to attain the plan's vision conceived in the landscape focus phase, and further developed across the entire planning cycle.

5

Recommendations on the Use of Landscape Metrics to Support the Planning of Sustainable Landscapes

The overarching goal of this handbook is to contribute to a fundamental goal of planning—to achieve a sustainable balance between human needs and the resources necessary to provide for those needs. Landscape ecology provides several perspectives and principles that have become fundamental for planners, one being a deeper understanding of the spatial dimension of landscape ecological processes. Planners should acquire an appropriate level of ecological literacy and numeracy as a prerequisite to understanding these fundamental principles of landscape ecology (Ahern et al. 1999). In this handbook we provide a working understanding of landscape metrics to assist planners in applying and interpreting pattern metrics to support the planning of sustainable landscapes. Additionally, this work intends to promote an interdisciplinary bridge between landscape ecologists and planners as well as a transdisciplinary link between the many academic areas and professional activities involved in planning.

In the following, we summarize a set of recommendations on the use of landscape metrics to support the planning of sustainable landscapes.

1. The absolute value of any landscape metric is often difficult or impossible to interpret in explicit ecological terms. Consequently, landscape metrics are best understood as comparative measures of landscape condition. In this manner, they can provide the basis for comparing alternative landscape scenarios or for understanding changes in landscape condition over time.

2. Each landscape metric provides only a partial description of landscape pattern, and is frequently insufficient to fully characterize one or more

206

landscape ecological processes. Using several metrics in combination, however, such as the core set of metrics described herein, can provide a more complete understanding of the pattern-process relationships under consideration.

3. The usefulness of landscape metrics for planning depends on the level of landscape analysis. Landscape-level metrics are useful for an initial overall analysis, class-level metrics for a more in-depth analysis, and patch-level metrics for further detailing planning solutions (Botequilha Leitão 2001). Moving window analysis is of great value to map local conditions more comprehensively.

4. There is no single "best" set of landscape metrics. Each metric has an appropriate use, and there are many complementary sets of metrics. Ultimately, the choice of metrics should reflect the particular pattern-process relationships under consideration. Thus, the proposed core set of metrics is not presented as the ultimate set. There will always be cases where other metrics may be more appropriate. Additionally, the ten metrics included in the core set are not recommended to be applied in all occasions. The use of these ten metrics needs to be further explored and tested to determine their applicability to all planning sectors and with each of the planning phases (as defined under the SLP framework).

5. Landscape metrics are only as good as the underlying model of landscape structure used to map the landscape. Defining the landscape in a meaningful manner is without doubt the most important step in the analysis. Particular attention should be given to the appropriateness of (1) the categorical model of landscape structure, (2) the map classification scheme, (3) the scale (i.e., grain and extent) of the landscape, and (4) the digital data model (i.e., vector vs. raster). Extreme caution must be exercised in comparing the values of metrics computed for landscapes that have been defined and scaled differently.

6. Landscape metrics can provide useful directions to planning, even in cases when they cannot provide definitive and quantitative data about exact landscape structure-function relationships. Metrics can provide comparative measurements and information to help gain insight about those relationships. "Until empirical evidence is available we need rough generalizations. Those may still be useful if they can rank planning options in terms of: option A is better than option B, for species function X" (Jongman 1999).

7. With metrics, it is crucial to appreciate that we have the power to measure and report more about landscape pattern than we can interpret in terms of effects on ecological processes. Thus, "there is a need to build a collective library of empirical studies in which ecological responses are related to particular landscape configurations" (Turner et al. 2001, 108). Unfortunately, planning decisions will continue to be made with and without specific information about landscapes and ecological processes. With proper use, landscape metrics can play an important role in adaptive management. Through the process of learning by doing (i.e., the implementation and monitoring of landscape plans), planners are particularly well positioned to produce the kind of empirical information needed to test predefined hypotheses on pattern-process relationships, and to adapt or modify plans accordingly.

8. Avoid automatism when applying metrics. "Rather than 'plugging' all available landscape indices (as calculated by computer programs) into statistical analyses, we recommend proposing hypothetical relationships followed by statistical tests. That means selecting those landscape indices that are likely to be relevant to the ecological process in question. This pre-selection requires understanding of mechanisms that would lead one to expect certain statistical relationships" (Tischendorf 2001). However, do not discard unexpected results; one may be surprised how much one can learn when trying to explain an unexpected outcome. Landscape simulations can raise non-formulated issues *a priori*, or provide information on small details apparently of no significant importance that may shed light onto a particular spatial process. Recall that creativity is an important part of not only artistic but also of scientific activities. In science, discoveries often result from a strenuous process of trial-and-error, and sometimes solutions (and insights) can emerge from unexpected events.

9. Always use metrics critically, being aware of their applicability and limitations. Metrics are tools that are most useful when they are properly framed by sound theoretical principles, providing a context in which the results can be interpreted and applied (Wiens 1999).

10. Landscape metrics are not a panacea for planners. Given uncertainty in the exact relationships between measured landscape patterns and landscape function, landscape metrics should be used with great intellectual and methodological care, and as only one of the many measures of landscape performance.

Wrapping Up

To grasp landscape wholeness, one needs to understand that varied and complementary information is needed to comprehend landscapes and their related phenomena. Both quantitative and qualitative approaches are needed to understand the holistic nature of landscapes, and to plan and manage landscapes for sustainability.

We realize that this handbook goes "out of the box" in both planning and landscape ecology. The integration of landscape ecology and planning, and particularly using landscape metrics, poses many challenges for planners and designers, but is needed to stimulate and nurture linkages between science and planning. One of the major challenges remaining is to link landscape structure with ecological function in a generalized way that makes it relevant for planners, and also at scales that are relevant for planners such as the ones at which detailed plans are made.

Our focus has been to provide examples of the potential usefulness of metrics to support planning, illustrating what general guidelines landscape ecology can provide to planning, explaining how metrics can be used in conjunction to interpret complex spatial processes in a specific planning context, and demonstrating these ideas for a relatively wide set of resources, and based on available and reliable scientific information. The approach adopted in this handbook can be characterized as an effort to advance the application of landscape ecological principles in landscape planning in support of the complex but critical goal of sustainability for all resources.

Glossary

Abiotic: Pertaining to the nonliving components of the environment.

Biological diversity: Broadly defined, the diversity of life at all levels of organization from the gene to the landscape, and all the interconnections that support life. More pragmatically, species and communities found in their natural places, distributed and functioning within their natural range of variability.

Class level: Pertaining to a single patch type (land cover type) in a categorically classified landscape or, as in a hierarchy, the aggregation of patches of the same type into classes.

Class metrics: Metrics integrated over all the patches of a given patch type (land cover type), representing the area and/or spatial configuration of the class.

Comprehensive planning: Planning that strives to address the majority of land use issues simultaneously.

Configuration: The specific arrangement of spatial elements in a landscape; specifically, the spatial character and arrangement, position, or orientation of patches within a class or landscape. Configuration is often used synonymously with spatial structure or landscape structure.

Connectivity: The spatial continuity of a patch type (or class) across a landscape (i.e., structural connectivity) or the degree to which specific ecological flows (e.g., movement of energy, materials, and organisms) across a landscape are facilitated or impeded (i.e., functional connectivity).

Corridor: A relatively narrow strip of a particular patch type (class or land cover type) that differs in at least one factor of interest from the areas adjacent on both sides, and as a consequence of its form and context, functions either to facilitate or impede ecological flows (e.g., movement of energy, materials or organisms) across a landscape.

Disturbance: Any relatively discrete event (natural or anthropogenic) in time that causes a significant change in the system under consideration, including destructive and catastrophic events (e.g., wildfire, urban development), as well as less notable, natural environmental fluctuations (e.g., beaver impoundment, tree-fall) (adapted from Pickett and White 1985).

Ecosystem management: Managing landscapes to bring human social and economic needs into closer agreement with ecological capabilities to ensure the sustainability of ecological and socioeconomic systems; a paradigm for the holistic management of landscapes.

Extent: The scope or domain of the data; typically defined in the spatial domain as the size of the study area or landscape, and in the temporal domain as the duration of time under consideration.

Fragmentation: Landscape process in which a patch type (e.g., habitat type or land cover type) is progressively subdivided into smaller, geometrically altered, and more isolated fragments, often as a result of both natural and human activities. Fragmentation refers specifically to the breaking up of a patch type into smaller, disconnected fragments, and is distinct from the loss of patch area per se, which may or may not occur concomitantly with fragmentation (adapted from McGarigal and McComb 1999).

Grain: The minimum resolution of data; typically defined in the spatial domain by the cell size (raster or grid data), quadrant size (field sample data), pixel size (imagery), or minimum polygon size (vector data); and in the temporal domain by the shortest unit of time under consideration.

Habitat: The local environment of an organism from which it gains the resources needed for survival and reproduction. Habitat is often variable in size, content, and location, changing with the phases in an organism's life cycle (adapted from Marsh 1998).

Heterogeneity: The quality or state of consisting of dissimilar elements, as with mixed habitats or cover types occurring on a landscape; opposite of homogeneity, in which elements are the same (adapted from Turner et al. 2001).

Hydrological: Of or pertaining to hydrology (see below).

Hydrology: The science dealing with the properties, distribution, and circulation of water on the surface of the land, in the soil and underlying rocks, and in the atmosphere (adapted from Webster's New Collegiate Dictionary).

Index: Variable that serves to reference the state of a system; typically a measured variable corresponding to a specific aspect of the system, as in a landscape metric (or landscape pattern index) that measures a particular aspect of landscape structure.

Indicator: Variable used to indicate the state or condition of a system; typically a measured property (e.g., the presence of species) used as a surrogate for other attributes or conditions that reflect the health of the system.

Land cover type (LCT): As used in this book, includes the different types or classes of both land cover and land use.

Landscape: An area that is spatially heterogeneous in at least one factor of interest (adopted from Turner et al. 2001). Here, the emphasis is on spatial heterogeneity at any scale or in any form (i.e., not necessarily repeated patterns at broad spatial extents). The landscape concept differs from the traditional ecosystem concept in that it focuses on groups of ecosystems and the interactions among them. There are landscape concepts with a wider perspective as the one provided in the European Landscape Convention (2000): "Landscape means an area, as perceived by people, whose character is the result of the action and interaction of natural and/or human factors."

Landscape ecological planning: Planning of ecologically sustainable landscapes; considering the spatial structure of the system, the flows of energy and materials among system components and between the system and its surroundings, and the evolution of the system over time—explicitly including the values, actions and impacts of humans.

Landscape level: Pertaining to the full spatial extent of the data or, as in a hierarchy, the entire patch mosaic (in a categorically classified landscape) comprised of patches aggregated into classes and classes aggregated into the landscape.

Landscape metrics: Algorithms that quantify specific landscape characteristics. Common usage refers to indices developed for categorical map patterns that describe the composition and/or spatial configuration of patches, classes of patches, or entire landscape mosaics.

Land use management: Management of human land uses; to exert control over the spatial and temporal distribution of human land use activities in order to achieve certain objectives.

Matrix: Background land cover type in a landscape, characterized by extensive cover and high connectivity, and typically playing a dominant role in the functioning of the landscape; not all landscapes at all times have a definable matrix.

Natural resource management: Management of natural resources; to exert control over the spatial and temporal distribution of natural resources (e.g., wildlife, water) and human activities in order to achieve certain objectives.

Patch: Surface area that differs from its surroundings in nature or appearance (adapted from Turner et al. 2001); the basic spatial unit or element in a categorically-classified landscape; relatively discrete areas of somewhat homogeneous conditions in which the patch boundaries are distinguished by discontinuities in character states from their surroundings by magnitudes that are perceived by or relevant to the phenomenon under consideration (adapted from Wiens 1976).

Patch level: Pertaining to individual patches in a categorically-classified landscape or, as in a hierarchy, the lowest level comprised of individual patches, which can be aggregated into classes (or land cover types), which in turn can be aggregated into the landscape.

Patch metrics: Metrics defined for individual patches, representing the area, spatial character, and/or spatial context of the patch.

Planning: The practice of organizing functions and space in such a way that it shows the best mutual relationship(s), or to develop human and natural potentials in a spatial framework in such a way that all can develop as well as possible (adapted from Buchwald and Engelhardt 1980).

Raster: The smallest discrete component of an image, usually representing a fixed surface area; a particular data format used to represent spatial (or geographic) information, consisting of a regular grid or lattice of rasters in which each raster is spatially explicit and can take on a unique value or set of values; synonymous with pixel.

Resolution: Precision of measurement; defined by the grain size, if spatial (adapted from Turner et al. 2001).

Riparian: The transition or ecotone between aquatic and terrestrial environments; usually used in reference to the terrestrial area under the ecological influence of an adjoining aquatic environment.

Scale: Spatial or temporal dimension of an object or process, characterized by both grain and extent (adapted from Turner et al. 2001).

Scientific paradigm: The constellation of achievements (concepts, values, techniques, etc.) shared by a scientific community and used by that community to define legitimate problems and solutions (adapted from Kuhn 1962).

Stormwater: Water that accumulates, and moves across, on land as a result of storms, particularly when the infiltration capacity of the land is exceeded.

Subpopulation: A population that is part of a larger population; usually referring to a geographically distinct population that is connected to other distinct populations through periodic movements of individuals between populations.

Sustainability: Meeting the needs of the present without compromising the ability of future generations to meet their needs.

Sustainable: The ability to maintain into perpetuity.

Sustainable land planning: Planning to achieve a long-term and productive balance between human land use and the environment (adapted from Marsh 1998).

Transdisciplinary: The collaboration of different disciplines in which boundaries between and beyond disciplines are transcended and knowledge and perspectives from different disciplines are integrated; an approach using shared perspectives informed by a range of disciplines and non-academic participants, such as land managers and the public (Tress, Tress and Fry 2005).

Urbanization: The process of urban development, including suburban residential and commercial development.

Vector: In the context of spatial data, a vector is a representation of a point, line or polygon; a particular data format used to represent spatial (or geographic) information, consisting of points, lines and/or polygons in which each element is spatially explicit and can take on a unique value or set of values.

Watershed management: The management of resources within a watershed; to exert control over the spatial and temporal distribution of resources (e.g., wildlife, water, humans) and human activities within a watershed in order to achieve certain objectives.

Wetland: An area in which the ground is seasonally or permanently wet and is occupied by water-loving (or tolerant) vegetation, such as cattails, mangrove, or cypress (adapted from Marsh 1998).

References

Agnes, Michael E. 2004. *Webster's new college dictionary.* Webster's New World. New York: John Wiley and Sons.

Ahern, J. and K. Kerkstra. 1994. Time space, ecology and design: Landscape aesthetics in an ecological framework in the Netherlands. In *Ecology, aesthetics and design,* ed. J. Hudson, 49–60. San Antonio, Texas: American Society of Landscape Architects.

Ahern, J. 1999. Spatial concepts, planning strategies and future scenarios: A framework method for integrating landscape ecology and landscape planning. In *Landscape ecological analysis: Issues and applications,* eds. J. Klopatek and R. Gardner, 175–201. New York: Springer-Verlag.

Ahern, J.F. 2002. Greenways as strategic landscape planning: Theory and applications. Wageningen, the Netherlands: Wageningen University. Doctoral thesis.

Ahern, J.F. 2004. Greenways in the USA: Theory, trends and prospects. In *Ecological networks and greenways: Concept, design, implementation,* eds. R.H.G. Jongman and G. Pungetti, 35–55. Cambridge, UK: Cambridge University Press.

Ahern, J., R. Neville, and LARP Studio IV students. 1998. The Mill River Watershed Study internal report. Amherst, MA: University of Massachusetts Department of Landscape Architecture and Regional Planning (LARP). Unpublished.

Ahern, J.F., A. Botequilha Leitão, J.N. Miller, E.A. Silva, A.O. Erbil, and K. Meinke. 1999. An adaptive framework method for landscape planning: A brief evaluation of potential planning tools. Snowmass, CO: The International Association for Landscape Ecology (IALE) 5th World Congress. Poster Presentation.

Alcamo, J. 2001. Scenarios as tools for international environmental assessments. Experts' corner report "Prospects and Scenarios No 5, Environmental Issue Report No 24." Copenhagen: European Environment Agency.

Alig, R.J., J.D. Kline, and M. Lichtenstein. 2004. Urbanization on the US landscape: Looking ahead in the 21st century. *Landscape and Urban Planning* 69: 219–234.

Allen, T. F. H., R. V. O'Neill, and T. W. Hoekstra. 1987. Interlevel relations in ecological research and management: Some working principles from hierarchy theory. *Journal of Applied Systems Analysis* 14: 63–79.

Andrén, H. 1994. Effects of habitat fragmentation on birds and mammals in land-scapes with different proportions of suitable habitat: A review. *Oikos* 71: 355–366.

Antrop, M. 1998. Landscape change: Plan or chaos? *Landscape and Urban Planning* 41: 155–161.

Antrop, M. 2000. Changing patterns in the urbanized countryside of Western Europe. *Landscape Ecology* 15: 257–270.

Antrop, M. 2001. The language of landscape ecologists and planners: A comparative content analysis of concepts used in landscape ecology. *Landscape and Urban Planning* 55: 163–173.

Atauri, J.A. and J.V. de Lucio. 2001. The role of landscape structure in species richness distribution of birds, amphibians, reptiles and lepidopterans in Mediterranean landscapes. *Landscape Ecology* 16: 147–159.

Baker, W. L., and Y. Cai. 1992. The r.le programs for multiscale analysis of landscape structure using the GRASS geographical information system. *Landscape Ecology* 7: 291–302.

Baldwin, D.J.B., K. Weaver, F. Schnekenburger, and A.H. Perera. 2004. Sensitivity of landscape pattern indices to input data characteristics on real landscapes: Implications for their use in natural disturbance emulation. *Landscape Ecology* 19: 255–271.

Barata, F.T. and J.M. Mascarenhas. 2002. Preservando a memória do território: O Parque Cultural de Tourega/Valverde. (Preserving the memory of the land: The Tourega/Valverde Cultural Park, in Portuguese.) évora: Universidade de Évora, Caderno n° 1 do Centro de Estudos de Ecosistemas Mediterrânicos.

Barten, P.K., T. Kyker-Snowman, P.J. Lyons, T. Mahlstedt, R. O'Connor, and B.A. Spencer. 1998. Massachusetts: Managing a watershed protection forest. *Journal of Forestry* (August) 96(8): 8–15.

Bartuska, A.M. 1999. Cross-boundary issues to manage for healthy forest ecosystems. In *Landscape ecological analysis: issues and applications*, eds. J. Klopatek and R. Gardner, 24–34. New York: Springer-Verlag.

Bastian, O. 2001. Landscape ecology—towards a unified discipline? *Landscape Ecology* 16: 757–766.

Baudry, J. and H.G. Merriam. 1988. Connectivity and connectedness: Functional versus structural patterns in landscapes. In *Connectivity in landscape ecology: Proceedings of the 2nd International Seminar of the International Association for Landscape Ecology*, ed. K.F. Schreiber, 23–38. Paderborn, Germany: Munstersche Geographische Arbeiten 29. Ferdinand Schoningh.

Bell, S. 1999. *Landscape: Pattern, perception and process*. London: Spon Press, and New York: Routledge.

Bender, D.J., T.A. Contreras, and L. Fahrig. 1998. Habitat loss and population decline: A meta-analysis of the patch size effect. *Ecology* 79(2): 517–533.

Bennett, A.F. 1990. Habitat corridors: Their role in wildlife management and conservation. Victoria, Australia: Department of Conservation and Environment.

Bennett, A.F. 1991. Roads, roadsides, and wildlife conservation: A review. In

Nature conservation 2: The role of corridors, eds. D.A. Saunders and R.J. Hobbs, 99–117. Chipping Norton, Australia: Surrey Beatty.

Bennett, A. F. 1999. Linkages in the landscape: The role of corridors and connectivity in wildlife conservation. Gland, Switzerland and Cambridge, UK: IUCN World Conservation Union.

Benson, B.J. and M.D. McKenzie. 1995. Effects of sensor spatial resolution on landscape structure parameters. *Landscape Ecology* 10(2): 113–120.

Berkowitz, A.R., C.H. Nilon, and K.S. Hollweg, eds. 2003. Understanding urban ecosystems: A new frontier for science and education. Millbrook, New York: Proceedings of the 8th Cary Conference held in April 1999 at the Institute of Ecosystem Studies.

Bogaert J., R. Rousseau, P. Van Hecke, and I. Impens. 2000. Alternative area-perimeter ratios for measurement of 2D-shape compactness of habitats. *Applied mathematics and computation* 111: 71–85.

Bolós, M., ed. 1992. Manual de ciencia del paisaje: Teoria, métodos y aplicaciones. Barcelona, Spain: Masson, S.A. Colección de Geografia.

Bormann, F.H., and G.E. Likens. 1979. *Pattern and process in a forested ecosystem.* New York: Springer-Verlag.

Botequilha Leitão, A. 1996. *Integração de Técnicas de Avaliaéão da Paisagem em Sistemas de Informação Geográfica* (Landscape evaluation techniques integration in geographical information systems, in Portuguese). Lisboa, Portugal: Instituto Superior Técnico. Dissertação para a obtenção do grau de Mestre (Dissertation thesis for Masters of Science).

Botequilha Leitão, A. 2001. *Sustainable land planning: Towards a planning framework. Exploring the role of spatial statistics as a planning tool.* Lisbon, Portugal: Technical University of Lisbon (Instituto Superior Técnico, Universidade Técnica de Lisboa). Doctoral dissertation.

Botequilha Leitão, A. and F. Muge. 2001. The role of landscape metrics in environmental planning and management of mining activities. In *Proceedings of APCOM 2001 29th international symposium on computer applications in the minerals industries held at the University of Mining and Technology*, eds. X. Heping, Wang, Yuehan and Y. Jiang, 713–718. Beijing: Balkema Publishers.

Botequilha Leitão, A. and J. Ahern. 2002. Applying landscape ecological concepts and metrics in sustainable landscape planning. *Landscape and Urban Planning* 59: 65–93.

Botequilha Leitão, A., H. Ferreira, L. Ribeiro, F. Muge, and J. Ahern. 2004. *2° relatório (e final) científico do Projecto PROBIO Entregue à Fundação da Ciência e tecnologia. (Final report for the Project Decision Support System for Planning and Management of Biodiversity in Protected Areas (PROBIO), in Portuguese, delivered to the Science and Technology Foundation, Ministry for Higher Education, Science and Technology).* Lisboa, Portugal: CVRM-Centro de Geossistemas do Instituto Superior Técnico (Lisbon, Portugal: CVRM Geo-Systems Center of Instituto Superior Técnico, Technical University of Lisbon). Available online at: http://alfa.ist.utl.pt/~cvrm/projects/probio.

Botkin, D. 1990. *Discordant harmonies: A new ecology for the twenty-first century.* New York: Oxford University Press.

Bradshaw, A. D. 2003. Natural ecosystems in cities: A model for cities as ecosystems. In *Understanding urban ecosystems: A new frontier for science and education*, eds. A.R. Berkowitz, C.H. Nilon and K.S. Hollweg, 77–94. Millbrook, New York: Proceedings of the 8th Cary Conference held in April 1999 at the Institute of Ecosystem Studies.

Brandt, J. 1998. New perspectives for landscape ecology. In Proceedings of the First National Landscape Ecology Workshop, Potuguese Association of Landscape Ecology (APED), *Challenges for Mediterranean landscape ecology: The future of cultural landscapes—examples from the Alentejo region*, eds. T. Pinto-Correia and M. Cancela de Abreu. Montemor-o-Novo, Portugal.

Brittingham, M.C., and S.A. Temple. 1983. Have cowbirds caused forest songbirds to decline? *BioScience* 33: 31–35.

Burkey, T.V. 1989. Extinction in nature reserves: The effect of fragmentation and the importance of migration between reserve fragments. *Oikos* 55: 75–81.

Burrough, P.A. 1986. *Principles of geographical information systems for land resources assessment*. Oxford: Claredon Press: Monograph on Soil and Resources Survey.

Capra, F. 1996. *The web of life: A new scientific understanding of living systems*. New York: Anchor Books.

Carlson, A., and G. Hartman. 2001. Tropical forest fragmentation and nest predation—an experimental study in an Eastern Arc montane forest, Tanzania. *Biodiversity Conservation* 10: 1077–1085.

Ceña, F. 1999. The farm and rural community as economic systems. In *Rural planning from an environmental systems perspective*, eds. F.B. Golley and J. Bellot, 229–286. New York: Springer-Verlag.

Center for Watershed Protection. 1998. Rapid watershed planning handbook: A comprehensive guide for managing urbanizing watersheds. Ellicott City, MD: CWP for the Office of Wetlands, Oceans and Watersheds and Region V, U.S. EPA.

Center for Watershed Protection. 2001. Guide for site planning for stream restoration. Elliot City, MD. Available online at: www.cwp.org.

Chapin, F.S. (III), O.E. Sala, I.C. Burke, J.P. Grime, D.U. Hooper, W.K. Lauenroth, A. Lombard, H.A. Mooney, A.R. Mosier, S. Naeem, S.W. Pacala, J. Roy, W.L. Steffen, and D. Tilman. 1998. Ecosystem consequences of changing biodiversity: Experimental evidence and a research agenda for the future. *Bioscience* 48(1): 45–52.

CO-DBP, 2001. *The European charter on water resources*. Bureau of the Committee for the activities of the Council of Europe in the field of biological and landscape diversity. Strasbourg, Germany: Directorate of Culture and Cultural and Natural Heritage, Council of Europe.

Corner, J. 1999. Introduction. In *Recovering landscape: Essays in contemporary landscape architecture*, ed. J. Corner. New York: Princeton Architectural Press.

Corry, R.C. and J. Nassauer. 2005. Limitations of using landscape pattern indices to evaluate the ecological consequences of alternative plans and designs. *Landscape and Urban Planning* 72: 265–280.

Costa Lobo, M. 1997. Sharing responsibilities. In *Environmental challenges in an expanding urban world and the role of emerging information technologies*, J. Reis

Machado and J. Ahern, 257–261. Costa da Caparica, Portugal: Centro Nacional de Informação Geográfica (CNIG).

Coulson, R.N., H. Saarenmaa, W.C. Daugherity, E.J. Rykiel Jr., M.C. Saunders, and J.W. Fitzgerald. 1999. A knowledge system environment for ecosystem management. In *Landscape ecological analysis: Issues and applications*, eds. J. Klopatek and R. Gardner, 57–79. New York: Springer-Verlag.

Council of Europe. 2000. European Landscape Convention. Florence, Italy. Proceedings available online at: http://www.coe.int/t/e/Cultural_Cooperation/Environment/Landscape.

Davis, F., D. Stoms, M. Bueno, A. Hollander, and J. Walsh. 1998. *Gap analysis of mainland California: An interactive atlas of terrestrial biodiversity and land management*. California GAP Analysis project—Interactive biodiversity atlas CD-ROM. University of California at Santa Barbara and the Natural Heritage Division, California Department of Fish and Game. Available online at: http://www.biogeog.ucsb.edu/projects/gap/gap_data.html.

De Leo, G. A., and S. Levin. 1997. The multifaceted aspects of ecosystem integrity. *Conservation Ecology* 1(1): 3. Available online at: http://www.consecol.org/vol1/iss1/art3.

Devillers, P. and R.C. Beudels. 2001. Bioindicators for biodiversity evaluation. Presented in "Monitoring and indicators" of the BioPlatform E-Conference *Biodiversity conservation in theory & practice* November 2001. Coordinated by the Belgian Biodiversity Platform, the Ministry of Environment, Government of Catalonia, Ecosystems Ltd., and the Centre for Ecology and Hydrology Banchory. Proceedings available online at: www.biodiversity.be/bbpf/econf/econfintro.html.

Devuyst, D., L. Hens, and W. De Lannoy, eds. 2001. *How green is the city? Sustainability assessment and the management of urban environments*. New York: Columbia University Press.

Diaz, N.M. 1996. Landscape metrics: A new tool for forest ecologists. *Journal of Forestry* 94(12): 12–16.

Dickman, C.R. 1987. Habitat fragmentation and vertebrate species richness in an urban environment. *Journal of Applied Ecology* 24: 337–351.

Dramstad, W.E., J.D. Olson, and R.T.T. Forman. 1996. *Landscape ecology principles in landscape architecture and land use planning*. Washington, D.C.: Island Press.

Dunn, C.P., D.M. Sharpe, G.R. Guntenspergen, F. Stearns, and Z. Yang. 1991. Methods for analyzing temporal changes in landscape pattern. In *Quantitative methods in landscape ecology: The analysis and interpretation of landscape heterogeneity*, eds. M.G. Turner and R.H. Gardner, 173–198. New York: Springer-Verlag.

Environmental Law Institute (ELI). 2003. *Conservation thresholds for land-use planners*. Washington, D.C. PDF file available online at: http://www.elistore.org.

Environmental Protection Agency (EPA). 1994. *Landscape monitoring and assessment research plan*. U.S. EPA 620/R-94/009. Las Vegas, NV: U.S. EPA Environmental Monitoring Systems Laboratory, Office of Research and Development.

Environmental Protection Agency (EPA). 1995. *Mid-Atlantic landscape indicators project plan Environmental Monitoring and Assessment Program (EMAP)*. U.S.

EPA 620/R-95/003. Research Triangle Park, NC: U.S. EPA National Exposure Research Laboratory, Office of Research and Development.

European Commission (EC). 2001. *From land cover to landscape diversity in the European Union.* Directorate-General for Agriculture, EUROSTAT and the Joint Research Centre (Ispra), and the European Environment Agency. Available online at: http://europa.eu.int/comm./agriculture/public/landscape/ch1.htm.

Fabos, J.G. 1985. *Land-use planning: From global to local challenge.* New York: Chapman and Hall.

Fahrig, L. 1997. Relative effects of habitat loss and fragmentation on population extinction. *Journal of Wildlife Management* 61(3): 603–610.

Fernandes, J.P. 2000. Landscape ecology and conservation management - evaluation of alternatives in a highway EIA process. *Environmental Impact Assessment Review* 20(6): 665–680.

Ferreira, H., A. Botequilha Leitão, R. Salgueiro, and L.F. Ribeiro. 2003. *Sustainable landscape planning as a tool to address water resource planning: A Portuguese case study on a coastal aquifer salination.* TIAC'03: Tecnologia de la intrusión de agua de mar en acuiferos costeros: Paises Mediterraneos. (Coastal aquifers intrusion technology: Mediterranean countries, in Spanish) Alicante, Spain: Instituto Geologico Minero de Espanha.

Ferreira, H.F., A. Botequilha Leitão, and L.F. Ribeiro. 2004. *Metodologias para o planeamento e gestão sustentáveis dos Recursos Hídricos. (Methodologies for sustainable planning and management of water resources,* in Portuguese with abstract in English.) Actas do 7º Congresso da Água (Proceedings of the 7th Water National Congress). Lisbon, Portugal: Civil Engineering National Laboratory (Laboratório Nacional de Engenharia Civil).

Ferreira, H. and A. Botequilha Leitão. 2006. Integrating landscape and water resources planning with focus on sustainability. In *From landscape research to landscape planning: Aspects of integration, education and application,* eds. B. Tress, G. Tress, G. Fry, and P. Opdam, 143–159. Heidelberg, Germany: Springer-Verlag.

Firmino, A. 1999. Agriculture and landscape in Portugal. *Landscape and Urban Planning* 46: 83–91.

Forman, R.T.T. 1995. *Land Mosaics: The ecology of landscapes and regions.* New York: Cambridge University Press.

Forman, R.T.T. 1999. Process, roads, suburbs, and society. In *Landscape ecological analysis: Issues and applications,* eds. J. Klopatek and R. Gardner, 35–53. New York: Springer-Verlag.

Forman, R.T.T. 2000. Estimate of the area affected ecologically by the road system in the United States. *Conservation Biology* 14(1): 31–36.

Forman, R.T.T., A.E. Galli, and C.F. Leck. 1976. Forest size and avian diversity in New Jersey woodlots with some land use implications. *Oecologia* 26: 1–8.

Forman, R.T.T. and M. Godron. 1986. *Landscape ecology.* New York: John Wiley and Sons.

Forman, R.T.T. and S.K. Collinge. 1995. The spatial solution to conserving biodiversity in landscapes and regions. In *Conservation of faunal diversity in forested landscapes,* eds. R.M. DeGraff and R.I. Miller. London: Chapman and Hall.

Forman, R.T.T. and R.D. Deblinger. 2000. The ecological road-effect zone of a Massachusetts (U.S.A.) suburban highway. *Conservation Biology* 14(1): 36–46.

Forman, R.T.T., D. Sperling, J.A. Bissonette, A.P. Clevenger, C.D. Cutshall, V.H. Dale, L. Fahrig, R. France, C.R. Goldman, K. Heanue, J.A. Jones, F.J. Swanson, T. Turrentine, and T.C. Winter. 2003. *Road ecology: Science and solutions*. Washington, D.C.: Island Press.

Foster, D.R. 1992. Land-use history (1730–1990) and vegetation dynamics in central New England, USA. *Journal of Ecology* 80: 753–772.

Foster, D.R. and E.R. Boose. 1992. Patterns of forest damage resulting from catastrophic wind in central New England, USA. *Journal of Ecology* 80: 79–98.

France, R.L., ed. 2002. *Handbook of water sensitive planning and design: Integrative studies in water management and land development*. Boca Raton, FL: Lewis Publishers.

Franklin, C. 1997. Fostering living landscapes. In *Ecological design and planning*, eds. G.F. Thompson and F.R. Steiner, 263–292. New York: John Wiley and Sons.

Franklin, J.F. and R.T.T. Forman. 1987. Creating landscape patterns by forest cutting: Ecological consequences and principles. *Landscape Ecology* 1(1): 5–18.

Freemark, K., C. Hummon, D. White, and D. Hulse. 1996. *Modeling risks to biodiversity in past, present and future landscapes*. Technical report No. 268. Ottawa, Canada: Environment Canada, Canadian Wildlife Service.

Fritz, R.S. 1979. Consequences of insular population structure: Distribution and extinction of spruce grouse populations. *Oecologia* 42: 57–65.

Galli, A.E., C.F. Leck, and R.T.T. Forman. 1976. Avian distribution patterns in forest islands of different sizes in central New Jersey. *Auk* 93: 356–64.

Garland, T. Jr., and W.G. Bradley. 1984. Effects of highway on Mojave Desert rodent populations. *American Midland Naturalist* 111: 1, 47–56.

Gates, J.E. 1991. Powerline corridors, edge effects, and wildlife in forested landscapes of the central Appalachians. In *Wildlife and Habitats in Managed Landscapes*, eds. J.E. Rodiek and E.G. Bolen. Washington, D.C.: Island Press.

Genelleti, D. and A. Pistocchi. 2001. Landscape ecology for sustainable land use planning: A GIS approach in a man-dominated landscape. In *Proceedings of the International Workshop on Geo-Spatial Knowledge Processing for Natural Resource Management*, eds. A. Ward, E. Binaghi, P.A. Brivio, G.A. Lazarone and G. Tosi, 244–248. Varense, Italy: Joint Research Centre, European Commission.

Gergel, S.E. and M.G. Turner. 2002. *Learning landscape ecology: A practical guide to concepts and techniques*. New York: Springer-Verlag.

Germaine, S.S., S.S. Rosenstock, R.E. Schweinsburg, and W.S. Richardson. 1998. Relationships among breeding birds, habitat, and residential development in greater Tucson, Arizona. *Ecological Applications*, 8(3): 680–691.

Gilpin, M.E. and I. Handki, eds. 1991. *Metapopulation dynamics: Empirical and theoretical investigations*. San Diego: Academic Press.

González Bernáldez, F.G. 1981. *Ecologia y paisaje*. Madrid: H. Blume Ediciones.

Graham, R.L., C.T. Hunsaker, R.V. O'Neill, and B.L. Jackson. 1991. Ecological risk assessment at the regional scale. *Ecological Applications* 1(2): 196–206.

Greeuw, S.C.H., M.B.A. van Asselt, J. Grosskurth, C.A.M.H. Storms, N. Riijkens-Klomp, D.S. Rothman, and J. Rotmans. 2000. Cloudy crystal balls: An assessment of recent European and global scenario studies and models.

Experts' corner report *Prospects and Scenarios No 4*, Environmental Issues Series No 17. Copenhagen: European Environment Agency.

Grossman, W.F. and J. Bellot. 1999. System analysis as a tool for rural planning. In *Rural Planning from an environmental systems perspective*, eds. F.B. Golley and J. Bellot, 315–343. New York: Springer-Verlag.

Grove, J.M. and W.R. Burch. 1997. A social ecology approach and applications of urban ecosystems and landscape analyses: A case study of Baltimore, Maryland. *Urban Ecosystems* 1: 259–275.

Groves, C.R., M.W. Beck, J.V. Higgins, and E.C. Saxon. 2003. *Drafting a conservation blueprint: A practitioner's guide to planning for biodiversity*. Washington, D.C.: Island Press.

Grumbine, R.E. 1994. What is ecosystem management? *Conservation Biology* 8(1): 27–38.

Gustafson, E.J. 1998. Quantifying landscape spatial pattern: What is the state of the art? *Ecosystems* 1: 143–156.

Gustafson, E.J. and G.R. Parker. 1992. Relationship between landcover proportion and indices of landscape spatial pattern. *Landscape Ecology* 7: 101–10.

Gustafson, E.J. and G.R. Parker. 1994. Using an index of habitat patch proximity for landscape design. *Landscape and Urban Planning* 29: 117–30.

Gutzwiller, K.J. and S.H. Anderson. 1992. Interception of moving organisms: Influences of patch shape, size, and orientation on community structure. *Landscape Ecology* 6(4): 293–303.

Hanna, K.C. and B. Kulpepper. 1998. *GIS in site design: new tools for design professionals*. New York: John Wiley and Sons.

Hanna, K.C. 1999. *GIS for landscape architects*. New York: ESRI Press.

Hansen, A. and F. di Castri. eds. 1992. *Landscape boundaries*. New York: Springer-Verlag.

Hanski, I. and M. Gilpin. 1991. Metapopulation dynamics - brief history and conceptual domain. *Biol. Journal of Linn Soc* 42: 3–16.

Hardt, R.A. and R.T.T. Forman. 1989. Boundary form effects on woody colonization of reclaimed surface mines. *Ecology* 70(5): 1252–1260.

Hargis, C.D., J.A. Bissonette, and J.L. David. 1998. The behaviour of landscape metrics commonly used in the study of habitat fragmentation. *Landscape Ecology* 13: 167–186.

Hayden, I.J., J. Faaborg, and R.L. Clawson. 1985. Estimates of minimum area requirements for Missouri forest birds. *Missouri Academy of Science* 19: 11–22.

Haynes-Young, R., D.R. Green, and S. Cousins. 1994. *Landscape ecology and geographic information systems*. London: Taylor and Francis.

Heinselman, M.L. 1973. Fire in the virgin forests of the Boundary Waters Canoe Area, Minnesota. *Quaternary Research* 3: 329–82.

Helliwell, D.R. 1976. The effects of size and isolation on the conservation value of wooded sites in Britain. *Journal of Biogeography* 3: 407–416.

Hobbs, R.J. 1993. Effects of landscape fragmentation on ecosystem processes in the Western Australian Wheatbelt. *Biological Conservation* 64: 193–210.

Holling, C.S. 1978. *Adaptive environmental assessment and management*. New York: John Wiley and Sons.

Hoover, J.P., M.C. Brittingham, and L.J. Goodrich. 1995. Effects of forest patch size on nesting success of wood thrushes. *Auk* 112: 146–155.

Hulschoff, R.M. 1995. Landscape indices describing a Dutch landscape. *Landscape Ecology* 10(2): 101–111.

Hulse, D., L. Goorjian, D. Richey, M. Flaxman, C. Hummon, D. White, K. Freemark, J. Eilers, J. Bernert, K. Vaché, J. Kaytes, and D. Diethlem. 1997. Possible futures for the Muddy Creek Watershed, Benton County, Oregon. Eugene, Oregon: University of Oregon.

Hulse, D., S. Gregory, and J. Baker, eds. Pacific Northwest Ecosystem Research Consortium. 2002. Willamette River Basin planning atlas: Trajectories of environmental and ecological change. Corvallis, Oregon: Oregon State University Press.

Hunziker, M. and F. Kienast. 1999. Potential impacts of changing agricultural activities on scenic beauty: A prototypical technique for automated rapid assessment. *Landscape Ecology* 14: 2, 161–176.

Iverson, L.R. 1988. Land use changes in Illinois, USA: The influence of landscape attributes on current and historic land use. *Landscape Ecology* 2(1): 45–61.

Jennings, M.D. 2000. Gap analysis: Concepts, methods, and recent results. *Landscape Ecology* 15: 5–20.

Jones, K.B., A.C. Neale, M.S. Nash, R.D. Remorte, J.D. van Wickham, K.H. Riitters, and R.V. O'Neill. 2001. Predicting nutrient and sediment loadings to streams from landscape metrics: A multiple watershed study from the United States Mid-Atlantic Region. *Landscape Ecology* 16: 301–312.

Jongman, R.G.H. 1999. Landscape ecology in land use planning. In *Issues in landscape ecology*, eds. J.A. Wiens and M.R. Moss, 112–118. Snowmass Village, Colorado: International Association for Landscape Ecology Fifth World Congress.

Jongman, R.G.H. 2002. Homogenization and fragmentation of the European landscape: Ecological consequences and solutions. *Landscape and Urban Planning* 58: 211–221.

Jongman, R.G.H. and G. Pungetti, eds. 2004. Ecological networks and greenways: Concept, design, implementation. Cambridge: Cambridge University Press.

Keitt, T.H., D.L. Urban, and B.T. Milne. 1997. Detecting critical scales in fragmented landscapes. *Conservation Ecology* [online]1(1): 4. Available online at: http://www.consecol.org/vol1/iss1/art4.

Kim, K.C. and R.D. Weaver, eds. 1994. *Biodiversity and landscapes: A paradox to humanity*. Cambridge: Cambridge University Press.

Kremsater, L. and F.L. Bunnell. 2000. Edge effects: Theory, evidence and implications to management of western North American forests. In *Forest Fragmentation: Wildlife and management implications*, eds. J.A. Rochelle, L.A. Lehmann, and J. Wisniewki, 117–153. Boston.

Kroodsma, R.L. 1982. Edge effect on breeding forest birds along a power-line corridor. *Journal of Applied Ecology* 19: 361–370.

Krummel, J. R., R. H. Gardner, G. Sugihara, R. V. O'Neill, and P. R. Coleman. 1987. Landscape patterns in a disturbed environment. *Oikos* 48: 321–324.

Kuhn, T. 1962. *The Structure of scientific revolutions.* Chicago: University of Chicago Press.

Lamberson, R.H., R. McKelvey, B.R. Noon, and C. Voss. 1992. A dynamic analysis of northern spotted owl viability in a fragmented forest landscape. *Conservation Biology* 6(4): 1–8.

Landis, J.D., J.P. Monzon, M. Reilly, and C. Cogan. 1998. *Development and pilot application of the California urban and biodiversity analysis (CURBA) model.* San Diego, CA: Proceedings of the ESRI '98 user Conference. Available online at: http://gis.esri.com/library/userconf/proc98/PROCEED.HTM.

Laurence, W.F., P. Delamonica, S. D'Angelo, A. Jerozolinski, and L. Pohl. 2001. Rain forest fragmentation and the structure of Amazonian liana communities. *Ecology* 82: 105–116.

Laurence, W.F., T.E. Lovejoy, H.L. Vasconcelos, E.M. Bruna, and R.K. Didham. 2002. Ecosystem decay of Amazonian forest fragments: A 22–year investigation. *Conservation Biology* 16: 605–618.

Lausch, A. and F. Herzog. 2002. Applicability of landscape metrics for the monitoring of landscape change: issues of scale, resolution and interpretability. *Ecological Indicators* 2: 3–15.

Lee, D. C. and G. A. Bradshaw. 1998. Making monitoring work for managers. U.S. Forest Service. Available online at: http://www.icbemp.gov/spatial/lee_monitor/begin.html.

Leopold, A. 1933. *Game management.* New York: Charles Scribner's Sons.

Levins, R. 1970. Extinctions. In *Some mathematical questions in biology,* ed. M. Gertebhaber, 77–107. Providence, R.I.: American Mathematical Society.

Li H. and J.F. Reynolds. 1993. A new contagion index to quantify spatial patterns of landscapes. *Landscape Ecology* 14: 2, 161–176.

Linehan, J.R., M. Gross, and J. Finn. 1995. Greenway planning: Developing a landscape ecological network approach. *Landscape and Urban Planning* 33: 179–193.

Linehan, J.R. and M. Gross. 1998. Back to the future, back to basics: The social ecology of landscapes and the future of landscape planning. *Landscape and Urban Planning* 42: 207–223.

Linton, R.B. et al. 1974. *Water in landscape: An aesthetic overview of the role of water in the landscape.* New York: Water Information Center.

Lubchenco, J., A.M. Olson, L.B. Brubaker, S.R. Carpenter, M.M. Holland, S.P. Hubbell, S.A. Levin, J.A. MacMahon, P.A. Matson, J.M. Melillo, H.A. Mooney, C.H. Peterson, H.R. Pulliam, L.A. Real, P.J. Regal, and P.G. Risser. 1991. The sustainable biosphere initiative: An ecological research agenda. *Ecology* 72(2): 371–412.

Lynch, J.F. and D.F. Whigham. 1984. Effects of forest fragmentation on breeding bird communities in Maryland, USA. *Biological Conservation* 28: 287–324.

Lynch, K. 1960. *The image of the city.* Cambridge, MA: Technology Press.

MacArthur, R.H. and E.O. Wilson. 1967. *The theory of island biogeography.* Princeton, NJ: Princeton University Press.

Magalhães, M.M.R. 2001. *A Arquitectura paisagista: Morfologia e complexidade.* Lisboa: Editorial Estampa.

Mandelbrot, B.B. 1977. *Fractals, form, chance and dimension.* New York: W.H. Freeman.

Mandelbrot, B.B. 1982. *The fractal geometry of nature.* New York: W.H. Freeman.

Mann, C.C. and M.L. Plummer. 1995. Are wildlife corridors the right path? *Science* 270: 1428–1430.

Marcucci, D.J. 2000. Landscape history as a planning tool. *Landscape and Urban Planning* 49: 67–81.

Marsh, W.M. 1998. *Landscape planning: Environmental applications, 3rd edition.* New York: John Wiley and Sons.

McDonnell, M.J. and S.T.A. Pickett. 1988. Connectivity and the theory of landscape ecology. In *Connectivity in landscape ecology*, ed. K.F. Schreiber, 17–21. Proceedings of the 2nd International Seminar of the International Association for Landscape Ecology. Paderborn, Germany: Munstersche Geographische Arbeiten 29. Ferdinand Schoningh.

McGarigal, K. 1998. Ecosystem management. Amherst, MA: University of Massachusetts at Amherst, Department of Forestry and Wildlife. Forestry 597b course notes.

McGarigal, K. and B.J. Marks. 1995. FRAGSTATS: Spatial pattern analysis program for quantifying landscape structure. Corvallis, Oregon: Oregon State University Forest Science Department.

McGarigal, K. and W.C. McComb. 1995. Relationships between landscape structure and breeding birds in the Oregon Coast Range. *Ecological Monographs*, 65(3): 235–260.

McGarigal, K. and W.C. McComb. 1999. Forest fragmentation effects on breeding birds in the Oregon Coast Range. In *Forest fragmentation: Wildlife and management implications*, eds. J.A. Rochelle, L.A. Lehman, and J. Wisniewski, 223–246. Leiden, The Netherlands: Koninklijke Brill NV.

McGarigal, K., S.A. Cushman, M.C. Neel, and E. Ene. 2002. FRAGSTATS: Spatial pattern analysis program for categorical maps. Computer software program. Amherst, MA: University of Massachusetts. Available online at: www.umass.edu/landeco/research/fragstats/fragstats.htm.

McGarigal, K. and S. A. Cushman. 2005. The gradient concept of landscape structure. In *Issues and perspectives in landscape ecology*, eds. J. Wiens and M. Moss, 112–119. Cambridge: Cambridge University Press.

McKelvey, K., B.R. Noon, and R. Lamberson. 1992. Conservation planning for species occupying fragmented landscapes: The case of the northern spotted owl. In *Biotic interactions and global change*, eds., J. Kingsolver, P. Kareiva and R. Hyey, 338–357. Sunderland, MA: Sinauer Associates.

Metropolitan District Commission (MDC). 1995. *Quabbin Watershed: MDC land management plan 1995 - 2004.* Commonwealth of Massachusetts: MDC Division of Watershed Management.

Miller, J.N. 2000. *A planning method for wildlife corridors in southwestern Massachusetts.* Amherst, MA: University of Massachusetts. Dissertation for Masters in Landscape Architecture.

Miller, J.N., R.P. Brooks, and M.J. Croonquist. 1997. Effects of landscape patterns on biotic communities. *Landscape Ecology* 12: 127–153.

Milne, B. T. 1988. Measuring the fractal geometry of landscapes. *Applied Mathematics and Computation* 27: 67–79.

Moore, N.W. and M.D. Hooper. 1975. On the number of bird species in British woods. *Biological Conservation*. 8: 239–250.

Moreira, F., F.C. Rego, and P.G. Ferreira. 2001. Temporal (1958–1995) pattern of change in a cultural landscape of northwestern Portugal: Implications for fire occurrence. *Landscape Ecology* 16: 557–567.

Moss, M. 2000. Interdisciplinarity, landscape ecology and the transformation of agricultural landscapes. *Landscape Ecology* 15: 303–311.

Müssner, R. and H. Plachter. 2002. Methodological standards for nature conservation: Case-study landscape planning. *Journal for Nature Conservation* 10: 3–23.

Naiman, R.J. 1996. Water, society and landscape ecology. *Landscape Ecology* 11(4): 193–196.

Nassauer, J.I. 1999. Culture as a means for experimentation and action. In *Issues in Landscape Ecology*, eds. J.A. Wiens and M.R. Moss, 129–133. Snowmass Village, Colorado: International Association for Landscape Ecology Fifth World Congress.

Naveh, Z. 1984. Towards a transdisciplinary conceptual framework of landscape ecology. In *Proceedings of the First International Seminar on Methodology in Landscape Ecological Research and Planning*, eds. J. Brandt and P. Agger. I.A.L.E., Roskilde, Denmark: International Association of Landscape Ecology.

Naveh, Z. 1991. Some remarks on recent developments in landscape ecology as a transdisciplinary ecological and geographical science. *Landscape Ecology* 5(2): 65–73.

Naveh, Z. 1994. Biodiversity and landscape management. In *Biodiversity and landscapes: A paradox to humanity*, eds. K.C. Kim and R.D. Weaver. 187–207. Cambridge: Cambridge University Press.

Naveh, Z. 1998. The role of landscape ecology in the Mediterranean. In Proceedings of the First National Workshop of Landscape Ecology: Portuguese Association of Landscape Ecology (APED), *Challenges for Mediterranean landscape ecology: The future of cultural landscapes—examples from the Alentejo region*, eds. T. Pinto-Correia and M. Cancela de Abreu. Montemor-o-Novo, Portugal.

Naveh, Z. 2001. Ten major premises for a holistic conception of multifunctional landscapes. *Landscape and Urban Planning* 57: 269–284.

Ndubisi, F. 2002. *Ecological planning: A historical and comparative synthesis*. Baltimore, Maryland: Johns Hopkins University Press.

Neel, M. C., K. McGarigal, and S. A. Cushman. 2004. Behavior of class-level landscape metrics across gradients of class aggregation and area. *Landscape Ecology* 19: 435–455.

Nelson, J.G., P. Grigoriew, P.G.R. Smith, and J.B. Theberge. 1997. The ABC resource survey method, the ESA concept, and comprehensive land use planning and management. In *Proceedings of the 3rd symposium of the Canadian Society for Landscape Ecology and Management*, ed. M. Moss, 143–175. Guelph, Canada: University of Guelph.

NIJOS and OECD. 2002. *Norwegian Institute of Land Inventory (NIJOS) and OECD expert meeting on indicators of agricultural impacts on landscapes: Summary and recommendations.* Oslo, Norway.

Nilsson, C., J.E. Pizzuto, G.E. Moglen, M.A. Palmer, E.H. Stanley, N.E. Bockstae, and L.C. Thompson. 2003. Ecological forecasting and the urbanization of stream ecosystems: Challenges for economists, hydrologists, geomorphologists, and ecologists. *Ecosystems* 6: 659–674.

Noss, R.F. 1988. *Effects of edge and internal patchiness on habitat use by birds in a Florida hardwood forest.* Gainesville, FL: University of Florida. PhD Thesis.

O'Callaghan, J.R. 1996. *Land use: The interaction of economics, ecology and hydrology.* London: Chapman and Hall.

O'Neill, R.V., B.T. Milne, M.G. Turner, and R.H. Gardner. 1988a. Resource utilization scales and landscape patterns. *Landscape Ecology* 2(1): 63–69.

O'Neill, R.V., J.R. Krummel, R.H. Gardner, G. Sugihara, B.L. Jackson, D.L. DeAngelis, B.T. Milne, M.G. Turner, B. Zygmunt, S.W. Christensen, V.H. Dale, and R.L. Graham. 1988. Indices of landscape pattern. *Landscape Ecology* 1(3): 153–162.

O'Neill, R.V., C.T. Hunsaker, K. Bruce Jones, K.H. Riitters, J.D. Wickham, P.M. Schwartz, I.A. Goodman, B.L. Jackson, and W.S. Baillargeon. 1997. Monitoring environmental quality at the landscape scale: Using landscape indicators to assess biotic diversity, watershed integrity, and landscape stability. *Bioscience* 47(8): 513–519.

Odum, E.P. 1971. *Fundamentos de Ecologia* (Portuguese translation of the original *Fundamentals of Ecology*). Lisboa: Fundação Calouste Gulbenkian.

Odum, E.P. 1989. Input management of production systems. *Science* 243 (4888): 177–182.

Opdam, P. 1991. Metapopulation theory and habitat fragmentation: A review of holarctic breeding bird studies. *Landscape Ecology* 3(2): 93–106.

Opdam, P. 1997. *Landeconet: The study of biodiversity in changing landscapes.* Available online at: http://www.nmw.ac.uk/ITE/econet/opdam.html.

Opdam, P., R. Van Apeldorn, A. Schotman, and J. Kalkhoven. 1993. Population responses to landscape fragmentation. In *Landscape ecology of a stressed environment*, eds. C.C. Vos and P. Opdam, 60–78. London: Chapman and Hall.

Opdam, P., R. Foppen, R. Reijnen, and A. Schotman. 1995. The landscape ecological approach in bird conservation: integrating the metapopulation concept into spatial planning. *Ibis* 137: S139–S146.

Opdam, P., R. Foppen, and C. Vos. 2002. Bridging the gap between ecology and spatial planning in landscape ecology. *Landscape Ecology* 16: 767–779.

Painho, M. and P. Antunes. 1997. Urban comfort indicators evaluated at statistical unit level. In *Environmental challenges in an expanding urban world and the role of emerging information technologies*, eds. J. Reis Machado and J. Ahern, 381–389. Costa da Caparica, Portugal: Centro Nacional de Informaç,ão Geográfica (CNIG).

Peck, S. 1998. *Planning for Biodiversity: Issues and examples.* Washington D.C.: Island Press.

Pereira, H.G. 2000. Geosystems as a conceptual framework for the trade-off between society needs and environmental issues in the extractive industries of the future. Preprints of Workshop Engineering and Technology (Engenharia e Tecnologia). Lisboa: Ordem dos Engenheiros.

Pickett, S.T.A. and P.S. White. 1985. *The ecology of natural disturbance and patch dynamics*. Orlando: Academic Press.

Pickett, S.T.A., W.R. Burch, S. Dalton, T.W. Foresman, J.M. Grove and R. Rowntree. 1997. A conceptual framework for the study of human ecosystems in urban areas. *Urban Ecosystems* 1: 185–199.

Pickover, C. A. 1990. *Computers, pattern, chaos and beauty: Graphics from an unseen world*. New York: St. Martin's Press.

Pimentel, D., O. Bayley, P. Kim, E. Mullaney, J. Calabrese, L. Walman, F. Nelson, and X. Yao. 1999. Will limits of the Earth's resources control human numbers? *Environment, Development and Sustainability* 1: 19–39.

Pino, J., F. Rodà, J. Ribas, and X. Pons. 2000. Landscape structure and bird species richness: Implications for conservation in rural areas between natural parks. *Landscape and Urban Planning* 49: 35–48.

Pinto-Correia, T. 1993. Threatened landscape in Alentejo, Portugal: The Montado and the other agro-silvo-pastoral systems. *Landscape and Urban Planning* 24: 43–48.

Pinto-Correia, T. and J. Mascarenhas. 1999. Contribution to the extensification/ intensification debate: New trends in the Portuguese montado. *Landscape and Urban Planning* 46: 125–131.

Platt, R.H. 1994. The ecological city: Introduction and overview. In *The ecological city: Preserving and restoring urban diversity*, eds. R.H. Platt, A.R. Rowntree, and P.C. Meick. Amherst, MA: The University of Massachusetts Press.

Powell, T.M. 1989. Physical and biological scales of variability in lakes, estuaries, and the coastal ocean. In *Perspectives in ecological theory*, eds. J. Roughgarden, R.M. May, and S.A. Levin. Princeton, NJ: Princeton University Press.

Rees, W.E. 2003. Understanding urban ecosystems: An ecological economics perspective. In *Understanding urban ecosystems: A new frontier for science and education*, eds. A.R. Berkowitz, C.H. Nilon and K.S. Hollweg, 115–136. Millbrook, NY: Institute of Ecosystems Studies. Proceedings of the 8th Cary Conference.

Reis Machado, J. and J. Ahern, eds. 1997. International conference in Environmental Challenges in an Expanding Urban World and the Role of Emerging Information Technologies. Costa da Caparica, Portugal: Centro Nacional de Informação Geográfica (CNIG).

Remmert, H. 1991. The mosaic-cycle concept of ecosystems: An overview. In *The mosaic-cycle concept of ecosystems*, ed. H. Remmert. *Ecological Studies* 85: 1–21. Berlin: Springer-Verlag.

Ribeiro Telles, G. 1998. Global landscape (Paisagem global). In Proceedings of the First National Landscape Ecology Workshop: Portuguese Association of Landscape Ecology (APED). *Challenges for Mediterranean landscape ecology: The future of cultural landscapes—examples from the Alentejo region*, eds. T. Pinto-Correia and M. Cancela de Abreu, 25–28. Montemor-o-Novo, Portugal.

Ribeiro, L.P.F. 1997. Historical and cultural resources: Strengthening a greenway network for landscape conservation in metropolitan areas. In *Environmental challenges in an expanding urban world and the role of emerging information technologies*, eds. J. Reis Machado and J. Ahern, 441–453. Costa da Caparica, Portugal: Centro Nacional de Informação Geográfica (CNIG).

Riitters, K.H., R.V. O'Neill, C.T. Hunsaker, J.D. Wickham, D.H. Yankee, S.P. Timmins, R.B. Jones, and B.L. Jackson. 1995. A factor analysis of landscape pattern and structure metrics. *Landscape Ecology* 10(1): 23–39.

Ripple,W.J., G.A. Bradshaw, and T.A. Spies. 1991. Measuring landscape pattern in the Cascade Range of Oregon, USA. *Biological Conservation* 57: 73–88.

Robbins, C.S., D.K. Dawson, and B.A. Dowell. 1989. Habitat area requirements of breeding forest birds of the middle Atlantic states. *Wildlife Monographs* 103: 1–34.

Rockwood, P. 1995. Landscape planning for biodiversity. *Landscape and Urban Planning* 31: 379–385.

Rogers, C.A. 1993. *Describing landscapes: Indices of structure*. Burnaby, B.C., Canada: Simon Fraser University. M.S. Thesis.

Rosen, C., ed. 2000. *World Resources 2000–2001: People and ecosystems*. Oxford: Elsevier Science.

Rosenburg, D. K., B. R. Noon, and E. C. Meslow. 1997. Biological corridors: Form, function, and efficacy. *BioScience* 47: 677–687.

Saraiva, M.G. 1999. O Rio como Paisagem. Gestão de corredores fluviais no quadro do ordenamento do território (The river as landscape: Management of fluvial corridors in the framework of landscape planning). Dissertação de Doutoramento em Arquitectura Paisagista (doctoral dissertation in Landscape Architecture, in Portuguese), Secção Autónoma de Arquitectura Paisagista, Instituto Superior de Agronomia, Universidade Técnica de Lisboa. Textos Universitários de Ciências Sociais e Humanas. Fundação Calouste Gulbenkian e Fundação para a Ciência e Tecnologia. Lisboa.

Saunders, D.A., R. Hobbs, and C.R. Margules. 1991. Biological consequences of ecosystem fragmentation: a review. *Conservation Biology* 5(1): 18–32.

Saura, S. 2004. Effects of remote sensor spatial resolution and data aggregation on selected fragmentation indices. *Landscape Ecology* 19: 197–209.

Saura, S. and J. Martinez-Millán. 2002. Sensitivity of landscape pattern metrics to map spatial extent. *Photogrammetric Engineering and Remote Sensing* 67 (9): 1027–1036.

Schumaker, N. 1996. Using landscape indices to predict habitat connectivity. *Ecology* 77(4): 1210–1225.

Scott, M.J., F. Davis, B. Csuti, R. Noss, B. Butterfield, C. Groves, H. Anderson, S. Caicco, F. D'Erchia, T.C. Edwards Jr., J. Ulliman, and G. Wright. 1993. GAP analysis: A geographical approach to protection of biological diversity. *Wildlife Monographs* 123.

Selman, P. and N. Doar. 1992. An investigation of the potential for landscape ecology to act as a basis for rural land use plans. *Journal of Environmental Management* 35: 281–299.

Shannon, C.E. and W. Weaver. 1949. *The mathematical theory of communications*. Urbana, IL: University of Illinois Press.

Sih, A., B.G. Jonsson, and G. Luikart. 2000. Habitat loss: Ecological, evolutionary and genetic consequences. *Tree* 15(4): 132–134.

Sijmons, D. ed. 2002. *Landscape: Plans, lectures, essays, and articles produced by H+N+S Landscape Architects.* Amsterdam: Architectura and Natura Press. (Revised version of *Landschap* 1998).

Simberloff, D. 1998. Flagships, umbrellas, and keystones: Is single-species management passé in the landscape era? *Biological Conservation* 83(3): 247–257.

Simberloff, D. and J. Cox. 1987. Consequences and costs of conservation corridors. *Conservation Biology* 1: 63–69.

Simberloff, D., J.A. Farr, J. Cox, and D.W. Mehlman. 1992. Movement corridors: Conservation bargains or poor investments? *Conservation Biology* 6(4): 493–504.

Sorrell, J.P. 1998. Using geographic information systems to evaluate forest fragmentation and identify wildlife corridor opportunities in the Cataraqui Watershed. Ontario, Canada: York University Faculty of Environmental Studies.

Soulé, M.E. 1991. Conservation corridors: Countering habitat fragmentation. In *Landscapes linkages and biodiversity*, ed. W.E. Hudson, 91–104. Washington D.C.: Island Press.

Steiner, F. 2002. *Human ecology: Following nature's lead.* Washington D.C.: Island Press.

Steinitz, C. 1990. A framework for theory applicable to the education of landscape architects (and other Environmental design professionals). *Landscape Journal* 9(2): 136–143.

Steinitz, C. 1993. *Geographical information systems: A personal historical perspective, the framework for a recent project, and some questions for the future.* Genoa, Italy. Proceedings of the European Conference on Geographical Information Systems.

Steinitz, C., ed., and the Students of the Fall 1996 Design Studio. 1997. *An alternative future for the region of Camp Pendleton, California.* Cambridge, MA: Harvard Graduate School of Design. Available online at: www.gsd.harvard.edu/depts/larchdep/research/pendleton/.

Steinitz, C., M. Flaxman, A. Mueller, S. Tepper, V. Tsurnamal, and D. Zyroff, eds., and the Students of the ISCAR Studio. 1998. *Alternative futures in the Western Galilee, Israel.* Cambridge, MA: Harvard Graduate School of Design.

Steinitz, C., et al. 2003. *Alternative futures for changing landscapes: The Upper San Pedro River Basin in Arizona and Sonora.* Washington, D.C.: Island Press.

Strelke, W.K. and J.G. Dickson. 1980. Effect of forest clearcut edge on breeding birds in Texas. *Journal of Wildlife Management* 44: 559–567.

Swenson, J.J. and Franklin, J. 2000. The effects of urban development on habitat fragmentation in the Santa Monica Mountains. *Landscape Ecology* 15(8): 713–730.

Szaro, R.C., W.T. Sexton, and C.R. Malone. 1998. The emergence of ecosystem management as a tool for meeting people's needs and sustaining ecosystems. *Landscape and Urban Planning* 40 (1–3): 1–7.

Taborda, C. 2000. Para uma ideia de espaço de paisagem (The space of landscape: Towards a concept, in Portuguese). In *Documentos de Arquitectura 03*, 22–29. Lisboa, Portugal: Associação de Estudos Documentos de Arquitectura.

Temple, S.A. 1986. Predicting impacts of habitat fragmentation on forest birds: A comparison of two models. In *Wildlife 2000: Modeling habitat relationships of terrestrial vertebrates*, eds. J. Verner, M. L. Morrison, and C. J. Ralph, 301–304. Madison, WI: University of Wisconsin Press.

Terborgh, J. 1989. *Where have all the birds gone?* Princeton, NJ: Princeton University Press.

Theobald, D.M., N.T. Hobbs, T. Bearly, J.A. Zack, T. Shenk, and W.E. Riebsame. 2000. Incorporating biological information in local land-use decision making: Designing a system for conservation planning. *Landscape Ecology* 15: 35–45.

Thompson, C. M. and K. McGarigal. 2002. The influence of research scale on bald eagle habitat selection along the lower Hudson River, New York. *Landscape Ecology* 17: 569–586.

Tinker, D.B., C.A.C. Resor, G.P. Beauvais, K.F. Kipfmueller, C.I. Fernandes, and W.L. Baker. 1998. Watershed analysis of forest fragmentation by clearcuts and roads in a Wyoming forest. *Landscape Ecology* 13: 149–165.

Tischendorf, L. 2001. Can landscape indices predict ecological processes consistently? *Landscape Ecology* 16: 235–254

Tress, B. and G. Tress. 2001. Capitalising on multiplicity: A transdisciplinary systems approach to landscape research. *Landscape and Urban Planning* 57: 143–157.

Tress, B., G. Tress, H. Décamps, and A.M. d' Hauteserre. 2001. Bridging human and natural sciences in landscape research. Editorial. *Landscape and Urban Planning* 57: 137–141.

Tress, B., G. Tress, and G. Fry. 2005. Integrative studies on rural landscapes: Policy expectations and research practice. *Landscape and Urban Planning* 70: 177–191.

Treweek, J. 1999. *Ecological impact assessment*. Oxford: Blackwell Science.

Turner, M.G. and C.L. Ruscher. 1988. Changes in landscape patterns in Georgia, USA. *Landscape Ecology* 1(4): 241–251.

Turner, M.G. 1987. Spatial simulation of landscape changes in Georgia: A comparison of three transition models. *Landscape Ecology* 1(1): 29–36.

Turner, M.G. 1989. Landscape ecology: The effect of pattern on process. *Ecological Systematics* 20: 171–197.

Turner, M.G., R.V. O' Neill, R.H. Gardner, and B.T. Milne. 1989. Effects of changing spatial scale on the analysis of landscape pattern. *Landscape Ecology* 3(3/4): 153–162.

Turner, M.G. 1990. Spatial and temporal analysis of landscape patterns. *Landscape Ecology* 4: 1, 21–30.

Turner, M.G., S.M. Pearson, W.H. Romme, and L.L. Wallace. 1997. Landscape heterogeneity and ungulate dynamics: What spatial scales are important? In *Wildlife and landscape ecology: Effects of pattern and scale*, ed. J.A. Bissonette, 331–348. New York: Springer-Verlag.

Turner, M.G., R.H. Gardner, and R.V. O'Neill. 2001. *Landscape ecology in theory and practice: Pattern and process*. New York: Springer-Verlag.

UNEP. 1995. *Global diversity assessment*. Washington D.C.: UNEP.

UNEP. 1997. *Recommendations for a core set of indicators of biological diversity* (UNEP/CBD/SBSTTA/3/Inf.13). Montreal, Canada. Third Meeting of the Subsidiary Body on Scientific, Technical and Technological Advice (SBTTA) of the Convention for Biological Diversity, UNEP.

Van Buuren, M. and K. Kerkstra. 1993. The framework concept and the hydrological landscape structure: A new perspective in the design of multifunctional landscapes. In *Landscape ecology of a stressed environment*, eds. C.C. Vos and P. Opdam, 219–243. London: Chapman and Hall.

Van Dorp, D. and P.F.M. Opdam. 1987. Effects of patch size, isolation and regional abundance on forest bird communities. *Landscape Ecology* 1(1): 59–73.

Van Lier, H.N. 1998a. Sustainable land use planning: An editorial commentary. *Landscape and Urban Planning* 41: 79–82.

Van Lier, H.N. 1998b. The role of land use planning in sustainable rural systems. *Landscape and Urban Planning* 41: 83–91.

Varela, E.R.D. 2005. *Landscape ecological planning with geographic information systems for the sustainability of landscapes. Application to the shire of A Mariña Oriental.* Santiago de Compostela, Spain: University of Santiago de Compostela Department of Agro-Forestry Engineering. Doctoral dissertation.

Verboom, J. 2001. *Biodiversity assessment tools for land-use scenario studies in fragmented landscapes.* In "Monitoring and indicators" and "Models" at the Bio-Platform E-Conference "Biodiversity Conservation in Theory and Practice" coordinated by the Belgian Biodiversity Platform, the Ministry of Environment, Government of Catalonia, Ecosystems Ltd.; and the Centre for Ecology and Hydrology Banchory. Available online at: www.biodiversity. be/bbpf/econf/econfintro.html.

Verboom, J. and W. Wamelink. 1999. Spatial modeling in landscape ecology. In *Issues in landscape ecology*, eds. J.A. Wiens and M.R. Moss, 38–44. Snowmass Village, CO: International Association for Landscape Ecology Fifth World Congress.

Vitousek, P.M., H.A. Mooney, J. Lubchenco, and J.M. Melilo. 1997. Human domination of earth's ecosystems. *Science* 277: 494–499.

Von Haaren, C. 2002. Landscape planning facing the challenge of the development of cultural landscapes. *Landscape and Urban Planning* 60: 73–80.

Vos, W. 1998. Europe's old agricultural landscape: Old and new perspectives. In Proceedings of the First National Landscape Ecology Workshop, Potuguese Association of Landscape Ecology (APED), *Challenges for Mediterranean landscape ecology: The future of cultural landscapes—examples from the Alentejo region*, eds. T. Pinto-Correia and M. Cancela de Abreu. Montemor-o-Novo, Portugal.

Wascher, D.M., ed. 2000. *Landscapes and sustainability.* Strasbourg, France: European Centre for Nature Conservation and the Countryside Agency. Proceedings of the European workshop on landscape assessment as a policy tool.

Wascher, D.M. 2004. Landscape-indicator development: Steps towards a European approach. In *The new dimensions of the European landscapes*, ed. R.H.G. Jongman, 237–252. Wageningen, The Netherlands: Wageningen UR, Frontis Series.

Wascher, D.M. and M. Pérez-Soba, eds. 2004. *Learning from transfrontier land-*

scapes: Project in support of the European Landscape Convention. Wageningen, The Netherlands: Alterra Wageningen UR.

Watt, A. S. 1947. Pattern and process in the plant community. *Journal of Ecology* 35: 1–22.

Wells, G. and J. Fogg et al., eds. 1998. *Stream river corridor restoration: Principles, processes, and practices.* Washington, D.C.: U.S.D.A. Natural Resources Conservation Service.

Whitcomb, R.F., C.S. Robbins, L.F. Lynch, et al. 1981. Effects of forest fragmentation on avifauna of the eastern deciduous forest. In *Forest island dynamics in man-dominated landscapes,* eds. R.L. Burgess and D.M. Sharpe, 125–205. New York: Springer-Verlag.

White, D., M. Preston, K.E. Freemark, and A.R. Kiester. 1999. A hierarchical framework for conserving biodiversity. In *Landscape ecological analysis: Issues and applications,* eds. J. Klopatek and R. Gardner, 127–153. New York: Springer-Verlag.

White, P. S. and S. T. A. Pickett. 1985. *Natural disturbance and patch dynamics: An introduction.* San Diego, CA: Academic Press.

Whittaker, R.H. 1953. A consideration of climax theory: The climax as a population and pattern. *Ecological Monographs* 23: 41–78.

Wickham, J.D. and K.H. Riitters. 1995. Sensitivity of landscape metrics to pixel size. *International Journal of Remote Sensing* 16: 3585–3594.

Wiens, J. A. 1976. Population responses to patchy environments. *Ecological Systems* 7: 81–120.

Wiens, J. 1999. The science and practice of landscape ecology. In *Landscape ecological analysis: Issues and applications,* eds. J. Klopatek and R. Gardner, 371–383. New York: Springer-Verlag.

Wiens, J.A., C.S. Crawford, and J.R. Gosz. 1985. Boundary dynamics: A conceptual framework for studying landscape ecosystems. *Oikos* 45: 421–427.

Wilcove, D.S. 1985. Nest predation in forest tracts and the decline of migratory songbirds. *Ecology* 66: 1211–1214.

With, K.A. 1997. The application of neutral landscape models in conservation biology. *Conservation Biology* 11(5): 1069–1080.

With, K.A. 1999. Landscape conservation: A new paradigm for the conservation of biodiversity. In *Issues in landscape ecology,* eds. J.A. Wiens and M.R. Moss, 78–82. Snowmass Village, CO: International Association for Landscape Ecology Fifth World Congress.

With, K.A. and T.O. Crist. 1995. Critical thresholds in species' responses to landscape structure. *Ecology* 76(8): 2446–2459.

Wu et al. 2002. Empirical patterns of the effects of changing scale on landscape metrics. *Landscape Ecology* 17: 761–782.

Yahner, R.H. 1988. Changes in wildlife communities near edges. *Conservation Biology* 2: 333–9.

Yahner, R.H. and D.P. Scott. 1988. Effects of forest fragmentation on depredation of artificial nests. *Journal of Wildlife Management* 52: 158–161.

Young, A. 1999. Is there really spare land? A critique of estimates of available cultivable land in developing countries. *Environment, Development and Sustainability* 1: 3–18.

Zonneveld, I.S. 1988. Landscape ecology and its application. In *Proceedings of the 3rd Symposium of the Canadian Society for Landscape Ecology and Management*, ed. M. Moss. Guelph, Canada: University of Guelph.

Zonneveld, I.S. 1990. Scope and concepts of landscape ecology as an emerging science. In *Changing landscapes: An ecological perspective*, eds. I.S. Zonneveld and R.T.T. Forman, 3–19. Berlin: Springer-Verlag.

Zonneveld, I.S. 1995. *Land ecology: An introduction to landscape ecology as a base for land evaluation, land management and conservation*. Amsterdam: SPB Publishing.

Zorn, P. and Upton, D. 1997. Ecological Integrity Monitoring Plan. Part 1: Ecological Indicators. Bruce Peninsula National Park and Fathom Five National Marine Park, Cornwall, Ontario, Canada: Canadian Heritage - Parks Canada, Ontario Regional Office, Ecosystem Management Section.

Author Bios

Jack Ahern is a licensed landscape architect and professor of landscape architecture at the Department of Landscape Architecture and Regional Planning (LARP) at UMass Amherst. He received his BS from UMass and his Masters of Landscape Architecture at the University of Pennsylvania in 1980 where he studied under the late Ian L. McHarg. He has worked in private landscape architectural practice in Philadelphia and upstate New York. He recently completed his PhD in Environmental Sciences from Wageningen University in the Netherlands. His teaching includes studios in landscape planning where students learn and apply ecological principles to local, regional and watershed plans.

André Botequilha Leitão is an Auxiliary Professor of Landscape Planning at the Faculty of Natural Resources Engineering, University of the Algarve, and a Researcher at the CVRM - Geosystems Center at the Instituto Superior Técnico, Technical University of Lisbon, Portugal. He received his MSc (1997) and his PhD in Environmental Engineering from IST - UTL (2003) where he focused on landscape ecology and sustainable planning. Since 1998, he has conducted his PhD and post doc research and other collaborations with the Landscape Architecture and Regional Planning Department, University of Massachusetts, Amherst. Here he developed his PhD and Post-Doctoral research, developed LP projects, and taught a studio with Professor Jack Ahern. His research and professional interests include ecologically sustainable landscape planning and inter- and transdisciplinarity.

Joseph N. Miller is a landscape ecologist and landscape architect in Annapolis, Maryland. He received his Masters of Science in ecology from Pennsylvania State University in 1991, where he performed landscape pattern research in comparative watershed studies. He received his

237

Masters of Landscape Architecture degree from the University of Massachusetts, Amherst in 2000, where his research focused on habitat corridor planning within suburban watersheds. His research and professional interests also include greenway planning and ecologically sustainable community planning.

Kevin McGarigal is an Associate Professor of Landscape Ecology at the University of Massachusetts Amherst, Department of Natural Resources Conservation. He received his PhD from Oregon State University. His overall professional goal, achieved through research, teaching, and outreach, is to improve our understanding of how landscapes are structured physically and biologically and the agents responsible for those patterns, how these patterns affect the distribution and dynamics of animal populations, how these patterns and processes change over time, and how to apply this information to better manage natural resources over multiple spatial and temporal scales.

Index